STRATEGIC COMMUNICATIONS

PLANNING FOR PUBLIC RELATIONS AND MARKETING

6TH EDITION

LAURIE J. WILSON, APR, Fellow PRSA
Brigham Young University

JOSEPH D. OGDEN
Brigham Young University

Kendall Hunt
publishing company

Cover images used under license from Shutterstock, Inc.

Kendall Hunt
publishing company

www.kendallhunt.com
Send all inquiries to:
4050 Westmark Drive
Dubuque, IA 52004-1840

CONTENTS

Chapter 3   COMMUNICATIONS RESEARCH METHODS   45

Chapter 4   USING RESEARCH FOR EFFECTIVE COMMUNICATIONS PLANNING   61

Chapter 5 SETTING GOALS AND OBJECTIVES   77

Chapter 6 CREATIVITY AND BIG IDEAS   91

Appendix A   TIPS FROM THE PROS   239

Appendix B   STRATEGY BRIEFS   241

PREFACE

So many things have changed in the world since the 5th edition of Strategic Communications Planning was released. Things that now seem common like the iPad, Instagram, Angry Birds and Justin Bieber's music career didn't exist when the last edition of this book was published. In fact, President Obama hadn't even been elected for the first time.

It was time to catch up . . .

The Boston Red Sox finally won another World Series in 2013, and it was time to make a giant leap forward with this book. As a result, the entire book has been overhauled. New chapters have been added, the matrix has evolved and the text is filled with social media cases and strategies. Despite an absolute explosion of mobile apps, social media sites and new networking platforms, one thing has remained constant: the need for a solid, adaptable strategic planning process. There are so many ways to segment publics now and so many new strategies and channels to reach them that the need for strategic analysis and planning has never been greater.

We believe that we've kept the elements that made this book one of the top-selling PR strategy and campaign texts for the past six years and added a vibrant, new digital and social media perspective. Here's some of what you can expect to find.

An updated and revised Strategic Communications Planning Matrix
- Includes the new "big idea" concept.
- Now simplified to eight steps.
- Follows each public through messages, strategies and tactics.

New chapter on creativity and big ideas
- Provides ideas and tools to harness creativity.
- Introduces the big idea concept — a creative and overarching strategy that appeals to all key publics and ties a campaign together.

New chapter on using social media for message delivery
- How to choose the best social media platforms.
- Branded content.
- Social media ROI.

New chapter on responding to requests for proposals
- Teaches students a matrix approach on how to respond to RFPs with a concise pitch.

We also removed the somewhat cumbersome teaching case and replaced it with "Matrix applied" sections which each introduce a different step in the strategic planning process. In addition, we've added to and updated the popular "Tips from the pros" found in each chapter. These provide students with relevant advice from practitioners who are at the top of their game.

Copy outlines have evolved into strategy briefs that include expanded digital and social media content. We even expanded the number of strategy briefs available in Appendix B to include such tactics as infographics, blog posts and YouTube videos.

Finally, we're particularly excited to introduce, for the first time with this edition, mini cases that demonstrate how some companies are applying strategic communications in winning ways and how others are completely losing. You can read about Target's blunders, T-Mobile's huge win and how WestJet won over holiday travelers and a few million others.

So as public relations and marketing advances in the digital age, so do we. The basic principles of researched-based strategic planning, however, remain unchanged. But the tools we use to conduct research, analyze data and communicate with our key publics have been revolutionized by advances in technology. We're confident this 6th edition will help you join the revolution.

ACKNOWLEDGMENTS

I would like to begin by acknowledging the extraordinary contributions of my co-author and longtime mentor, Laurie J. Wilson, who retired from full-time teaching in December 2013. Laurie first wrote down the Strategic Communications Planning Matrix for publication some 20 years ago after stitching together the best ideas and different planning approaches of the BYU PR faculty. She, of course, also added her legendary discipline to the matrix process — making it a cohesive and useful tool. There is no doubt that "the matrix," as it has come to be known by students and practitioners across the country, would not have been published without Laurie's diligent efforts.

Still, we acknowledge the contributions of all those early BYU PR faculty members. Lacking an analytical tool for students to use in solving public relations problems within the RACE model, faculty collaborated on a process that specifically outlined the type of research needed and how that research and its subsequent analysis should direct the planning and communication steps. Early contributors to the matrix also included: Bruce Olsen, Ray Beckham, Brad Hainsworth, Larry Macfarlane and JoAnn Valenti.

Today, the matrix approach is used by more than 200 universities and colleges around the world to train budding professionals in the art and science of strategic communications. The matrix provides a structure for effective communication that inherently teaches analytical skills that are too often missing from education today.

In addition to the pioneering BYU faculty members mentioned, I express gratitude to the thousands of graduates, practitioners and professors across the country who have learned, applied and helped shape the matrix into its current form. I welcome your continued feedback as the matrix advances to remain relevant in a rapidly changing communications landscape.

For this edition, Laurie and I would like to gratefully acknowledge the contributions of senior practitioners from across the nation whose advice and counsel is found in every chapter. We appreciate these professionals for taking the time and effort to share their experience and wisdom. We also wish to acknowledge the many contributions of two very fine research assistants and BYU students, Jakob Walker and Dylan Ellsworth. Next, I want to thank our talented editor, Jennifer Mathis, and exceptional graphic designer, Jon Woidka, for their work on the book. They both made the content more memorable and accessible. Lastly, I wish to express appreciation to Angela Willenbring, our patient project manager at Kendall Hunt publishing, and to the composition team that pulled all the elements together.

As the Strategic Communications Planning Matrix continues to evolve and moves into a new era of communications marketing and social media, I salute those who first had the vision to create the process so many years ago.

Joseph D. Ogden
Lindon, Utah
December 2014

ABOUT THE AUTHORS

Laurie J. Wilson

Laurie J. Wilson is a recently retired, award-winning professor of communications at Brigham Young University. In 2001, she was recognized by PRSA as the nation's Outstanding Educator. In 1990, she was recognized as the Public Relations Student Society of America Outstanding Faculty Adviser and subsequently served four years as the national faculty adviser. She received a Utah Golden Spike award as Professional of the Year in 2010. In 1995, she was inducted into the PRSSA Hall of Fame. Wilson has also received the prestigious Karl G. Maeser Teaching Award and three Student Alumni Association Excellence in Teaching Awards from BYU.

Wilson received her Ph.D. from American University in Washington, D.C., after working in public relations and marketing for several years. She joined the BYU faculty in 1989, where she has served as chair of the communications department and of the public relations program. She also served six years as the university's director of internships. At the same time, Wilson co-chaired a national PRSA task force on internships, which created the first-ever standards for quality public relations internships. She has served as national chair for a number of education initiatives and task forces in PRSA, has served in the public relations division of the Association for Education in Journalism and Mass Communication, and has served on the diversity task force of the Association of Schools of Journalism and Mass Communication. She represented PRSA on the Joint Commission on Public Relations Education, chairing the undergraduate curriculum committee. She has served on site teams accrediting communications programs for the Accrediting Council on Education in Journalism and Mass Communications and leads site visit teams certifying schools in public relations education for PRSA. She is on the editorial boards of the "Journal of Public Relations Research" and the "Journal of Promotion Management."

Wilson's areas of expertise, research and publication include strategic planning and issue management, corporate social responsibility and building community partnerships. She consults regularly in those areas and is an educational consultant to communications programs. In addition to this book, Wilson has co-authored three other communications books. She also serves in the local United Way where she was a member of the executive board for 20 years.

Joseph D. Ogden

Joseph D. Ogden is an associate professor of communications at Brigham Young University. His areas of expertise include message design, persuasive writing, media relations, strategic planning and marketing. He teaches introduction to public relations, PR case studies, advanced media writing and communications management. He has also taught marketing, international business and business ethics. In addition, he has guest lectured at several colleges and universities across the country.

He was previously assistant dean of the Marriott School of Management at BYU and executive director of the school's National Advisory Council. He has also directed many business study abroad programs in Asia and founded the global marketing study abroad program at BYU. In 2010, Ogden received the N. Eldon Tanner award, the school's highest administrative honor. In 2013 he received a Brigham Young Outstanding Service award.

Ogden is also founder and president of JDO Communications Strategists, a strategic marketing and communications consulting firm. The firm has worked nationally and internationally with companies in hospitality, travel, entertainment, finance and technology.

Before coming to BYU, Ogden worked as corporate communications director for a nearly $1 billion-a-year personal care and nutrition products company. He was the company's spokesman, oversaw public relations and marketing in Asia and managed investor communications for the publicly traded firm.

Ogden earned an MBA from the Marriott School of Management. He also earned a bachelor's degree in communications with minors in music and business from BYU. He completed a non-degree program in negotiation at Harvard and MIT.

In addition to his academic and professional pursuits, he is an active musician, avid skier, experimental cook and architecture enthusiast.

CHAPTER 1

THE RELATIONSHIP-BUILDING APPROACH TO COMMUNICATIONS

"Trust is the most basic element of social contact — the great intangible at the heart of truly long-term success."

—Al Golin

FOUNDER OF GOLIN/HARRIS INTERNATIONAL

LEARNING IMPERATIVES

- To understand that an organization's survival is dependent upon establishing trust among key publics.

- To understand the characteristics of a relationship-building approach to organizational communications.

- To be introduced to the Strategic Communications Planning Matrix as a tool for planning and implementing organizational communications.

On March 8, 2014, Malaysia Airlines Flight 370 departed Kuala Lumpur for Beijing. An hour after takeoff, ground control lost contact with the Boeing 777-200, and it disappeared from radar.

On the day the flight disappeared, Malaysian officials offered very little information about what went wrong. Not until four days into the international search did Malaysian officials reveal that they had radar evidence suggesting the plane had turned around midflight. Countries from around the world that had joined the search were frustrated that they had been looking in the wrong place. Some experts say the delay was so critical that it may now mean the plane might never be found because of ocean currents.

Malaysia Airlines and government officials were so reluctant to release information related to the investigation into the missing aircraft that they completely lost the **trust** of the international community as well as of the families and friends of those missing on the flight.

The very act of trying to withhold information that might make the national airline look bad made it and the country look worse and hindered the investigation. Airline and government officials including the prime minister of Malaysia were not transparent. They almost appeared criminal in not wanting to: 1) talk about how and why two passengers got on the plane with stolen passports, 2) admit that the plane's data transmitter appeared to have been deliberately turned off, and 3) talk about the pilots' backgrounds and investigate ulterior motives.

As Malaysian officials continued to release halting information related to the search, the international community turned their trust to Australian Prime Minister Tony Abbott whose government was managing search efforts some 1,500 miles off the coast of Perth, Australia.

The MH370 tragedy, which cost the lives of all 239 passengers and crew onboard, is an example of just how much governments, businesses and others have to learn about the importance of building and maintaining trust.

TRUST
An emotional judgment of one's credibility and performance on issues of importance.

People write messages and prayers for victims of Malaysia Airlines flight 370 in IIUM Library, Kuantan Pahang, Malaysia.

© Shahrul Azman/Shutterstock.com

Trust

As we began a new century, corporate America discovered through sad experience that trust was the primary issue of concern. In fact, it had always been the primary issue. Now, more than a decade into the new century, with aggressive relationship-building strategies, businesses seem to be recovering somewhat. But it took the events of the early part of this century — 9/11 and its effect on the economy; the demise of Enron, Worldcom, Arthur Andersen and others; the security brokers' scandal; mismanagement by mutual fund managers and many other similar events — for all sectors of our economy to realize that trust among an organization's publics is the single most important factor in organizational survival.

In a crisis of trust, organizations looked to professional communicators for counsel on rebuilding relationships with the publics upon whom their survival depended. Finally, leaders in all kinds of organizations began to recognize the need for an integrated approach to communication to build — or rebuild — relationships key to an organization's success.

Al Golin is a respected senior public relations professional and founder of GolinHarris, an international communications firm with offices in 34 countries. In 2004, he published a significant book, "Trust or Consequences," in which he wrote about his decades-long career as a counselor to CEOs of major corporations intimately involved in building relationships with their publics. He asserts that trust is the key element of strong relationships and the only way to ensure organizational success in the long run. Golin's results with CEOs have been mixed. Many, like Ray Kroc of McDonald's, followed his advice, making regular deposits in the "trust bank" and reaping significant benefits over the long term. Others have disregarded his counsel in favor of short-term gains, leaving them ill-prepared and at risk when crises hit.

© Radu Bercan/Shutterstock.com

Most trusted groups

While recent **research** shows trust in business has rebounded some, trust in governments around the globe continues to decline. For the last 14 years, Edelman, one of the world's largest public relations firms, has conducted an annual global survey of public trust in institutions. In 2014 the gap between trust in business (58 percent) and trust in government (44 percent) was 14 points — the largest in the history of the Edelman Trust Barometer (see Figure 1.1).

RESEARCH-BASED
When decision-making in the planning and implementation process is based on the acquisition, interpretation and application of relevant facts.

Figure 1.1
Edelman Trust Barometer Timeline

Fall of the celebrity CEO — Nongovernmental organizations approach parity in credibility with business and government; trust in business wanes in the aftermath of 9/11.

Shift in credibility — "A person like me" emerged as the most credible spokesperson in the U.S. and in the top three globally. Trust in employees was significantly higher than in CEOs.

Trust is now an essential line of business — Trust and transparency became as vital to a company's reputation as quality of its products and services.

Business to lead the debate for change — Business holds the trust advantage over government in the majority of markets. NGOs are still the most trusted institution. The public expects businesses to engage in developing and supporting regulations alongside government.

2002 years   2004   2006   2008   2010   2012   2014

Global trust disparity — Although trust in business and government increased globally, major U.S. companies in Europe and Asia suffered from loss of trust while European and Asian companies within the U.S. continued to flourish.

Young influencers have more trust in business — Younger elites (25–34) were more trusting of virtually every source of information on a company compared with older elites (35–64). Trust in Chinese companies reached an all-time low.

Fall of government — With many countries being plagued with financial crises, trust in government rapidly declined. Most countries surveyed don't trust government to do what is right.

Source: 2002–2014 Edelman Trust Barometers

TIPS FROM THE PROS

Who do you trust?

Richard Edelman, CEO of Edelman, the world's largest public relations firm, tips you off on who is most trusted.

Knowing who people turn to for information is invaluable as a PR practitioner. Over the past 15 years, the Edelman Trust Barometer has measured trust levels in 27 nations, both among opinion elites and the general population. The important trends we observe are the dispersion of authority, skepticism of information without repetition and the emergence of a new set of values that builds trust.

NGOs ARE MOST TRUSTED

Around the globe, the most trusted institution is now the nongovernmental organization. This is a recognition of the importance of environment and proper treatment of employees. But it also signifies a protest against failure by business and government. The most stunning rise of civil society is in China, where NGOs now rank ahead of government in trust, up from 30 percent in 2006 to 84 percent today.

Business is the second most trusted group, followed by media, with government trailing badly. In some markets such as the U.S., the gap between business and government trust is 20 points or more, a record chasm. But business should take little comfort; by a three-to-one margin, respondents ask for more government regulation in fast-evolving industries such as energy, financial services and food.

STRONG CONFIDENCE IN EXPERTS AND FRIENDS

The reordering of authority is best described by a loss of trust in traditional leaders, including heads of government and chief executive officers, who respectively rank ninth and tenth as sources of credible information. In fact, only 20 percent of respondents believe these leaders will tell the truth in a difficult or complex situation. Instead, there is confidence in experts such as academics or engineers, plus a reliance on a friend or person like yourself.

KEYS TO BUILDING TRUST

The failure of the establishment has caused a shift in the trust equation, from value to values. Specifically, respondents now place low importance on excellent financial results, outstanding CEOs and top rankings. Rather, they trust companies that treat employees well, place customers ahead of profit and communicate frequently and honestly.

Businesses should establish a new compact with stakeholders based on:

- **Open advocacy of its interests** — Offer a strategy that begins with the context of how a proposed change will improve the lives of customers, as well as the bottom line.
- **Willingness to modify policy** — Seek input from a wide range of stakeholders, and partner with NGOs in drafting goals which offer both a business case and a pro-society rationale.
- **Clear metrics to measure progress** — Report frequently on progress against metrics. Acknowledge where delivery is under expectation and have a path to improved performance.

The trend toward growing trust in business is encouraging; still, nearly half of those surveyed want more government regulation, especially in industries such as financial services, energy and food and beverage. Small, medium and family-owned businesses tend to be more trusted than large enterprises. However, there is still a crisis of trust among business leaders. Only one in five people trust a business leader to tell the truth. A CEO has much lower credibility than a technical expert, an academic or a person like you.

These data have huge implications for communicating with today's publics. It would seem formal and informal opinion leaders are more important than ever before. Bloggers with considerable followers can hold more sway over a public on many issues than the CEO of Toyota.

Trust in media sources has also shifted dramatically in the past decade. While traditional media still hold a slight edge over online search engines, the trust gap is down to only 2 percent, with 65 percent of respondents trusting traditional media sources and 63 percent trusting online sources. Trust in social media (45 percent) has jumped significantly in the past two years and now surpasses owned media/advertising (44 percent).

Toyota CEO, Akio Toyoda, speaks to reporters prior to testifying on Capitol Hill about the company's safety issues.

© Haruyoshi Yamaguchi/Corbis

Leveraging the array of available media makes it easier for publics to engage in discourse and increases the number of times individuals are exposed to a story. We know this can enhance trust as people often need to hear things multiple times before accepting and believing.

Trust becomes actionable when it is built on a foundation of honesty and openness. It must permeate the entire organization from the top executives to front-line support and service employees.

An integrated approach

Public relations scholars have been researching and advocating **relationship building** for years. Rather than being fragmented by key publics as organizational functions have been in the past, we recommend an integrated approach

RELATIONSHIP BUILDING
A return to the roots of human communication and persuasion that focuses on personal trust and mutual cooperation.

to reach all publics and stakeholders in order for the organization to thrive over the long term. The importance and role of trust-based relationship building are rooted in PR research and practice.

When **public relations** emerged from the journalism profession as press representation for corporations in the early 1900s, the public relations counselor was positioned as a key adviser to the CEO. Over time, that status was lost to attorneys and accountants because the PR profession was unable to demonstrate a concrete contribution to the bottom line. Even when business entered an era of keen market competition for products and services where communication now plays a primary role in sales, relationship building was seen as unimportant.

For the last three decades, public relations professionals have been waging a battle to regain a strategic role. Part of that effort is a strong emphasis on research and evaluation to justify communication efforts in terms of their specific benefits to the accomplishment of the organizational mission. Another emerging value to organizations is the ability of PR practitioners to manage issues that affect an organization's focus on its primary business.

Corporate management is recognizing the ability of communicators to manage certain organizational issues that do not respond to traditional economic and business principles and practices (Wilson, 1996; Wilson, 1994a and 1994b). As a result of the crisis of trust, we have finally demonstrated the bottom-line impact of building strong relationships with publics. And we have justified our argument that ultimate organizational survival depends upon building relationships over the long term.

PUBLIC RELATIONS
Strategically managing communication to build relationships and influence behavior.

What does it mean to be "strategic?"

In this chapter, we introduce the strategic planning process that drives the tactical decisions made by communications professionals. But first, we must understand what it means to be a **strategic function**.

Very simply, strategy is a well-coordinated approach to reaching an overall goal. It may be helpful to draw an analogy to military strategy. In a given battle, the overall goal may be to secure a certain piece of ground or a particular town. The strategy is the coordinated effort of all participants to achieve that goal. When an organization sets a particular goal in support of its mission, strategy serves to integrate the efforts of all departments to achieve the goal. Communications is strategic when it aids in formulating the organization's approach to accomplishing overall goals and then supports those efforts in a coordinated and consistent manner, working in concert with all other organizational entities.

To effectively function in that role requires solid research that drives decision-making. It requires vision or a long-term, rather than short-term, mentality. Strategic functioning necessitates a broad perspective of the organizational environment and all contributing members. It demands incisive understanding of the organizational

STRATEGIC FUNCTION
One that contributes significantly to the accomplishment of an organization's mission and goals.

TIPS FROM THE PROS

Strategic communication

John Paluszek, APR, Fellow PRSA, senior counsel at Ketchum, former PRSA president, founder and executive producer of "Business In Society" and Global Alliance for Public Relations and Communication Management chair, tips you off on the importance of strategic communication.

There's great news on strategic communications: It's going global and social with the potential to positively impact virtually all institutions as well as aspiring strategic communications professionals.

You see, strategic communications universals — building reciprocal relationships based on trust, accountability, transparency, ethical behavior and symmetrical communication — are increasingly being applied around the world to address many new stakeholders.

A full description of these epic trends would require several volumes, but a very top-line summary may be instructive:

1. Public relations — i.e., strategic communications — is now a global profession. It has proven protean, adaptable to a wide range of economic, political and cultural systems and traditions. In my Global Alliance service, I have seen it function successfully in some 20 countries spanning the globe. It is being applied in support of organizational objectives ranging from marketing and internal communications to investor relations and public affairs.
2. After decades of evolution, "sustainable development," aka "corporate social responsibility," is now morphing from quasi-philanthropy to a *truly integrated, high-priority commitment* to help achieve organizational (mainly business) objectives while addressing society's macro challenges. Its many elements range from progressive environmental/energy policies to cause-related marketing.

These seminal developments present unprecedented opportunities for the inclusion of strategic communications at the highest levels of management. Prudent practitioners will bear in mind — and manifest — the famous epigram of publisher-philanthropist Walter Annenberg: "Every human advancement or reversal can be understood through communication."

mission and the goals that directly support the accomplishment of that mission. Finally, strategic functioning means that the communications and marketing efforts are driven by an understanding of the organization and where communications fits and coordinates with all other organizational functions. Strategic managers are analytical, pragmatic, visionary and perspicacious.

The development of communications and PR functions in business

Business organizations began giving serious attention to communication with publics in the early 1900s. Journalists began serving as press agents and publicists for major corporations such as Ford Motors and AT&T. By midcentury, public relations practitioners were organizational counselors. They responded to traditional American business management practices by manipulating the organization's environment, oftentimes in ways that might now be considered ethically questionable. By the 1960s, conflicts over issues important to key organizational publics gave birth to **crisis management** as a key function of communicators. Rather than just reacting to crises, good managers began to anticipate problems and mediate them before they could affect the organization's environment and profitability, and **issue management** was born as a long-term approach to identifying and resolving issues.

The very concept of issue management fit well into traditional American business management techniques, based almost entirely on economic principles. Nevertheless, there was obvious conflict between the long-term nature of issue management and the short-term profit orientation of American businesses. Further, there was a more critical conflict between the self-interested rather than public-interested approach of American businesses and the publics who were beginning to demand accountability.

In spite of the conflict, issue management techniques became popular in business communications practice and gave birth to the role of communication in **strategic management**. This meant evaluating all proposed action through a focus on organizational goals, usually defined in short-term contributions to the bottom line. Even though issues must be identified far in advance to be effectively mediated, as depicted in Hainsworth's issue cycle (1990), the purpose is to save the organization future difficulty, not to address the needs of organizational publics because they are intrinsically valued. This focus brought communicators squarely into the camp of purely economically-based, rationalist business management.

It is not surprising that organizational communications ended up here. Throughout its history, public relations and business communications have consistently moved away from a "relations" orientation. Even with all of our technological advances, we have been slow to recognize the limitations of mass communications and mass media. We resisted a shift from using mass media to more targeted media, which means we have not been accessing appropriate message channels to reach many of our publics. Some still tend to see publics as an inert mass, hypnotized by mass media, mindlessly absorbing our messages and acting on them. The dynamic emergence of social media, however, has forever altered the landscape as users customize all sources of information and selectively choose their engagement. The latest research and mass adoption of social media should convince practitioners of the need to carefully understand and strategically target publics.

Partially as a reaction to the economic (bottom-line) orientation of strategic management and partially as a result of international trends in business, some scholars in the 1990s attempted to shift public relations focus to relationship building (Creedon, 1991; Kruckeberg and Starck, 1988; Wilson, 1996 and 2001; Ledingham and Bruning, 2000).

CRISIS MANAGEMENT
The process of anticipating and mediating problems that could affect an organization's environment and profitability.

ISSUE MANAGEMENT
A long-term approach to identifying and resolving issues before they become problems or crises.

STRATEGIC MANAGEMENT
The process of evaluating all proposed actions by focusing on organizational goals, usually defined in short-term contributions to the bottom line.

Scholars and practitioners have returned to the roots of human communication and persuasion in devising approaches that build more personal relationships based on trust and cooperation. We must view segmenting and personalizing communication as a more viable approach to publics than mass communications.

Societal trends

Five trends in society should have led us to our roots in communication and relationships long ago.

The **first** trend is increasingly segmented publics requiring alternatives to traditional media channels for the dissemination of messages. TV provides a clear example. Less than half the population watches television shows live. That number drops even lower when looking specifically at millennials. Technology has made it easier and easier to choose when and what you want to view. Sitting down every Wednesday at 8 p.m. to catch a new episode of ABC's "Modern Family" is almost laughable. A large portion of "Modern Family" viewers probably don't even know when it airs.

In fact, our study of audience has indicated that even within the groups segmented by demographics and psychographics, we find smaller segments which have been labeled interpretive communities (Lindloff, 1988) because of differences among them in the ways they receive, interpret and act upon messages. These shared interest groups are evidenced now in the user communities fostered through Internet channels, particularly social media.

The **second** trend is dramatically escalating social problems that no longer affect only fringe or marginalized groups in society. The productivity of the workforce is seriously jeopardized by problems affecting families such as drug abuse, physical abuse, gangs, teen pregnancy and the declining quality of education. When such problems begin to affect the workforce they threaten productivity and profits and must be addressed.

The **third** trend is an increased reliance on organizational communicators to establish relationships with publics to mediate issues. The business environment has become increasingly burdened with social issues and problems that corporations have failed to control using traditional management techniques. Companies are forming alliances with communities, governments and special interest groups to address societal problems. These actions are ostensibly in the name of social responsibility, but a more accurate justification of the establishment of cooperative efforts is probably that corporations have been unable to solve those problems unilaterally.

The **fourth** trend leading us to a relationship-based approach to business management and communications is that business entities in the U.S. now face a more knowledgeable and business-savvy public that demands corporate commitment of resources to solve the problems affecting the community as well as employees and their families. In fact, some would say that the public understands just enough about the operation of business to be dangerous. They are aware of corporate profits, although not always cognizant of net profits versus gross revenues, and apply pressure for organizations to use their resources in socially responsible ways.

The **fifth** trend requiring mutually beneficial relationships with our publics is their previously mentioned control over access to information. Whereas limited channels of mass media previously placed control of information in the hands of

Can shoppers trust Target?

BACKSTORY

As Target customers made purchases on the busiest shopping day of the year — Black Friday 2013 — little did they know their credit/debit card information was being stolen. In what was the second-largest data breach in U.S. history, Target later disclosed that more than 40 million customers' card details — names, card numbers, expiration dates and CVV verification codes — had been stolen by cyber attackers.

It took Target several weeks to acknowledge its system had been hacked despite several threat alerts from the company's own security software. More than two months after the original incident, Target officials revealed that an additional 70 million customers' personal information had also been compromised. The incident severely damaged Target's reputation and dissolved much of the trust it had built over the years.

KEY FACTS

- The hackers used point-of-sale malware to immediately transfer personal data as customers were checking out in more than 1,700 Target stores between Nov. 27 and Dec. 15.
- In addition to credit card information, hackers also obtained customers' names and phone numbers as well as home and email addresses.
- Target issued its first news release about the incident more than three weeks after the initial breach.
- The security breach was eventually traced to a criminal group in Eastern Europe.
- Fraudulent charges appeared on about three million credit and debit cards, as a result of information stolen from Target.
- Target faced more than 40 pending lawsuits as well as an FTC investigation.

© Sergey Yechikov/Shutterstock.com

How would you respond?

TARGET'S STRATEGY

Target, although still unsure of the full extent of the incident, acknowledged the data breach on Dec. 19, 2013. The company informed customers of the actions it was taking to address the issue, assured them that a full investigation was taking place and provided a comprehensive website offering resources and daily updates related to the breach. Customers were also provided with updates and information through email, Facebook and Twitter. Copies of Target's official email communications were posted online so customers could validate the authenticity of the emails.

To encourage customer spending and foster goodwill, Target announced on Dec. 20 that they would be offering an employee discount to all in-store shoppers on Dec. 21 and 22. They also provided a year's free credit monitoring for all affected customers.

Along with hiring a new chief information officer, Target began a search for a newly created chief information security officer and a new chief compliance officer. Target also announced that it would spend upwards of $100 million to upgrade payment terminals to accept the more secure Chip-and-PIN cards.

RESULTS

- Target's online and in-store shopping traffic hit a three-year low following the breach — only 33 percent of U.S. households shopped at Target in January 2014 compared to 43 percent in January 2013.
- The cyberattack has already cost the retailer at least $61 million.
- Fourth-quarter 2013 profits fell 46 percent to $520 million from $960 million in 2012.
- Target has yet to fully bounce back from the Black Friday security breach. Should and could they have done more to regain customers' trust?

LINK
http://www.businessweek.com/articles/2014-03-13/target-missed-alarms-in-epic-hack-of-credit-card-data

WORKS CITED

Anonymous. (2014). The Target breach, by the numbers. Krebs on Security. Retrieved from http://krebsonsecurity.com/2014/05/the-target-breach-by-the-numbers/

Bloomberg. (2014). Hacking timeline: What did Target know and when? *Bloomberg Businessweek.* Retrieved from http://www.businessweek.com/videos/2014-03-13/hacking-timeline-what-did-target-know-and-when

Finkle, J., & Skariachan, D. (2014). Target breach worse than thought, states launch joint probe. Reuters. Retrieved from http://www.reuters.com/article/2014/01/10/us-target-breach-idUSBREA090L120140110

Grueter, E. (2014). Deciphering the Target data breach, how POS systems are compromised. docTrackr. Retrieved from http://www.doctrackr.com/blog/bid/368859/Deciphering-the-Target-Data-Breach-How-POS-Systems-are-Compromised

Hsu, T. (2014). Target CEO resigns as fallout from data breach continues. *LA Times.* Retrieved from http://www.latimes.com/business/la-fi-target-ceo-20140506-story.html

Jayakumar, A. (2014). Data breach hits Target's profits, but that's only the tip of the iceberg. *The Washington Post.* Retrieved from http://www.washingtonpost.com/business/economy/data-breach-hits-targets-profits-but-thats-only-the-tip-of-the-iceberg/2014/02/26/159f6846-9d60-11e3-9ba6-800d1192d08b_story.html

Kaiser, T. (2013). Target data breach compromises 40 million customer credit/debit cards. *DailyTech.* Retrieved from http://www.dailytech.com/Target+Data+Breach+Compromises+40+Million+Customer+CreditDebit+Cards/article33963.htm

Malcolm, H. (2014). Target sees drop in customer visits after breach. *USA Today.* Retrieved from http://www.usatoday.com/story/money/business/2014/03/11/target-customer-traffic/6262059

Schleicher, M. (2014). Data breach case study: Lessons from Target data heist. TechInsurance. Retrieved from http://www.techinsurance.com/blog/cyber-liability/data-breach-lessons-from-target/

Target. (2013). Data breach FAQ. Target. Retrieved from https://corporate.target.com/about/shopping-experience/payment-card-issue-FAQ

the organization, the proliferation of social media has put much more control in the hands of users.

Withholding information in today's technological society is virtually impossible. Controlling information or the "spin" on information is also unlikely when publics have many sources from which to validate and source information. This makes **misinformation** and **disinformation** from external sources a significant concern for organizations. Building trust-based relationships with publics is the only approach that results in sustained credibility.

Essentially, then, we in communications and marketing must think of our publics in terms of strategic communities. Wilson (1996 and 2001) contends we must approach our publics as **strategic cooperative communities,** focusing on relationship-based interaction among all members of a community to achieve individual and collective goals.

Building relationships with publics

From the synthesis of the business-based strategic management approach to public relations and the strategic cooperative communities model, five characteristics emerge to typify organizations operating within this style of management.

The **first** characteristic is long-range vision. Rather than selecting key publics and critical issues by their immediate effect on the organization, companies identify all potential organizational publics and systematically establish relationships. They are using their relationships to identify the issues that will be critical in the next century, not just the next decade. They have a respect for people and work toward a consensus for action.

The **second** is a commitment to community, not just to profit. Companies involved in the community are often led by a CEO who is personally committed to charitable work. Commitment at this high level gives the organization's community involvement strength and integrity because it is based on a sincere desire to serve rather than to manipulate for the sake of profit alone. It is understood that what is good for or improves the community almost always benefits the company, as well.

The **third** characteristic, underlying this community commitment, is an organizational value orientation emphasizing the importance of people. Progressive policies and initiatives based on trust of and respect for employees are usually evidence of a people-first orientation. Human dignity is highly valued, and policies and procedures are designed accordingly.

The **fourth** characteristic is cooperative problem-solving. The company values employees who will work together to solve problems. Employees are given the latitude to design and implement solutions within their work areas, relying on management to provide an overall vision. In such an environment, employees are not afraid to make a mistake because management understands that mistakes are indicative of an effort to progressively solve problems.

Lastly, the **fifth** characteristic is that such organizations build relationships with all of their publics based on mutual respect, trust and human dignity — not just on self-interested gain. These relationships engender an environment in which

MISINFORMATION
Information that is unintentionally inaccurate or misleading.

DISINFORMATION
Information that is intentionally inaccurate or misleading.

STRATEGIC COOPERATIVE COMMUNITIES
Relationship-based interaction among all members of a community to achieve individual and collective goals.

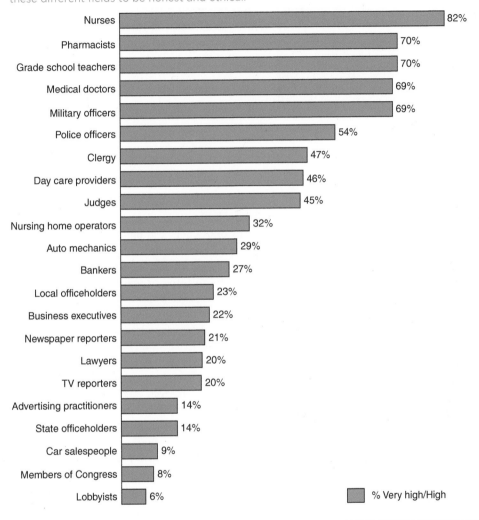

Figure 1.2
The most honest/ethical professions

The results of this poll show the percentage of respondents that considered people in these different fields to be honest and ethical.

Profession	%
Nurses	82%
Pharmacists	70%
Grade school teachers	70%
Medical doctors	69%
Military officers	69%
Police officers	54%
Clergy	47%
Day care providers	46%
Judges	45%
Nursing home operators	32%
Auto mechanics	29%
Bankers	27%
Local officeholders	23%
Business executives	22%
Newspaper reporters	21%
Lawyers	20%
TV reporters	20%
Advertising practitioners	14%
State officeholders	14%
Car salespeople	9%
Members of Congress	8%
Lobbyists	6%

■ % Very high/High

Source: © Gallup Organization

community members seek solutions where all participants win. The community begins to look out for the best interests of the organization because it is in the community's best interest for the organization to thrive.

Relationships with an organization's publics are based on critical values that have little to do with profit motivation. The values of service, respect and concern for community are at the base of the relationships we establish with people. This is evidenced in a 2013 Gallup poll, listing nurses as the most honest and ethical professionals (see Figure 1.2). Whether we build a relationship with an individual, or with an individual representing an organization, does not change the fact

that the strength of the association is determined by the salience of shared values that place a priority on people.

It is important to note that durable relationships are not created out of rationalist, bottom-line business management techniques. They are created and strengthened through mutual trust, respect, cooperation and benefit. Trust is based on honest communication and is a prerequisite of cooperative relationships as well as a tangible result.

The strategic communications planning matrix

Now that we have established a strategic role for communications in developing relationships, we are able to implement the planning that will accomplish specific objectives and is targeted at publics immediately important to the organization. If we have worked to identify and assess our strategic relationships, the selection of key publics for any particular communication or marketing effort will be simplified and much more accurate. We have less chance of omitting a critical public, and we know more about all of our publics. Part of our research is already done. We are also better prepared to send messages because our relationships with organizational publics have been maintained and strengthened in our overall approach to marketing and communication.

A strategic, **analytical** approach to an organization's communication is absolutely requisite. Public relations has used the four-step RACE model — research, action planning, communications and evaluation — but making that process truly analytical, so that each step is determined by the information acquired and decisions made in previous steps, is a challenge. Incorporating feedback during implementation and making needed alterations to ensure success is even more difficult.

Effective practitioners are doing the kinds of research and measurement that helps to make wise decisions. But doing so requires a framework for applying what we have learned through research.

It is not enough to discover the attitudes, values and beliefs of a segmented demographic public; we must interpret those in terms of the issue or problem at hand and predict future behavior. Determining that a public's self-interest regarding a certain issue is the health and welfare of its children is of no use unless we then formulate messages that emphasize the health and welfare of the target public's children. Identifying certain targeted media as the best channels to deliver messages to a segmented public does us no good if we then shotgun the message through mass media.

The 8-Step Strategic Communications Planning Matrix introduced in this chapter was inspired in the early 1990s by the faculty at Brigham Young University in Provo, Utah. It was designed to direct problem solving analytically, using research to

ANALYTICAL PROCESS

A process in which action in each step is determined by the information acquired and decisions made in previous steps.

make decisions in each step of communication planning and implementation. The matrix is the tool we use throughout this book to support the **strategic communications planning** process. The process begins with the identification of a problem or opportunity that sets the stage for background research and a situation analysis based on the research. It outlines additional research necessary for decision-making that will take place in the planning and implementation processes.

The planning process then starts with setting a goal that directly resolves the identified challenge. This goal may or may not be a tangible, measurable outcome. You next move forward to determine objectives — specific and measurable outcomes — that will ensure the accomplishment of the goal. Next you will want to think creatively about a "big idea." This will be an overarching strategy and message that will appeal to all publics. Specific key publics are then selected, messages determined and strategies and tactics designed to send those messages. Calendaring, budgeting and evaluation are also addressed in a strategic way, using research as the foundation for decisions in each step.

The Strategic Communications Planning Matrix enables professionals in communication and marketing to address problems and issues of concern to organizations in a strategic way, in concert with the overall organizational goals and objectives. It is enhanced by the understanding of how each organizational public forms a strategic relationship. Planning is simplified because of the nature and direction of the cooperative relationships already established, and implementation is made easier because of established channels of interaction and a predisposition on the part of the publics within cooperative communities to give heed to the organization's messages.

STRATEGIC COMMUNICATIONS PLANNING
An approach to communications planning that focuses actions on the accomplishment of organizational goals.

Summary

The global business community is rebounding from a crisis of trust. The crisis was precipitated by neglecting the relationships that are key to our success. We neglected those relationships because we were so focused on short-term profit measures that we were unable to see the necessity of strong, trust-based relationships as crucial to long-term survival.

In the past 25 to 30 years, public relations scholars and communication professionals have been struggling to return the practice of the organization's communication to its strategic role and function. Recognizing that we evolved away from, rather than toward, the strategic counseling role we should be serving, we have examined our roots in communication as well as current trends in business, society and technology.

Essentially, we are now in a better position than ever in terms of driving relationship building within organizations. We must systematically track the status of those relationships to ensure appropriate allocation of resources over the long term. Within the context of those relationships, we can more effectively use traditional analytical and strategic planning to solve organizational problems. The Strategic Communications Planning Matrix provides one of the best tools available to approach all communications challenges and opportunities within the trust-based relationship framework of today's successful organizations.

8-STEP STRATEGIC COMMUNICATIONS PLANNING MATRIX

RESEARCH

1. BACKGROUND

Planning begins with a synthesis of primary and secondary research. It provides background information on the industry, external environment, client, product, service or issue. It includes a market analysis and segmentation study that identifies current trends in opinions, attitudes and behaviors. Resources such as staffing, facilities and intervening publics are also identified.

2. SITUATION ANALYSIS

The situation analysis consists of two paragraphs. The first paragraph is a statement of the current situation and a description of the challenge or opportunity based on research. The second paragraph identifies potential difficulties that could impede success.

3. CORE PROBLEM/ OPPORTUNITY

The core problem/opportunity is a one-sentence statement of the main difficulty or prospect including likely consequences if not resolved or realized.

ACTION PLANNING

4. GOAL AND OBJECTIVES

Goal — The goal is a one-sentence statement of the overall result needed to solve the problem or seize the opportunity. The goal does not have to be quantified.

Objectives — Objectives are numbered or bulleted statements of specific results that will lead to the achievement of the goal. Objectives must be specific, written, measurable, attainable, time-bound, cost-conscious, efficient and mission-driven. If objectives are clear, key publics become obvious.

5. BIG IDEA, KEY PUBLICS, MESSAGES, STRATEGIES AND TACTICS

Big Idea — A "big idea" is a creative, overarching strategy and message that appeals to all publics you will target. Describe your big idea in one sentence. Then include a bullet for each of these three components: Big idea strategy, message and visual representation of the idea. An optional fourth bullet could be a slogan that encapsulates the big idea message and strategy.

Key Publics — Key publics include a description of each group that must be reached to achieve the goal and objectives. Identify:

- Objectives accomplished by key publics
- Demographics and psychographics
- Relationship with organization or issue
- Opinion leaders
- Motivating self-interests
- Viable communication channels

Plan specific messages, strategies and tactics for one public before moving to the next public.

ACTION PLANNING

Messages   Message design is public-specific and focuses on self-interests. Create a small number of primary and a larger number of secondary messages for each public.

Primary messages are short summary statements similar to sound bites. They identify a category of information and/or communicate what action you want a public to take. They also tie the desired action to a public's self-interest(s).

Secondary messages are bulleted statements that give credibility to the primary message with facts, testimonials, examples and stories. They provide the ethos, pathos and logos of persuasion.

Strategies   Strategies identify what a public must do to fulfill an objective and the channel(s) through which messages will be sent to motivate that action. Multiple strategies may be required for each public.

Tactics   Tactics are the creative elements and tools used to deliver messages through specific channels. A number of tactics are required to support each strategy. Examples are story placements, YouTube videos, Twitter posts, special events, infographics, websites or blogs.

6. CALENDAR AND BUDGET

Calendar   Calendars show when each tactic begins and ends and the relationship of tactics to each other in a time continuum. Calendars are organized by public and strategy to show the work required. A Gantt chart is recommended.

Budget   Budgets are also organized by public and strategy. The budget projects the cost of each tactic. It also indicates where costs will be offset by donations or sponsorships. Subtotals are provided for each strategy and public.

COMMUNICATION

7. COMMUNICATION CONFIRMATION

The confirmation table checks the logic of your analysis in formulating a persuasive plan. The action plan is reduced to a format that shows the alignment of strategies and tactics with key publics and opinion leaders; messages with self-interests; and all of these components with the objectives. The completed table becomes a tool to manage implementation of the campaign.

Key Public	Objectives	Self-interests	Primary Messages	Opinion Leaders	Strategies	Tactics

EVALUATION

8. EVALUATION CRITERIA AND TOOLS

Evaluation criteria are the desired results established by the objectives.

Evaluation tools are the methodologies you use to gather the data. These tools must be included in the calendar and budget.

Exercises

1. Discuss the corporations in your community and the national and international issues they have become active in resolving. Why do you think they selected those particular issues to address?

2. Select one or two local corporations actively doing business in your locality. Imagine yourself in the position of the corporate communications counselor, identify the strategic relationships of those organizations and assess the status of those relationships.

3. Discuss what factors have contributed to nurses being the most honest and ethical professionals today. What could be done to improve trust among PR practitioners?

References and additional readings

Creedon, P. J. (1991). Public relations and 'women's work:' Toward a feminist analysis of public relations roles. *Public Relations Research Annual, 3*, 67-84.

Cutlip, S., Center, A., Broom, G., & Sha, B. (2012). *Effective public relations* (11th ed.). Englewood Cliffs, NJ: Prentice-Hall, Inc.

Edelman Worldwide (2014, May 3). 2014 Edelman Trust Barometer. Retrieved from http://www.edelman.com/insights/intellectual-property/2014-edelman-trust-barometer/

Gallup. (2013, December 5). [Graphs Dec. 5-8, 2013]. *Honesty/Ethics in Professions.* Retrieved from http://www.gallup.com/poll/1654/honesty-ethics-professions.aspx

Golin, A. (2004). *Trust or consequences: Build trust today or lose your market tomorrow.* New York: AMACOM.

Grunig, J. E., & Hunt, T. (1984). *Managing public relations.* Fort Worth, TX: Holt Rinehart & Winston.

Grunig, J. E., & Repper, F. (1992). "Strategic management, publics, and issues." In J. E. Grunig (Ed.), *Excellence in public relations and communication management* (pp. 117-158). Hillsdale, NJ: Lawrence Erlbaum Associates.

Hainsworth, B. E. (1990). The distribution of advantages and disadvantages. *Public Relations Review*, 16(1), 33-39.

Hainsworth, B. E., & Wilson, L. J. (1992). Strategic program planning. *Public Relations Review*, 18(1), 9-15.

Heath, R. L., & Cousino, K. R. (1990). Issues management: End of first decade progress report. *Public Relations Review*, 16(1), 6-18.

Kruckeberg. D. & Starck, K. (1988). *Public relations and community: A reconstructed theory.* New York: Praeger.

Ledingham, J., and Bruning, S. (2000). *Public relations as relationship management: A relational approach to the study and practice of public relations.* Mahwah, NJ: Lawrence Erlbaum Associates.

Lindloff, T. R. (1988). Media audiences as interpretive communities. In NJ Anderson (Ed.), *Communication yearbook 11* (pp. 81-107). Newbury Park, CA: Sage Publications.

Lukaszewski, J. E., & Serie, T. L. (1993b). Relationships built on understanding core values. *Waste Age*, March, 83-94.

Newsom, D., Turk, J. V., & Kruckeberg, D. (2007). *This is PR: The realities of public relations* (9th ed.). Belmont, CA: Wadsworth Publishing Company.

Norris, J. S. (1984). *Public relations*. Englewood Cliffs, NJ: Prentice-Hall, Inc.

Wilcox, D. L., Cameron, G. T., & Reber, B. H. (2014). *Public relations: Strategies and tactics* (11th ed.). Upper Saddle River, NJ: Pearson Education.

Weiner-Bronner, D. (2014, March 21). A complete timeline of the search for Malaysia Airlines Flight 370. *The Wire*. Retrieved from http://www.thewire.com/global/2014/03/heres-every-mh370-theory-weve-considered-so-far/359355

Wilson, L. J. (1994a). Excellent companies and coalition-building among the Fortune 500: A value- and relationship-based theory. *Public Relations Review, 20*(4), 333-343.

Wilson, L. J. (1994b). The return to gemeinschaft: Toward a theory of public relations and corporate community relations as relationship-building. In A. F. Alkhafaji (Ed.), *Business research yearbook: Global business perspectives, Vol. I* (pp. 135-141). Lanham, MD: International Academy of Business Disciplines and University Press of America.

Wilson, L. J. (1996). Strategic cooperative communities: A synthesis of strategic, issue management, and relationship-building approaches in public relations. In H. M. Culbertson and N. Chen (Eds.), *International public relations: A comparative analysis*. Hillsdale, NJ: Lawrence Erlbaum Associates.

Wilson, L. J. (2001). Relationships within communities: Public relations for the next century. In R. Heath (Ed.), *Handbook of public relations* (pp. 521-526). Newbury Park, CA: Sage Publications.

CHAPTER 2

PUBLIC INFORMATION AND PERSUASIVE COMMUNICATION

"Public sentiment is everything. With public sentiment, nothing can fail; without it, nothing can succeed."

—Abraham Lincoln
16TH PRESIDENT OF THE UNITED STATES

LEARNING IMPERATIVES

- To understand the role of public opinion and its impact on successful communication with an organization's publics.

- To understand the theory and principles underlying persuasion and how to use them to change behavior.

- To understand how to use persuasive appeals.

- To understand the legitimate role of advocacy in a free market economy and the ethical standards that apply to persuasive communication.

As communications professionals, we are in the public information and persuasion business. The ethical basis of marketing and public relations is in advocacy. Advocacy is an essential societal value deeply rooted in the U.S. Constitution. Notice, for instance, the citizen's right in the U.S. legal system to an attorney or "advocate." In our organizational function as advocates, we play a critical role in a democratic society with a free marketplace of ideas and a free market economy as we provide information and advocate products, services or issues honestly, responsibly and in accordance with public and consumer interest. That advocacy is a crucial public service that allows people to make informed decisions for their lives.

Because we are engaged in public information and **persuasion**, what we do is inextricably tied to **public opinion**. What publics think and believe directly affects how they behave. As we established in the previous chapter, an organization that ignores the opinions of its publics simply will not build sufficient trust to survive in today's society. Although this text is not designed to be a comprehensive treatment of the theories and models of public opinion and persuasion, understanding some of the basic and seemingly timeless principles of persuasion is requisite to effective advocacy.

PERSUASION
Disseminating information to appeal for a change in attitudes, opinions and/or behavior.

PUBLIC OPINION
What most people in a particular public express about an issue that affects them.

Behavior: the ultimate objective

Civilizations have been engaged in public information and persuasion since the beginning of time. While much more is now known about what techniques work and why, not much has fundamentally changed in the processes used to motivate people to act. What has changed is our precision in applying research to shape specific persuasion techniques to more effectively reach and motivate well-defined publics. In modern times, Walter Lippmann published his seminal work, "Public Opinion," in 1922. His work and the work of subsequent scholars in the field essentially define public opinion as what most people in a particular group think, feel and express about an issue or event of importance to them.

In 1923, public relations practitioner Edward Bernays published "Crystallizing Public Opinion," asserting that knowing what people think isn't enough. To make a difference, we have to get them to act on their opinions and **attitudes**. As important as public opinion is, the savvy communications professional will always remember that behavior is the final evaluation. According to practitioner Larry Newman, in public relations we are ultimately trying to get people to do something we want them to do, not do something we don't want them to do or let us do something we want to do.

ATTITUDES
Collections of beliefs organized around an issue or event that predispose behavior.

Knowing what our publics think is only useful insofar as it leads us to accurately predict what they will do. Even when we simply disseminate information in the public interest, we typically do so with some behavioral expectation in mind. A public information campaign about the risk of influenza isn't just informing people; its purpose is to motivate people to practice preventive behaviors like getting a flu shot or using hand sanitizer. We must determine what behavior we are trying to influence, and then lay the groundwork to get there.

Shaping attitudes to change behavior

According to Milton Rokeach (1968), behavior is based on attitude, which he called a predisposition to behave. Working in the 1960s and 70s, he created a theory of beliefs, values and attitudes (see Figure 2.1), which was further developed by Martin Fishbein and Icek Ajzen as the theory of reasoned action and, subsequently, the theory of planned behavior. Rokeach asserted that the fundamental building blocks of our cognitive system are **beliefs**. Beliefs are inferences we make about ourselves and about the world around us. From observation, we infer that the sky is blue, that dark clouds result in rain, that leaves on trees are green. Rokeach said that some beliefs are more central to an individual's cognitive system than others. These core beliefs, or **values**, are typically well established and relatively stable. They are difficult to change because they are fundamental to the individual and his/her belief system. They function as "life guides," determining both our daily behavior and our life goals.

BELIEFS

Inferences we make about ourselves and the world around us.

VALUES

Core beliefs or beliefs central to an individual's cognitive system.

For example, if someone challenges our belief that leaves are green by pointing out red leaves on certain trees, it doesn't really shake our world. But if someone challenges our value that a supreme being created those trees, it causes dissonance and discomfort because that "value" is central to our cognitions.

According to Rokeach, collections of beliefs and values organize around a focal point, such as an issue, an event or a person, to form an attitude. He defines attitudes as predispositions to behave. Attitudes determine an individual's behavior in any given situation. Rokeach uses gardening as an example. The collection of an individual's beliefs — that gardening is fun, that it saves money, that it releases tension and that it produces beautiful flowers — will result in a favorable attitude toward gardening. Given the absence of intervening attitudes, a person's collection of beliefs and resultant attitudes will motivate his/her gardening behavior.

For communications professionals to motivate behavior then, they must understand and tap into core beliefs and values that shape attitudes. Rokeach found that changing the collection of beliefs and values surrounding an issue or event could change the attitude and resultant behavior. Remembering that core beliefs are difficult to change, we may try to tap into a value and base the alteration of peripheral beliefs on that central belief. We may also need to motivate people to change the relative importance of a belief or value to help us build a foundation for attitude change. Or we may introduce beliefs and values into the collection that hadn't before been considered relevant. At any rate, it is important for us to recognize that people do not do something just because we want them to do it or because we think they should consider it in their self-interest. People behave in their self-interest as

Figure 2.1
Rokeach's theory of beliefs, values and attitudes

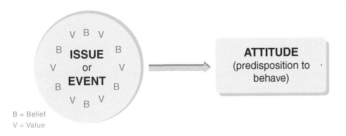

B = Belief
V = Value

Figure 2.2
Theory of reasoned action, adapted from Fishbein and Ajzen

they define it, according to their own beliefs and attitudes. Changing behavior requires addressing those beliefs and attitudes.

In the 1970s, Fishbein and Ajzen (1980) developed Rokeach's work further to help us understand attitudes and to predict and change behavior. They asserted that behavior was not just a result of the influence of attitudes (collections of beliefs and values), but also of **subjective norms** (see Figure 2.2.) Subjective norms are how we perceive others expect us to behave. Subjective norms may also be how we perceive society expects us to behave. Even more critical may be how we think people important to us, such as peers and parents, would like us to behave. Fishbein and Ajzen's theory of reasoned action advanced Rokeach's model using both attitudes and subjective norms as the foundation of intended behavior, which then becomes behavior. Subsequently, Ajzen (1991) added one additional factor — perceived behavioral control — to create the theory of planned behavior.

Rokeach's work primarily addressed the beliefs and values that are the building blocks of attitudes which predispose our behavior. Fishbein and Ajzen studied subjective norms as an addition to attitudes to formulate behavioral intention. In 1990, social scientist and public relations practitioner Pat Jackson developed a behavioral model of public relations (Figure 2.3) that focuses on converting attitudes or

SUBJECTIVE NORMS
Perceived behavioral expectations.

Figure 2.3
Pat Jackson's behavioral public relations model

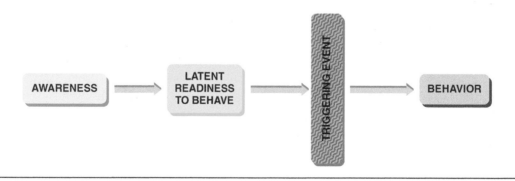

behavioral intentions into actual behavior. His model addresses a public's progression from awareness to actual behavior change as a result of communication efforts.

In Jackson's model, the awareness stage is the public information process. Word-of-mouth, publicity, online posting, publications and other communication tools create awareness and reinforcement of an issue. They should be designed to tie the message into people's existing perceptions and attitudes, or to adjust those attitudes if necessary. Awareness efforts must be based on quality research to determine the attitudes and perceptions that are the foundation for a certain public's behavior or potential behavior. From this awareness, people begin to formulate a readiness to act — an attitude, predisposition to behave or behavioral intention. Converting the attitude into action requires some kind of **triggering event** such as an election in a political campaign or a sale at a clothing store. The event thus transforms readiness into actual behavior.

TRIGGERING EVENT
An event that transforms readiness to act into actual behavior.

Using Rokeach's initial formulation and Fishbein and Ajzen's development of the theory, combined with Jackson's behavioral model, we know that understanding attitudes is essential in understanding and predicting behavior. And we know that influencing and changing the beliefs and values that shape attitudes will allow us to influence and change attitudes, which then changes behavior. For example, research shows that efforts to stop smoking among Hispanic males are far more successful when the appeals focus on family relationships and responsibilities. Smoking behavior among Hispanic males is facilitated by attitudes comprised of beliefs regarding the pleasure and peer acceptance associated with smoking. When beliefs and values are introduced regarding relationships with family and children, and how smoking affects their health and futures, stop-smoking appeals are dramatically more effective. Taking the three models together, we understand that the attitudes underlying behavior must be influenced and changed (by altering the set of beliefs), and then a triggering event, for example, a workplace "smoke out," must be used to motivate the behavior change.

Another set of theories that aids us in understanding how to change attitudes is the balance or cognitive consistency theories. Basically this body of research has found that people are comfortable when their beliefs, attitudes, knowledge and behaviors are consistent. The presence of conflict among those cognitive elements creates discomfort or dissonance. Leon Festinger (1957) contends that when the cognitive elements are in conflict, people tend to reduce or eliminate the dissonance by changing the elements or introducing new elements (such as new information).

The classic example is that of a smoker. In today's environment with today's information, smoking behavior potentially causes great dissonance or conflict in the cognitive processes. The smoker will try to reduce the dissonance. One way would be to change one or more of the cognitive elements, such as behavior, by stopping smoking. Another way would be to add a new element, like switching to an e-cigarette, which is perceived to be less harmful. A third way is to see the cognitive elements as less important than they used to be (e.g., longer life isn't such a desirable belief if I have to give up pleasure to achieve it). A fourth method would be to seek consonant information, such as evidence contradicting the health hazard studies. Fifth, you might reduce the conflict among cognitive elements by distorting or misinterpreting (misperceiving) the information

Barack Obama gives campaign speech in Charlotte, N.C.

available on the ill effects of smoking. Finally, you have the option to flee the situation, or simply refuse to contemplate the conflict, thereby avoiding the dissonance.

If we understand these cognitive processes, we are better able to work with people to bring about cognitive consonance — or the absence of conflict. The process of changing the cognitive elements is the process of persuasion.

Using behavior to segment publics

While demographic data has always been useful in segmenting publics, much more useful is psychographic data that includes the values, beliefs and lifestyles of publics. Knowing the behavior of publics — in purchasing, recreation and other activities — helps us segment them and design more effective messages for specifically targeted communication channels.

Studies done by James Grunig (1983) in the early 1980s concluded that publics can be identified by similarities in their communication behavior, but that the behavioral characteristics transcended the use of demographics to define them. In his research, he consistently identified four types of situational behavioral publics:

- All-issue publics (active on any and all issues).
- Apathetic publics (inactive and disinterested).
- Single-issue publics (active on one or a few issues).
- Hot-issue publics (bandwagon jumpers).

The notion that publics coalesce and emerge from situations is an important one, particularly as we deal with crisis communication and crisis management. Psychographics may be of more help in profiling these kinds of publics than demographics, but even psychographics may be of limited worth when segmenting publics by issue.

As we will see in the next several chapters, behavior is the ultimate objective. The matrix leads us through the steps to motivate behavior. It helps to determine which publics we need to target and what messages will shape their latent readiness to act (attitudes). It also aids in designing the specific strategies and tactics to deliver those messages and to provide triggering events.

Public opinion

Now that we understand that attitudes determine the behavior of an individual and, by extension, a group of individuals or public, let's examine how we discover the attitudes held by our publics. Essentially, public opinion is the expression of the attitudes of a particular public. Extensive psychological and sociological studies have been done on the phenomenon of public opinion. Its measurement — in an attempt to predict behavior — has become not only a science but also a highly profitable career track. Most of the descriptions of the phenomenon contain similar elements and can be synthesized into a straightforward definition: Public opinion is the collection of beliefs, attitudes and opinions expressed by the majority of individuals within a particular group or public about an issue or topic of interest to them.

Let's examine the elements of this definition:

- Public opinion is collective. It is not what just one individual thinks; it is the collection of what several people think.
- The beliefs and ideas must be expressed to be public opinion. Public discussion usually crystallizes or solidifies opinion into something that can be expressed.
- The opinion must be held by the majority of individuals within the group.
- The opinion is identified with a certain group or public, not the mass or "whoever" is out there. The particular public holding the opinion is identifiable from the mass. Opinion research uses demographics and psychographics to identify the specific publics expressing the particular opinion.
- The opinion is focused on a particular issue or topic.
- The masses are segmented into publics differently from topic to topic. The issue of embryonic stem cell research will create within the mass audience certain public segmentations that will be different than those created by the issue of Palestinian sovereignty in Israel.
- The topic must hold a particular interest to the individuals within the group. In other words, it must involve their self-interest.
- Interest is typically aroused and sustained by events relating to the topic or issue. The stem cell debate heats up as we begin to lose scientists to other nations that have advanced such research. At some point, other news takes precedence and attention wanes. But the debate is again fueled when someone famous contracts a disease that could potentially be cured through stem cell research.

Opinion formation

Because public opinion is a collection of individual opinions, the logical place for us to begin in determining how public opinion is formed is with the individual. A review of the basic models and principles of human communication will aid us in determining how individuals form opinions.

Opinion is basically a thought process. We attach meaning to the world around us based on the collective influence of our past experience, knowledge, culture and environment. This collective influence is often referred to as our **frame of reference**. Within this frame of reference we establish our own personal beliefs, values and attitudes which were previously discussed as the foundation of our behavior. All of our thoughts, ideas and communicative acts are processed through our frame of reference, and no two individual frames of reference are identical. Our frame of reference determines how we perceive or sense our world as well as the communication of others directed toward us.

In the mid-1940s, Hadley Cantril (1944) proposed 15 "laws" of public opinion that demonstrate the influence of an individual's frame of reference. Those laws can be synthesized into a few basic observations that serve as guides in shaping public opinion.

- Opinions are more easily influenced by events than words, but opinion changed by events requires subsequent reinforcement.
- Opinion is basically determined by self-interest, and persuasion is only effective if it maintains a consistent appeal to self-interest over time. Opinion rooted in self-interest is extremely difficult to change.

FRAME OF REFERENCE
The collective influence of experiences, knowledge, culture and environment that forms our perceptual screen.

- Information is most effective when opinion is in formative stages.
- If people already trust their leaders, they will allow them the opportunity to handle sensitive situations. People trust their leaders' decision-making more when they feel they (the people) have had a part in shaping the decision.
- Public opinion is focused more on expected results than on methods to achieve those results. People care more about an outcome than the process to reach the outcome.

TIPS FROM THE PROS

Shaping public opinion

Phil Bussey, senior vice president and chief customer officer at Puget Sound Energy, former president and CEO of the Greater Seattle Chamber of Commerce, tips you off on informing your publics.

With three decades in the public affairs and public relations business, I've learned that within the phrase, "there's a sucker born every minute," lies the temptation and ultimate undoing of those who intend to unethically persuade or mislead publics. Practitioners have a crucial and valued responsibility to inform the public on behalf of the organization. Disseminating factual information in a timely and persuasive manner helps the public make better informed decisions. Our job is not to take advantage of the uninformed; it is to educate them.

Three principles have brought me success in the world of public information and public opinion.

Honesty IS the best policy. The public will tolerate a fool, but not a liar. Don't say it if you can't back it up with evidence or facts. The only thing worse than inaccurate or misleading statements are retractions or confessions published when they are discovered. You lose not only momentum, but far worse, you lose credibility.

Speed kills. Getting your message out first "kills" the competition. Most importantly, it puts you in control. Even with bad news it limits the damage and keeps communication lines open. Remember, bad news doesn't get better with time. To be effective: be first, be fast and be factual.

Know thy customer. A major problem in dealing with public opinion is that "you don't know what you don't know." Successful practitioners work hard to understand their publics' desires, concerns and opinions and then craft their message accordingly. Use every tool and gather available research to know your audience, and be sure to focus on the grass-roots level. Know your customer, and you'll know what to say, how to say it and when to say it.

Elisabeth Noelle-Neumann (1984) has identified another phenomenon of public opinion we characterize as the "sleeper" effect. An individual's fear of social rejection or isolation may cause him/her not to verbalize an opinion he/she perceives to be in the minority. In other words, vocal groups may suppress mainstream or majority opinions because the majority believes itself to be in the minority and, therefore, remains silent. This "spiral of silence" as Noelle-Neumann termed it, or the "silent majority" as former President Richard Nixon called it, is a sleeper factor usually unaccounted for in our research unless we dig for it. Noelle-Neumann identified mass media as an accomplice in the spiral of silence because their own voice may often reflect the minority opinion, but it has become one of the loudest and most dominant voices in the free marketplace of ideas. Once the spiral of silence is broken, however, the silenced opinion flows forth like water from a breached dam. People quickly discover that others think as they do and no longer remain silent.

The phenomenon of perception

Perception is an unpredictable phenomenon, largely because it is so individually determined. Unless you have a solid understanding of an individual's frame of reference, it is impossible to predict how he/she will perceive an event, experience or message. In communication we sometimes forget that meaning is in people. Our words and messages do not transfer meaning; they can only evoke images in the minds of our public that we hope will have similar individual meanings.

In addition to being very individual, perception also carries with it the power of truth. What is perceived by an individual is what he/she believes to be true. We express this in clichés such as "seeing is believing," but the impact of perception is far greater than we usually realize. Whether or not a perception is accurate has no bearing on its power as truth to the perceiver. When police question witnesses of a traffic accident, they get as many different stories as there are observers, each absolutely certain his/her version is the truth.

Sometimes perception is so intimately tied to an individual's belief and value system that it is difficult, if not impossible, to alter it even when it is flawed. Norris calls these "cast-iron" perceptions. Such perceptions are almost impossible to change.

Some perceptions are shared with others in a group and are "preformed." We have already decided how certain things should be and that is the way we perceive them. We call these stereotypes. We often stereotype people (e.g., dumb blondes or computer geeks), but other phenomena can be stereotyped as well (e.g., government is wasteful or political revolution is bad.) Stereotypes are often useful in helping us deal with the world around us, but they become dangerous when they prevent us from perceiving things as they really are. They are also dangerous when they create an environment in which people are denied the opportunity to reach their potential.

As public relations professionals, we should be aware of Klapper's concepts of selective exposure, **selective perception** and **selective retention**. Because of the barrage of stimuli we receive from our environment, including increasing numbers of messages from

SELECTIVE PERCEPTION
The subconscious function of selecting from the millions of daily stimuli only those messages one chooses to perceive.

SELECTIVE RETENTION
The function of selecting from the stimuli perceived only those messages one chooses to retain.

Shoppers walking in Mong Kok, one of Hong Kong's busiest shopping places.

people trying to persuade us, our perceptual mechanism also works as a screen or a filter to keep us from experiencing overload. As we learn from the uses and gratifications theory of mass media, we choose the media and channels we pay attention to, and we choose those messages we want to perceive as well as those we want to retain. This is a critical principle in marketing, advertising and public relations. Our professions depend on channels to get messages to key publics, but if those publics are not paying attention to the channels through which we send messages, or are electing not to perceive or retain our messages, our efforts are useless.

For example, think about how you get your news. Few people read every story in their newsfeed from start to finish. As you scroll through an app, you read headlines and look at pictures to decide which stories you want to read. You do the same with email. You check the sender and the subject and often delete without opening. Individuals selectively perceive far fewer messages than are targeted at them in a given day, and they actually retain even less of the content once those messages have been filtered through the perceptual screen to determine whether they are useful. In fact, studies of selective perception in advertising demonstrated that people actually pay more attention to ads and consume more information about a product after they have purchased it than before. Just as agenda-setting theory predicts, they are looking for reinforcement of their purchase decision rather than using the information to actually make a decision.

Selective perception becomes an even more poignant phenomenon when we consider how new technologies have given the consumer, or public, control over how and if he/she receives information. As people seek information less from mass media and more from increasingly specialized and segmented sources, we must become more sophisticated in appealing to their self-interests. Uses and gratifications theory (1973-74) identifies three motives for media use: environmental surveillance, environmental diversion and environmental interaction. A basic assumption of the theory is that people choose how media will serve them and use media for their own purposes.

A problem with this user-driven access to information — and with social media in general — is the variable reliability of the information. Now, more than ever, misinformation abounds. Anyone with a story to tell, accurate or not, can post it. Blogs, YouTube, Facebook, Twitter, Pinterest, Snapchat all provide a soapbox for expression. Most people know all online information should be verified for accuracy, but how many actually do that? Just like we typically believe what we read from traditional media news sources, so also do we believe what is online — except online information is much more suspect than information filtered through journalists.

What all this means for communications professionals is that we must make a greater effort to understand the frames of reference of our key publics, use good research to try to predict how messages and events will be perceived by those publics and design messages that those publics will select, retain and act upon. But we must also constantly monitor traditional and social media to find out the information and misinformation reaching our publics and respond accordingly.

Opinion leaders

OPINION LEADER
A trusted individual to whom one turns for advice because of his/her greater knowledge or experience regarding the issue at hand.

One of the most important influences in the phenomena of public opinion and persuasion is an **opinion leader**. An opinion leader is someone we turn to for advice and counsel, typically because he/she has more knowledge or information about the issue in question. We all have a number of opinion leaders in our lives. They may be authority figures of some kind, or they may be your next-door neighbor. When you get ready to buy a car, to whom do you talk about the best value? Before voting on a local referendum, with whom do you usually discuss it? What blogs or websites do you go to when trying to decide on a purchase or a vote or other kind of action? All of these sources are opinion leaders for those particular issues or decisions. Whether their knowledge and information comes from personal experience, special training, extensive reading or any other source, you trust their judgment.

Studies of opinion leaders show that they are usually heavy consumers of media. In the 1940s, Elihu Katz and Paul Lazarsfeld conducted studies of voting behavior that led to their seminal two-step flow theory of opinion leadership. They found that certain individuals within a community search out information from mass media and other channels and pass it on to others. (Subsequent research has altered this hypothesis to a multiple-step flow, finding that the number of relays between the media and the final receiver varies.)

Because of their possession of more information, we consider opinion leaders better informed and rely on their advice and counsel. We trust a mechanic because he/she consumes the most credible, reliable and current information on automobiles and auto repair. The mechanic also has much more experience identifying problems and making repairs than we do. We trust a doctor to be informed and know where to go to get the best information on medical diagnosis and treatment. We might know a neighbor who has a particular interest in the plants and flowers that grow best in our area. We trust the neighbor's advice because he or she has acquired knowledge and experience with plants that grow well. Plus the neighbor's yard probably looks very nice.

As these examples show, opinion leaders can be formal or informal. They are specialists on particular issues or topics and are better informed on those topics. Research also shows that opinion leaders tend to be early adopters of new ideas and products. As noted in the first chapter, some of the most effective opinion leaders are peers, and the Internet is the great equalizer for peer-to-peer communication. Viral campaigns using opinion leaders are a new reality because people trust others who are "just like" them. While the ethics of such viral campaigns are not yet fully sorted out, they are already being used with notable success.

Measuring public opinion

"Saturday Review"/world columnist Charles Frankel said, "Majority opinion is a curious and elusive thing." It is certainly not stable. It changes from moment to moment as circumstances are constantly changing. For that reason alone, any measure of public opinion is never absolutely accurate. The moment the survey is completed, the interview is concluded or the focus groups are dismissed, the results are dated material.

James Stimson (1991), a well-known scholar in the field of public opinion measurement, contends that most measures are not accurate predictors of behavior because they measure attitudes and opinions in isolation from other members of the social group. He points out that individuals may formulate opinions on issues when approached, but those opinions are altered, refined and crystallized

Goodluz/Shutterstock.com

through discussion and interaction with others. Additionally, people do not behave in isolation; they are part of social systems that strongly influence behavior.

The Coca-Cola Company learned this lesson the hard way when introducing New Coke in 1985 (Schindler, 1992). The new formulation came about in response to the wildly successful Pepsi Challenge advertising campaign that had been eroding Coca-Cola's market share. Pepsi pitted itself against Coke in head-to-head taste tests at malls and grocery stores across the country. A Pepsi representative would set up a table with two unmarked cups: one containing Pepsi, and one with Coca-Cola. Shoppers were encouraged to taste both colas and then select which drink they preferred. The representative would then reveal the identity of the two colas with a consensus choosing the sweeter Pepsi over Coke. As a result, Coca-Cola officials commissioned "Project Kansas," a secret effort to reformulate the company's flagship soda.

Taste tests for the new formula showed a strong preference for it over Coke and Pepsi. In opinion surveys, people expressed the belief that if the majority preferred the new formula, then Coke should change to it. But a curious phenomenon occurred in the focus groups. When the groups began discussion, participants favored a formula change as they did in the opinion surveys. Then, as some members of the groups began to voice their preference for the old formula, the overriding value of personal choice caused individuals within the focus groups to change their attitudes in support of the rights of those who preferred the old formula (because of taste or out of habit).

However, because quantitative opinion surveys were judged, at the time, to provide more credible data than qualitative research, Coca-Cola trusted them instead of the focus groups, changed the formula and scheduled a phasing out of the old.

For the first couple of weeks people accepted the new formula; then the outcry of the masses for the rights of diehard Coke loyalists to continue purchasing the original formula forced the company to create Coca-Cola Classic — leaving the old formula on the market but also scaling back production of New Coke. That is exactly what should have been predicted from observing the focus groups. Opinion surveys that measure opinion and predict behavior in isolation from the group may be inherently flawed. Coke found out that Americans value the right of personal choice more than they value the majority's rule. New Coke was eventually renamed Coca-Cola 2 and was ultimately discontinued in 2002.

Further, the opinion expressed by individuals in a public may reflect a number of realities other than the opinion on that particular issue. The expression may be indicative of party or organizational loyalty, peer group pressure to conform or a reflection of the opinion of an influential whose judgment the respondent may trust more than his/her own. And the combination of beliefs and attitudes that are the basis for behavior are far more complex and multidimensional than a singular opinion on a particular topic. Singular opinions on an issue do not necessarily directly lead to behavior. Too many other factors, events and attitudes intervene. Unless the measuring device is carefully designed and implemented, it may not measure the most salient opinion and resultant behavior. The results will be misleading, causing costly strategic errors.

In spite of the difficulties, we must still do our best to measure public attitudes and opinions as a foundation for persuasive efforts. Measurement problems are identified to aid us in designing research that corrects for and minimizes difficulties. This is done to help us understand and better interpret results, as well as to design programs that are flexible enough to respond to changing opinions. The methods for measuring public attitudes and opinion are described more fully in the next chapter. The most typical are survey research, which yields statistical results, and personal interviews and focus group research, which typically provide qualitative results.

Methods of persuasion

More often than not in today's environment, public relations engages in disseminating information rather than in heavy-handed persuasion. Knowledge and information are key cognitive elements that help shape attitudes and opinion. Further, public information provides the awareness foundation necessary for persuasion to effectively motivate publics. Nevertheless, sometimes even objective information of benefit to a public must be designed and delivered in such a way as to draw the attention of publics accustomed to filtering out messages to prevent overload. The message itself may not be designed to persuade, but the targeted publics may need to be persuaded to pay attention to the message.

Newsom, Turk and Kruckeberg (2013) contend that people are motivated to action through power, patronage or persuasion. Power may be legitimate authority, peer group pressure or informal status. Patronage is simply paying for the desired behavior, either monetarily, in kind or by favor. Persuasion, the method most used by public relations, typically involves information dissemination and devises appeals to change attitudes and opinions to achieve the desired behavior.

Methods and approaches to persuading typically focus on getting a public to pay attention to a message, accept it and retain it. Yet persuasive attempts fall short if they do not address motivating behavior. Carl Hovland's Yale Approach suffers from just such a shortfall. His four-step approach addresses persuading people to a particular opinion through gaining attention, designing the message for comprehension (understanding), creating acceptance through appeal to self-interest, and finally, ensuring retention through well-organized and presented arguments. Hovland believed attitudes change if you change opinion. But, as we have seen, merely changing opinions is insufficient. Unless attitudes and opinions are changed in such a way that they motivate the behavior we are seeking, we have expended valuable resources (time and money) to no avail. Behavior change is not only the ultimate measure of success but also provides the reinforcement necessary to retain an attitude change. And as Jackson asserted, changing attitudes is not sufficient; behavior must be triggered in some way.

As noted earlier, opinion leaders are tremendously effective in motivating behavior. A public's reliance on known and trusted opinion leaders is often the key to motivating behavior. Reaching opinion leaders with media messages is one of the most effective persuasive methods used in public relations today.

Using mass media to influence publics

It is important to consider the effect of mass media in persuasion. McCombs and Shaw's agenda-setting theory contends that mass media do not tell people what to think; rather, they tell people what to think about. Media sets the agenda or determines what is important, and, as Lazarsfeld reiterates, they serve to reinforce existing attitudes and opinions. Uses and gratifications theory affirms that people choose the media they pay attention to based on their own needs. Agenda-setting studies have also shown that people select what they pay attention to for the purpose of reinforcing the decisions they have already made. People who had already purchased a car were the heaviest consumers of car ads. The same phenomenon is true across the board. People choose news channels that project their same political and social opinions. The vast majority of Sean Hannity's listeners are people who agree with his political, social and economic attitudes. For all of these reasons, media have not traditionally been considered persuaders.

Nevertheless, additional research has discovered what are called second-level agenda-setting effects (also known as **media framing**) that do have persuasive power. In their delivery of a story, media "frame" it with a set of attributes that affect how the audience perceives the story. In an extreme example, media may report that a man drank the water from a well and died. The impression is that the water was contaminated and killed him. But detail omitted from the brief media report may have changed the perception had it been included. Suppose the man was suffering from terminal cancer and had returned to the farm of his youth to drink once more from its pure water before he died. That changes the story entirely. There is no question that media frame stories and thereby inject bias, whether intentionally or not. In public relations, we "frame" messages to persuade publics. But we must always use care to never frame messages in deceptive or manipulative ways.

We live in a changing world where some media personalities seem to have transcended the role of information provider and agenda setter; certain commentators and newscasters have obtained a celebrity status that has made them as influential as opinion leaders in shaping public opinion. The riots in Los Angeles following the verdict in the Rodney King case in the 1990s are a poignant warning that media, and the 30-second sound bite, may have more power than previously thought in shaping opinion. Although a jury in a trusted judicial system weighed all the available evidence and rendered its conclusion, most of America had already determined guilt based on more limited information provided by newscasters, newsmagazines and talk show hosts. As advancing technology exacerbates the isolation of individuals in our publics, media celebrities like Oprah Winfrey, Matt Lauer and Anderson Cooper have become increasingly influential.

Out of mass media research have come other theories that prove useful to our persuasive efforts. **Media priming** is one such theory. Research has shown the power of media to "prime" publics at crucial points in a political or social process. The salience or importance of issues is affected by the amount of media coverage those issues receive. While priming effects diminish over time, new stories can be introduced to revive the issue at key points in a debate, election or other decision

FRAMING
Designing a message to influence how an issue or event is perceived.

PRIMING
Increasing the salience of a public issue through strategically timed media coverage.

Is he an "American treasure?"

MINI CASE

ALEC BALDWIN

BACKSTORY

While on the tarmac before departing from LAX, actor Alec Baldwin was asked by American Airlines' crew members to stop playing the game Words with Friends. According to flight attendants, Baldwin became violent and aggressive. Baldwin then tweeted angrily about American Airlines' staff as the plane made its way back to the gate. He was subsequently removed from the flight and continued to tweet insults aimed at the crew. His antics gained national media attention, threatening his image and potentially jeopardizing his career as a TV and film actor.

KEY FACTS

- Baldwin was removed from an American Airlines flight on Tuesday, Dec. 6, 2011.
- Baldwin's tweets berated American Airlines. One said it was "where Catholic-school gym teachers from the 1950s find jobs as flight attendants."
- In the media frenzy that followed, nearly 90 news stories reported his removal from the flight, calling him a "hothead" and "plane crazy."
- Zynga, the creators of Words With Friends, showed support for Baldwin by tweeting "Let Alec Play."

How would you respond?

ALEC BALDWIN'S STRATEGY

Baldwin's rep, Matthew Hiltzik, responded quickly on the actor's behalf. This helped diffuse the situation and gave the story a shorter life, but it could've been better. Hiltzik explained that "Alec was asked to leave the flight for playing 'Words with Friends' while parked at the gate. He loves WWF so much that he was willing to leave a plane for it, but he has already boarded another AA flight."

The day after the incident, Baldwin issued an apology to the other passengers. He admitted on *The Huffington Post* blog that he let the situation "get the better" of him. This was a good move to shorten the life of the story; however, Baldwin continued to rant about the airline's low-quality service, comparing it to riding a Greyhound bus. Undoubtedly at his agent's recommendation, Baldwin deleted his Twitter account. Hiltzik claimed that this was in an attempt to better focus on his role in NBC's "30 Rock."

NBC/NBCUniversal/Getty Images

(Continued)

Is he an "American treasure?" (*continued*)

Finally, he made a brilliant cameo appearance on "Saturday Night Live" the week of the incident. Playing the role of an American Airlines pilot, he issued an apology to Mr. Baldwin, justified playing a game "for smart people" and referred to himself as "an American treasure."

RESULTS

- Baldwin maintained his popularity, and NBC signed a new two-year contract with him in March 2012.
- "30 Rock" viewership ratings for Baldwin's season six premiere on January 12, 2012, remained strong, bringing in more than 4.47 million viewers.
- Baldwin's popularity ranking on IMDB's STARmeter reached the highest point during the incident since mid-April 2011.

WORKS CITED:

Alec Baldwin. (n.d.). In IMDb Pro. Retrieved from https://pro-labs.imdb.com/name/nm0000285/graph

American Airlines. (2011, December 7). In Facebook [Fan page]. Retrieved February 20, 2014, from https://www.facebook.com/AmericanAirlines/posts/10150397380436078

Baldwin, A. (n.d.). In IMDb Pro. Retrieved from http://pro.imdb.com/name/nm0000285/news?year=2011;start=241

Baldwin, A. (2011, December 7). My flying lesson. *The Huffington Post*. Retrieved from http://www.huffingtonpost.com/alec-baldwin/american-airlines-service-_b_1135201.html

Calabrese, E. (2011, December 7). 'Plane crazy' Alec grounded. *New York Post*. Retrieved from http://nypost.com/2011/12/07/plane-crazy-alec-grounded/

Derschowitz, J. (2011, December 12). Alec Baldwin mocks American Airlines incident on "Saturday Night Live." *CBS News*. Retrieved from http://www.cbsnews.com/news/alec-baldwin-mocks-american-airlines-incident-on-saturday-night-live/

Peterson, K., & Daily, M. (2011, November 29). American Airlines files for bankruptcy. *Reuters*. Retrieved from http://www.reuters.com/article/2011/11/30/us-americanairlines-idUSTRE7AS0T220111130

Puente, M. (2011, December 8). Alec Baldwin's Twitter rant: A 140-character cautionary tale. *USA Today*. Retrieved from http://usatoday30.usatoday.com/life/people/story/2011-12-07/Alec-Baldwin-Twitter-rant/51713766/1

Seidman, R. (2012, January 13). Thursday final ratings: 'Big Bang Theory' adjusted up; 'Private Practice' adjusted down. *TV by the Numbers*. Retrieved from http://tvbythenumbers.zap2it.com/2012/01/13/thursday-final-ratings-big-bang-theory-adjusted-up-private-practice-adjusted-down/116462/

Turnier, C. (n.d.) American Airlines, Greyhound, or Alec Baldwin: Which brand is at stake? *Talentzoo.com*. Retrieved from http://www.talentzoo.com/beneath-the-brand/blog_news.php?articleID=12484

(2011, December 7). Alec Baldwin kicked off plane, American Airlines responds. *The Huffington Post*. Retrieved from http://www.huffingtonpost.com/2011/12/07/alec-baldwin-kicked-off-p_n_1133909.html

(2011, December 8). Alec Baldwin apologizes to passengers, not to American Airlines. *CBS News*. Retrieved from http://www.cbsnews.com/news/alec-baldwin-apologizes-to-passengers-not-american-airlines/

(2012, December 3). Alex Baldwin signs new Universal TV deal. *The Huffington Post*. Retrieved from http://www.huffingtonpost.com/2012/12/03/alec-baldwin-universal-tv-nbc-deal_n_2232735.html

process. As skilled public relations practitioners place truly newsworthy stories in mass media, we can activate priming to our persuasive advantage.

A powerful example of this occurred in the Elizabeth Smart case. Elizabeth was abducted at age 14 from her family's Salt Lake City home on June 5, 2002. The story made national news, but the search for Elizabeth turned up nothing in the days that followed. Nonetheless, an adept public relations expert hired by the Smart family kept the story alive locally, releasing new information and details about the investigation every few days or weeks until Elizabeth was found nine months later on March 12, 2003, in Sandy, Utah, 18 miles from the site of her abduction. This is an extraordinary example of media priming — being able to keep the story alive for nine long months. Elizabeth was found because members of the public recognized her captors Brian Mitchell and Wanda Barzee from news pictures they had seen — despite the fact that they were all wearing wigs at the time of their capture.

Persuasive appeals

Effective persuasion always requires some kind of appeal to self-interest. As will be fully explored in a later chapter, self-interest should not imply selfishness. Often the most effective **persuasive appeals** are to our publics' better nature: for the benefit of community or society or disadvantaged populations. Appealing to the self-interest of those you are trying to motivate is an essential element of all persuasive messages.

Perhaps the most effective formula for persuasive appeals dates back more than two millennia to the philosopher and rhetorician Aristotle. His classic logos (logical argument), pathos (emotional appeal) and ethos (source credibility) are as salient today as they were in ancient Greece. These three appeals constitute the majority of persuasive appeals used in communications, either singly or in combination. These appeals should be carefully selected to address your public's overriding self-interest.

The message itself is a key element of persuasive appeal. It should appeal to an individual's self-interest and use other appropriate appeals based on key public research. Equally as important, the medium or channel for delivery must be carefully selected. The medium must be credible and believable, capable of reaching the target public and technologically suited to the message itself. For example, television has high credibility and mass viewership, but it is typically suitable only for short, simple messages. Detailed messages are better conveyed through print and online media.

Robert Cialdini has developed an intriguing persuasion strategy he calls self-persuasion. He identifies five key elements:

1. *Consistency*. Once committed to an opinion, people behave accordingly. And those commitments are reinforced through behavior. Studies show that volunteers serving a cause are much more likely to donate to that cause than those who are not involved.
2. *Reciprocity*. People will actively support something if they feel they owe something to the person or organization inviting their support.
3. *Social validation*. This is the bandwagon effect. People are influenced by others' beliefs and behaviors. Get a lot of people to use a product, and everyone thinks they have to have it.

PERSUASIVE APPEALS
Appeals to self-interest to enhance persuasion and motivate behavior.

4. ***Authority (opinion leaders)***. People follow the advice of someone they trust who has knowledge on the subject.
5. ***Scarcity***. People rush to support or obtain something that is disappearing. If the availability is limited, people want to get it before it is gone.

Research-based persuasion efforts

As you can see from preceding discussion, while much research has been done to understand and perfect the persuasion process, there are too many variables in the human psyche and behavior for persuasion to be an exact science. Every public, every situation, every purpose is different and requires extensive examination and analysis. No perfect formula exists. Every effort to persuade is different; no two are alike, although some similarities may exist. Each effort will require fresh thought and new ideas, based on solid research. We need to do research to understand our publics intimately. We need to know their demographics and psychographics and refrain from relying on old research for that information. Fresh data and ongoing research is necessary to understand the continually changing publics we address.

Further, new research into persuasion techniques and appeals is constantly emerging. For example, we know from research that widespread use of product-warning labels may be responsible for consumer desensitization to their safety information. They are no longer an effective communication tactic to convey safety procedures. Research also tells us that when we want to get a public to adopt a preventive behavior such as getting a flu shot, that a gain-framed message is more effective (e.g., avoid getting sick this winter.) But when trying to motivate screening behavior such as getting a mammogram, loss-framed messages work best (e.g., failure to detect tumors early limits your treatment options.)

Similarly, much research has been conducted on different public segments. We have extensive data on the attitudes, lifestyles, values, behaviors, preferences and media use of every conceivable public segment. We have available to us extensive and continually updated profiles of publics based on age, ethnicity, religion, recreation, political leanings, special interests, hobbies, professions and every other possible segmentation. We know their media habits, their information preferences, their opinion leaders. In today's data-rich environment there is no need for guesswork. We have information literally at our fingertips to construct persuasive efforts that have high probabilities of success. If we fail, we probably didn't do the research.

The point is that we need to access the most current data and studies to select our channels and tactics and to construct our messages and appeals so they are the most effective. The techniques shown in Figure 2.4 are only a sample of the kinds of tips we can glean with a little careful research.

The ethics of persuasion

At the heart of much of the conflict between journalists and marketing, advertising and public relations professionals is the question of ethical practice. Whereas ethical codes for journalists are based in objectivity, the ethical basis for our communication efforts is in advocacy. That foundation does not make the practice of persuasive communication less ethical. In fact, advocacy is key to the effective functioning of a democratic society and a free market economy.

Figure 2.4
Guidelines for changing attitudes and opinions

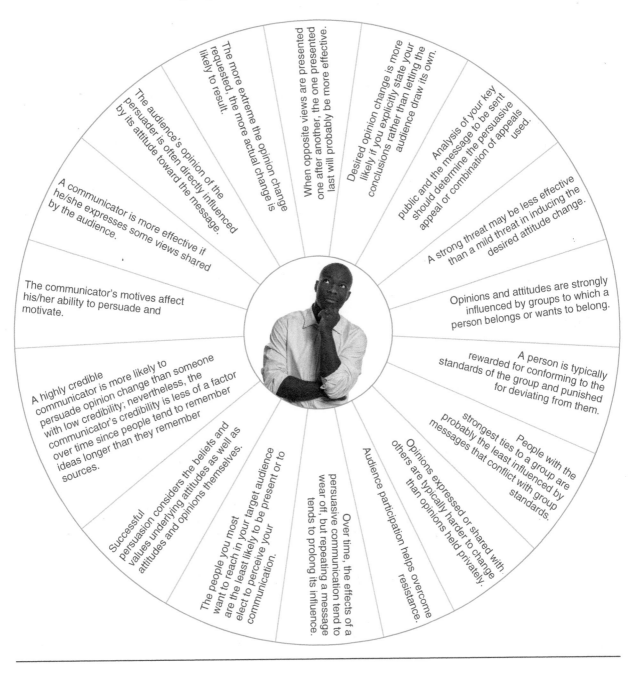

⬡ Figure 2.5
Persuasive appeals or propaganda devices

NAME-CALLING. Giving an idea a label, either good or bad, to encourage the public to accept and praise or reject and condemn the idea without examining evidence.

GLITTERING GENERALITY. Associating something with a "virtue word" that is designed to encourage the public to accept and approve the idea without examining the evidence.

TRANSFER. Transferring the aura of authority and prestige of a celebrity or opinion leader to a product, person or idea to persuade the public to accept or reject it.

TESTIMONIAL. Endorsement of a product by a celebrity or opinion leader who actually uses it.

PLAIN FOLKS. Attempting to convince the public that a speaker's (often a politician's) ideas are good because he/she is "of the people" or "one of us."

CARD-STACKING. Selective use of facts to tell only one side of the story, often obscuring the other side.

BANDWAGON. An appeal to conformity with the majority, this method tries to persuade by encouraging people to join their friends and neighbors because "everybody's doing it."

EMOTIONAL STEREOTYPES. Evoking an emotional image like the "ugly American" or a "PR flack."

ILLICIT SILENCE. Withholding information that would clarify a situation or correct an incorrect impression or assumption.

SUBVERSIVE RHETORIC. A device frequently used in political campaigns, this appeal involves attacking the spokesperson rather than the idea.

Source: The Institute for Propaganda Analysis

Because of the influence of marketing, advertising and public relations in our society, it is of primary importance that persuasive appeals be used in an honest and ethical manner. The Institute for Propaganda Analysis has formulated a list of persuasive appeals designed to mislead (Figure 2.5). Sometimes called "propaganda devices," these appeals raise the question, is there a difference between persuasion and propaganda? Some consider persuasion ethical and propaganda unethical because of its attempt to distort or mislead. Others contend they are the same, the judgment of propriety being a matter of perception.

Whereas some of the "propaganda devices" in Figure 2.5 are clearly unethical, others are used quite ethically in persuasive campaigns. For example, "name-calling" is widely used as labeling an issue or event for ease in reference. A short label reference is selected based on the perception or image it conveys. The same revolutionaries in a third-world nation are alternately considered both terrorists and freedom fighters, depending on your point of view. The label is consistent with the labeler's perception, not necessarily intended to mislead. To detractors, such a label is considered "propaganda;" to supporters it is an accurate depiction of reality.

In fact, persuasion actually began as propaganda and was not considered "evil" until World War II when Nazi Germany engaged in the practice. In the 17th century, Pope Gregory XV established the College of Propaganda to train priests to proselyte to propagate the faith. The United States itself engaged in propaganda efforts in both world wars, not only directed at the populations of Europe but also at Americans. Perhaps the most reasonable approach to evaluating persuasive methods and appeals is to avoid the persuasion versus propaganda debate and to simply follow ethical standards that prevent us from manipulating information and publics. Appendix C contains the codes of ethics from a number of research and advocacy-based professional associations such as the American Marketing Association, the American Advertising Federation, the Association of Institutional Research and the Public Relations Society of America. Following those ethical codes will help us ethically engage in persuasive communication.

According to retired television commentator Bill Moyers, the challenge for communications professionals engaged in persuasion is to do so ethically. Although many practitioners are held to ethical codes of conduct either through their employers or professions, anyone using persuasive devices should meticulously examine the integrity of his/her methods. In his book, "Persuasion: Reception and Responsibility" (1983), Charles Larson identifies a number of ethical criteria that can guide the communications professional. They can be reduced to the following guidelines:

- Do not use false, distorted or irrelevant evidence or reasoning or diversionary tactics.
- Do not deceive or mislead your audience or conceal your purpose.
- Do not oversimplify complex issues or minimize detrimental effects.
- Do not engage in advocacy for something or someone you do not trust or believe in personally.

Ethical decision-making is critical to our reputation as professionals. Although ethical codes and behavior are addressed more fully in a later chapter, it should be noted here that all decisions we make as communications professionals affect the profession itself, as well as our own status and reputation. No decisions are free from ethical considerations; every decision we make as practitioners has ethical consequences. Being aware of those consequences and carefully examining our proposed plans and behaviors according to sound ethical principles will help us avoid the ethical land mines that some of our colleagues unwittingly encounter.

Persuasion in and of itself is not unethical. Advocacy has a strong history and important role in our free society. Nevertheless, it must be conducted according to principles that support not only the public interest but also the public's right to know and choose.

Summary

Marketing and public relations is the business of disseminating information, persuading opinion change and motivating behavior. Since behavior is based on values, beliefs and attitudes, it is imperative we understand how to influence those cognitive elements or we will not meet with success. Sometimes providing public information is enough; often it is not. Persuasive methods, used ethically and responsibly, are inextricable elements of advocacy communication.

Exercises

1. Examine a local fundraising effort for persuasive appeals. What types of appeals are being used? How effective are they in this instance? What recommendations would you make for improving the effectiveness of the persuasive appeals?

2. Describe some of your basic beliefs, values and attitudes. Then, identify how they influence and motivate your behavior.

3. Identify an issue of importance in your community. Select three publics directly affected by that issue and the opinion leaders for those publics.

4. Compile a database of sources from which to draw data and information that will be useful in profiling specific segmented publics such as government websites, trade associations, research institutes and media services.

References and additional readings

Ajzen, I. (1991). The theory of planned behavior. *Organizational behavior and human decision processes*, 50, 179-211.

Baran, S. J., & Davis, D. K. (1995). *Mass communication theory: Foundations, ferment, and future.*

Broom, G. M., & Sha, B. (2013). *Cutlip and Center's effective public relations* (11th ed.). Upper Saddle River NJ: Pearson Education.

Cantril, H. (1944). *Gauging public opinion.* Princeton, NJ: Princeton University Press.

Cialdini, R. (1993). Strategic management in PR practice. In Newsom, D., Scott, A., & Turk, J. V. (2004). *This is PR: The realities of public relations* (5th ed.) (pp. 205-206). Belmont, CA: Wadsworth Publishing Company.

Dillard, J. P. & Pfau, M. (2002). *The persuasion handbook: Developments in theory and practice.* Thousand Oaks, CA: Sage Publications.

Dillard, J. P. & Shen, L. (2013). *The SAGE handbook of persuasion: Developments in theory and practice.* Thousand Oaks, CA: Sage Publications.

Festinger, L. (1957). *A theory of cognitive dissonance.* Stanford, CA: Stanford University Press.

Fishbein, M. & Ajzen, I. (1980). Predicting and understanding consumer behavior: Attitude-behavior correspondence. In Ajzen, I. & Fishbein, M. (eds.), *Understanding attitudes and predicting social behavior* (pp. 148-172). Englewood Cliffs, NJ: Prentice Hall.

Grunig, J. E. (1993). Communication behaviors and attitudes of environmental publics: two studies. *Journalism Monographs*, 81 (March), 40-41.

Jackson, P. (1990). Behavioral public relations model. *PR Reporter*, 33(30), 1-2.

Katz, E, Blumler, J. G. & Gurevitch, M. (1973-1974). Uses and gratifications research. *The Public Opinion Quarterly, 37*(4), 509-523.

Larson, C. (1983). *Persuasion: Reception and responsibility*. Belmont, CA: Wadsworth Publishing Company.

Littlejohn, S. W. & Foss, K. A. (2010). *Theories of human communication* (10th ed.). Long Grove, IL: Waveland Press, Inc.

Newsom, D., Turk, J. V., & Kruckeberg, D. (2013). *This is PR: The realities of public relations* (11th ed.). Independence, KY: Cengage Learning.

Noelle-Neumann, E. (1984). *The spiral of silence*. Chicago: University of Chicago Press.

Norris, J. S. (1984). *Public relations*. Englewood Cliffs, NJ: Prentice-Hall, Inc.

Rokeach, M. (1968). *Beliefs, attitudes and values: A theory of organization and change*. San Francisco, CA: Jossey-Bass.

Schindler, R. M. (1992). "The real lesson of new Coke: the value of focus groups for predicting the effects of social influence." *Marketing Research,* December, 22-27.

Stimson, J. A. (1991). *Public opinion in America: Moods, cycles, and swings*. Boulder, CO: Westview Press.

Wilcox, D. L., Cameron, G. T., & Reber, B. H. (2014). *Public relations: Strategies and tactics* (11th ed.). New York: Allyn & Bacon.

CHAPTER 3

COMMUNICATIONS RESEARCH METHODS

". . . digital media collectively provide searchable access to a wealth of experiences and insights, the quantity and diversity of which seems likely to increase substantially."

— Jonathan M. Levitt

<small>CONTRIBUTOR TO THE *JOURNAL OF DIGITAL INFORMATION*</small>

LEARNING IMPERATIVES

- To understand the necessity of research as a foundation for decision-making.

- To recognize the variety and sources of information available.

- To understand the basic research methodologies for effective communication research.

RESEARCH
Gathering and using information to clarify an issue and solve a problem.

In the last decade, **research** in the communications field has exploded. Before this time, it was often considered an unaffordable luxury. Now we seem to abound in data, so much so that we sometimes drown in it. The key, now, is to sort through and synthesize data into usable information to help us make wise decisions.

Not only do most successful organizations now do research, but there are a plethora of specialized consultants and research firms which have taken market, social media, environmental, communications and organizational research to levels of sophistication never before dreamed. Whereas in the past, communications practitioners found themselves begging for a pittance to find out what their publics thought, they now have executives whose first question is, "What does the research say?"

As a result, our challenge is no longer to convince practitioners to do research. At this point in your education or career, you have learned the value of research and measurement and how to do it or how to buy it. Further, there are now dozens of texts and handbooks as well as online resources for conducting research. The challenge is to provide the basic framework for thinking about and organizing research and analysis, and then, in the next chapter, to apply it in the strategic-planning process.

The role of research in communication

Research is only as good as its application to the problem-solving process. To be research-oriented means gathering and basing decisions on information as part of your daily routine. To be effective in communicating with an organization's publics, we must be constantly listening and scanning the environment for information. We should establish good communication channels so information is constantly flowing to us — resulting in adjustments and refinements of our efforts as plans proceed. Research helps us to:

- Save time and money.
- Understand our publics.
- Make sound decisions.
- Avoid mistakes.
- Discover new ideas.
- Identify potential publics.
- Identify communication channels.
- Justify plans.
- Connect with communities.

As professional communicators we should be wary of "gut reactions," knowing what we know about how people perceive and misperceive. Always test the information that leads to conclusions, and especially to key decisions. The next chapter provides a checklist of the information you need to meet the various challenges of an organization and to plan strategically to seize opportunities. In this chapter, we identify some of the best sources of information and the methodologies used to obtain it.

Research methods and the diversity of tools

Research methods are often categorized as formal and informal, quantitative and qualitative, and primary and secondary. Nevertheless, these categorizations are not parallel. For example, **formal research** is not necessarily **quantitative research**, nor is it always **primary research**. A few definitions regarding research will help to avoid confusion.

> *Formal and informal research.* Formal research implies a structured study. It is governed by rules of research that include previously identifying what you hope to learn, how and from whom. Because it follows universal rules of research, the findings are more accurate and reliable. **Informal research** is less structured and more exploratory. It does not follow specific rules. Nevertheless, it often provides valuable insight to lead us in directions of more formal discovery.
>
> *Quantitative and qualitative research.* Quantitative research gathers statistical data for analysis. **Qualitative research** is focused on individuals and groups not statistically representative of a given population. While qualitative research may be supported by some statistical data analysis, it is not governed by laws of probability. It may, however, be governed by rules of research. Focus groups, for example, are a qualitative tool. They may be informal discussions, but are more often formal research yielding important insights into a public's perceptions, attitudes and motivations. Now that focus group methodology has actually become a dominant method of market research, the rules of research governing this methodology are meticulously followed to ensure accurate insights. Although the method is classified as formal research because it follows rules and structure, it is still typically a qualitative approach that yields in-depth understanding but no statistical data.
>
> *Primary and secondary research.* Primary research implies gathering the information firsthand for a specifically identified purpose. It doesn't necessarily refer to survey research. Personal interviews as well as mail and telephone analysis also yield primary information. Primary research is research that you implement yourself or contract out for a particular purpose. **Secondary research** is primary research data originally collected for a different purpose that is now being drawn upon for a new use. Typically, it is cheaper and faster to use secondary research. In this era of omnipresent data, you should exhaust secondary sources before embarking on any costly primary research efforts.

Given these definitions, the research tools become more difficult to categorize. Focus groups may be formal or informal. They are typically qualitative, but if enough groups are conducted, some quantitative data analysis may be done on the results. Results are primary research when you organize and conduct them for the immediate purpose, but reviewing transcripts and analyses of focus groups conducted for other purposes is secondary research that may shed light on the problem you are trying to solve.

FORMAL RESEARCH
Data gathering structured according to accepted rules of research.

QUANTITATIVE RESEARCH
Using research methods that yield reliable statistical data.

PRIMARY RESEARCH
Firsthand information gathered specifically for your current purpose.

INFORMAL RESEARCH
Less-structured exploratory information gathering.

QUALITATIVE RESEARCH
Using research methods that provide deeper insight into attitudes and motivations but don't provide statistical significance.

SECONDARY RESEARCH
Information previously assimilated for other purposes that can be adapted for your needs.

Similarly, personal interviews may be informal and qualitative research. They may be one of your "listening" techniques. Or, given more structure and an appropriate design, they may be formal and quantitative, allowing statistical analysis with a high degree of confidence. They would be a primary research tool if conducted for the project at hand, yet may be useful as secondary data in subsequent programs.

Whether the research you do is formal or informal, quantitative or qualitative, primary or secondary, depends largely on what you need and how you structure it. You should determine your purpose (what you are hoping to accomplish with the research) and what you are trying to find out from whom, before you decide on the best tools to use and how to structure the effort.

Secondary research

Organizational research

The first place to begin in gathering information is within the organization itself. Many kinds of research tools are available to help gather and assess the information available to you. A communication audit examines all of the organization's communication to see if it supports the organization's mission and message. Environmental scanning within an organization monitors the mood and feelings that exist among the workers, customers, investors, suppliers and many other publics of the organization. Online, mail and telephone analysis helps you track what issues cause concern among your publics. Social media analytics help to monitor your reach and relationships. Certainly customer service and complaint sites help you track opinion trends and potential problems.

Important background information about your company or your client is found in the publications and websites of the organization. Employee publications, blogs, digital communications, annual reports, brochures and marketing materials, policy and procedures manuals, organizational charts, sales and accounting records, histories and any other material available from the organization, either in hard copy or electronically, can be valuable information. Keep in mind that such material usually possesses an inherent bias, and you need to look outside the organization as well as inside to make sure you have the complete picture. Organizations do not often open their closets to display the skeletons through their own printed and electronic material. You will get rich information about the organization through its material, but you will not usually get the bad news. And, not knowing the bad news may sabotage your communication efforts. While the organization itself is the place to start your research, it should never be your only source.

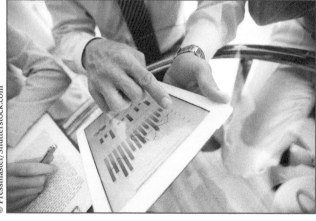
© Pressmaster/Shutterstock.com

The organization may also have data from past surveys or research. You may need some primary research to determine the mood and opinion of employees. Most organizations would benefit by taking a searching look inside before focusing research efforts externally.

Internet and library research

Information technology and the computer revolution have given us access to incredible resources for research. Information that would take weeks or months to find from original sources is now readily available at our fingertips. The communication professional of today and of the future must understand how to get good data from the Internet to compete in this new environment.

Online research has, in most cases, replaced a personal visit to the library. It gives the researcher access to the collections held by thousands of libraries and organizations and to databases full of information and references. Nevertheless, much is available in library documents that may be difficult to find or expensive to secure elsewhere. Most of us underestimate the value of the data available in our local college and public libraries. And unless you actually take the time to investigate, to talk to a resource librarian or to just explore the collection, you will not appreciate the vast amount of information at your fingertips.

Remember the latest census? It's available on the Internet. In that census, some people received a more in-depth questionnaire than the rest of us, and the psychographic data are accessible as well. Further, the census is continually updated with interim studies. Also accessible is a host of government documents and studies published every year, along with many private research studies. You can find national and local newspapers and magazines that date back years, sometimes to the beginning of publication. Often the results of opinion polls can be found and rich economic data on local, state, national and international markets.

Some universities have separate libraries for their business schools. In that case, the business library probably contains detailed market analysis and other such valuable information. While most of this information may be available electronically, there are volumes of information that can only be accessed by visiting a library in person. The more current the information, the more likely you will be able to get it via the Internet. Nevertheless, there may be significant risks in ignoring the deeper background that older documents contain.

Organizational information is also readily available on the Internet. And increasingly, you will find many independent websites, blogs and other Internet sites that contain valuable information. Be careful of the source of the information, and seek secondary confirmation when possible. The information may be credible, such as that from an industry analyst with a professional responsibility to provide such information, or it may be a site constructed by a disgruntled customer or employee containing extremely biased or inaccurate information, rumor and innuendo.

External organizations

Our tax dollars support local, state and national government offices that have a charge to operate in the public interest. Providing public information is often an integral part of that responsibility. Much of the information is now available over the Internet, but some of the valuable information you seek may only be available upon request, or by digging through studies and papers. Sometimes the bureaucracy can be difficult, and getting information can take weeks or even months. Nevertheless, the information available is often critical.

Most cities and states have economic development offices of some kind that collect invaluable information on industries and markets. State, and sometimes local, governments have information on population, wages, education, unemployment, health and just about everything else you can imagine. Environmental data is readily available from area chambers of commerce and travel councils. Be persistent; the information you want may be part of something else. You will have to do most of the searching, so start specific but be ready to broaden your search until you find documents and reports that will provide the information you need. You have to ask broad and searching questions to get to the right documents and studies. For example, asking a clerk for any studies on how much college students spend on e-books might not get you the information you want. But studies of online use or income and expenditures of 18- to 24-year-olds or the costs of a college education would all contain information on e-book expenditures.

Inherent in the missions of associations, advocacy groups or professional societies is gathering and disseminating information. One of the most valuable benefits of membership may be access to the research they gather. You may be able to access the information you want from them through their publications or resource libraries. You may have to pay a search or use fee to access the material. In some cases, you may need to get the material through an association member. But the data available is generally very rich, current and valuable.

A word of caution: When you receive data from these kinds of organizations, especially from activist groups, check the sources and methodologies used. Be aware that any information published by an interest group of any kind will be inherently biased to some degree. Make sure you understand and allow for that bias, and seek confirming and/or disputing information from other sources, or carefully examine the research methodology used and adjust for distortion.

Media research

Media research straddles the line between secondary and primary research. Depending on the purpose, it could be either. Nevertheless, it is crucial in today's media environment. A number of publishing houses produce Internet-accessible media guides and services that provide current and valuable information about media throughout the nation by category: newspapers, magazines, radio stations, television stations, cable stations and so on. Media services such as PR Newswire, CisionPoint, which is based on Bacon's media database, and BurrellsLuce media monitoring track editors and reporters by assignment, how to submit pieces and what is typically accepted. The guides also indicate readership, viewership or listenership and will sometimes provide additional **demographic** information that may be of help in profiling key publics. They at least provide a way to contact the media organization to request more detailed information. Most media organizations can provide detailed viewer, listener or reader profiles because they sell advertising. And, advertisers want to know who they're buying access to.

Media and Internet analysis and clips are a critical part of communications research and evaluation. Whether in-house or a contracted service, tracking such coverage is essential. Nevertheless, because of the time it takes to be thorough, you will usually get more comprehensive and cost-effective clipping and analysis if you contract a clipping service. Clipping services may do as little as simply clip anything (print, broadcast and other electronic media) that mentions the company or an issue of interest to the company. At the other end of the spectrum, they may engage in extensive analysis and evaluate the positive or negative impact of the pieces that discuss the organization and its competitors or any of the

DEMOGRAPHIC DATA
Information used to segment publics according to tangible characteristics such as age, gender and socioeconomic status.

issues faced by the industry. You can specify the level of service you want and pay accordingly.

Monitoring the Internet is particularly important to organizations today. And the methodology has become more sophisticated as tracking tools have been developed and refined. Most organizations have given up trying to monitor all the online conversations, but a selective approach to online listening related to issues of concern to your organization is imperative.

Primary research

Focus groups

Focus group research has become an important and reliable source of data to understand our publics. A focus group is a moderator-led discussion with four to 14 participants. The moderator asks open-ended questions to garner qualitative responses on attitudes and behavior. The moderator must be careful not to bias the discussion by injecting personal opinion or information into the group. He/she should encourage participation from all members of the group and probe for in-depth understanding. The moderator must also create an atmosphere of openness, honesty, safety and confidentiality in order to engender free and open discussion. With the permission and knowledge of the participants, the session is usually recorded (audio or video), and the discussion transcribed for further evaluation and data tabulation.

Focus group research is generally easier to conduct than survey research and provides rapid results along with depth of opinion and attitudes within the group. The discussion nature of focus groups shapes, refines and crystallizes opinions and attitudes (see Figure 3.1). Further, while not always less expensive than other kinds of research, it is often more cost-effective. Focus groups used to be conducted in communications and marketing research primarily as discussion forums for advisory committees or idea panels to supplement quantitative research. The information was often used as a precursor to survey research to assist in developing a questionnaire that adequately probed attitudes and opinions. In today's research-oriented marketplace, many practitioners recognize that, while survey research is becoming less credible as an accurate representation of publics, focus groups provide the kind of information needed to immediately address and resolve problems.

As discussed in the previous chapter, people do not behave in isolation. The discussion and refinement of opinions and attitudes which occur in focus groups often provide problem-solving behavioral information that surveys cannot. The example cited in the previous chapter of the introduction of new Coke is a case in point. Both research techniques were used, yielding opposite results. Yet because of the reputation for validity of survey research over focus-group responses, the company chose to rely on predictions of behavior based on attitudes expressed in isolation. They should have more carefully considered the group behavior that emerged from the focus groups.

Further, focus group research can demonstrate the process of opinion formation. While not representative, the group is a social microcosm of a larger public. The analysis of how attitudes and opinions change based on the flow of the dis-

FOCUS GROUP RESEARCH Moderator-led discussions with fewer than 15 participants providing in-depth information on attitudes and behaviors.

Figure 3.1 _____
Uses and abuses of focus group research

Uses

Immediate results. Focus group research is relatively easy to organize, implement and analyze. That often makes it much less costly as well.

Comfort in numbers. A small group is usually less intimidating than a personal interview. People feel more comfortable expressing opinions.

Flexible and response-oriented. Because the structure is less rigid, the group takes the discussion where it wants to go, and a broader investigation of the topic is possible. The focus is on responses (attitudes and opinions), not on the questions, so information emerges on salient topics through the natural flow of discussion.

Gauge of group behavior. Rather than researching individual behavior or potential behavior, focus groups explore attitudes and behavior influenced by the group or society, a far more reliable measure and predictor.

Issues explored and opinions crystallized. Because the group is discovering and examining attitudes and behaviors they may not have thought about before, it allows time for discussion and rumination to discover motivations.

Sensitive issues addressed. When members of the group can empathize with one another because of similar experiences, they are more open in the discussion of sensitive, value-laden issues like stem cell research or spouse/child abuse.

Attitudes of activists included. A focus group provides a cooperative atmosphere which may encourage the participation of activists and organizational detractors not willing to participate in other kinds of research.

Issues and jargon identified. The responses from a focus group identify the issues of most concern to the group as well as the language they use and can understand in discussing those topics. Such a foundation provides solid ground for subsequent research and message development.

Abuses

Weak moderator. If the moderator is weak, he/she may allow some members of the group to dominate, and others may be intimidated or refrain from offering opinions. The group result will be biased and probably useless.

Dominant moderator. If the moderator dominates the group, he/she will impose opinions and attitudes rather than probing the attitudes of the group.

Not homogenous. A focus group should be homogenous, or the members will be intimidated and uncomfortable with sharing their attitudes. Broad representation is achieved by conducting multiple focus groups among several homogenous publics, rather than mixing representation within a single group.

Too few groups. For the research to be valid, a number of groups must be conducted among various homogenous publics. Then the information can be consolidated to provide a more comprehensive look.

Generalizing to a population. Focus group research is qualitative, not statistical. You cannot generalize your conclusions to any "general public." Your conclusions are very much issue- and group-specific. They may be indications that will lead you in problem-solving or in designing quantitative research, but they do not represent public opinion.

cussion can help us know what information people need to make sound decisions and what appeals will be most effective in the larger arena. Innovations in focus group research now allow quantification of results if certain conditions are met. Conducting large numbers of groups and employing some content analysis techniques can make the data statistically reliable.

The Internet provides an interesting resource for traditional focus group research. Scheduled online chats can produce similar results without the geographic restrictions. Nevertheless, care must be taken that participants are invited and known. Otherwise, the data may not be useful for the researcher's purpose. Face-to-face group discussion is still preferable but can be simulated using tools such as Skype.

Copy and product testing

One classic use of focus groups is for copy and/or product testing. But this is not the only method by which to test. Copy testing simply selects individuals within your target publics and requests their review of copy, whether survey copy or communication copy (brochures, advertising and the like). In product testing, individuals are asked to examine and use a product and provide feedback on everything from packaging and sales methods to product quality. Product tests may be done individually by personal interview, by mail, in focus groups or online.

Honest responses in copy and product testing help avoid costly mistakes. Survey research instruments should always be tested before being implemented. Testing copy helps ensure that the messages are coming across in such a way as to produce the desired result. Marketers test promotional campaigns or products in areas representative of the overall market. Sometimes, two or three different versions of a product or a campaign will be tested in similar areas to determine which will be the most effective to roll out nationwide. Copy and product testing is one of the most valuable kinds of research available to the practitioner. Its greatest value lies in its ability to prevent mistakes — saving money, effort and time.

Psychographic studies

Values and Lifestyles Segmenting, developed by SRI International in 1978, is research methodology that classifies publics not just by demographics, but also by psychographics or attitudes, beliefs and lifestyles. Found to be far more effective in segmenting publics than demographics alone, psychographic studies help us to know what motivates individuals within a particular public. The VALS categories — achievers, survivors, sustainers, belongers and so on — have been used extensively in advertising and marketing to segment and tailor messages to specific target publics. They provide the same valuable segmentation for communication with all the organization's publics. Communicators should know the VALS categories, both the original and the more recently revised segmentations, and understand the motivations tied to the differences in attitudes and lifestyles.

Other market research firms have subsequently developed similar categorizations. In the 1990s, Claritas developed PRIZM, segmenting American consumers into 14 groups with 66 demographically and behaviorally distinct types like "Cosmopolitans" and "Kids & Cul-de-Sacs." PRIZM was subsequently purchased by Nielsen, the company known for rating what people watch on television.

Oftentimes, local media and other similar organizations will have segmented and profiled their own target audiences using a combination of demographic and **psychographic data**. Whereas some will be unwilling to disclose the information, which is quite costly to compile, others may be persuaded to share the data, especially if the request comes from a nonprofit organization or is for a charitable purpose.

Another valuable tool for understanding key publics is Values in Strategy Assessment, a process developed by Wirthlin Worldwide and purchased by Harris Interactive, which has now also joined forces with Nielsen. This tool's premise is that values are the fundamental determinant of an individual's behavior and decisions. Understanding the fundamental values of a public provides the strategy to motivate action.

Social media analytics

A new reality of today's communication environment is pervasive social media. With the range of networks available today, organizations must carefully choose those with which they will engage — those most appropriate for building relationships with key publics. Facebook was perhaps the first to become an essential presence for the organization. Now Twitter, Pinterest, Instagram, Snapchat and a host of other social media networks have become channels through which we interact with our publics. Since the effort to build and manage a social media presence is so costly and time-consuming, it is critical that organizations employ research methods to ensure the effectiveness of their social media efforts in delivering the messages of the organization, building relationships with key publics and providing the interactions key publics desire.

Quite simply, social media analytics are the tools used to measure, analyze and interpret the interactions and relationships with our key publics. It, in large part, is essentially "online listening" to help us better meet the needs of publics. The Eastman Kodak Company used online listening several years ago to determine what features consumers wanted in a digital camera. They discovered through their research that no existing camera offered the combination of features consumers were buzzing about on Facebook. Kodak engineers quickly went to work and within a few months were able to bring a new product to market that contained all of the features people wanted most at an affordable price. The new camera sold extremely well, but unfortunately wasn't enough to save the struggling company from bankruptcy in 2012.

This kind of measurement is so important that many of the social media networks, like Facebook and Google, have imbedded their own monitoring and analytical tools to track social media efforts. In addition, a host of external tools — some free, some for a fee — integrate measurement of all social media efforts. It is essential, nevertheless, that you are careful about what you are measuring. Measuring the number of "likes" or "friends" or "followers" doesn't measure whether publics are actually retaining and acting on your message. Don't confuse coverage with success. Remember that behavior — or action — is the final evaluation. It doesn't matter how many "followers" you have if they don't actually perform the action that will satisfy your objectives.

PSYCHOGRAPHIC DATA

Information used to segment publics according to values, attitudes and lifestyles.

Survey research and opinion sampling

A popular quantitative research method is survey research, although its credibility has declined somewhat in recent years because of the difficulty in securing a truly random sample. Several events have affected the ability of researchers to secure truly random and representative samples. Mail surveys have always been extremely unreliable, not only because of low response rates but also because of skewing. Only certain kinds of people will take the time to respond to a mail survey, making it anything but representative.

Telephone surveys have also declined in credibility for the same reason. And the "do not call" registry has made telephone surveying more difficult than ever. Although telephone surveys are not prohibited by the registry, the very existence of a "do not call" list seems to have given people the courage to refuse calls they would have previously endured.

Nevertheless, survey research has been a popular research technique in communications and will probably continue to be in some form or another. For example, researchers may find the personal drop-off method to still be effective because of the personal contact involved in dropping off and/or picking up a survey. It is not as easy to turn down someone face to face as it is to say "no" over the telephone. Online programs like Qualtrics make surveying easier but still face the challenge of securing representative samples. Professional research firms have developed other techniques that can also improve response rates.

Survey research is a difficult and exacting approach. It requires meticulous attention to detail at every step of the process: questionnaire design, sample selection, survey implementation, data processing and data analysis. A mistake or misjudgment at any point will skew the results, often without the researcher knowing the data is skewed.

To be valid and reliable, survey research must follow strict rules of research. The idea behind survey research is to take a sample from a population, or universe. If we follow good statistical procedures, we should be able to make that sample relatively representative of the universe, although we can never be absolutely sure of our accuracy unless we survey every individual in the population (a census). The total number of individuals surveyed in the population and the way they are selected will determine how accurately the results reflect the universe.

Statistical research on very critical issues, or in close political campaigns, needs to have a high level of confidence and a low **sampling error**, also known as margin of error. The **confidence level** reflects the researcher's percentage of certainty that the results would be the same (within the margin of error) upon replication of the survey. The margin of error reflects the percentage points that the sample results, on any given question, may vary from the population as a whole. Increasing the sample size increases the confidence level, and decreases the margin of error. The only way to be 100 percent confident and eliminate the margin of error would be to survey the entire population or take a census. Research regarding an organization's publics generally requires at least a 95 percent confidence level and a margin of error of 5 percent or less. Further, the more important or controversial the issue, the greater the need for a lower margin of error.

There are two basic kinds of survey sampling: probability and nonprobability. Probability sampling is scientifically random; every individual in the population has an equal chance of being selected. Nonprobability samples survey whoever is available, for example, intercepting students during the lunch hour as they

SAMPLING ERROR
Measured as margin of error, it indicates the possible percentage variation of the sample data from the whole population.

CONFIDENCE LEVEL
The percentage of certainty that the results of a survey would be the same if replicated.

TIPS FROM THE PROS

Beyond sampling error

Dee Allsop, Ph.D., CEO of Heart+Mind Strategies and former president of Harris Interactive Solutions Groups — producers of the Harris Poll — tips you off on understanding key factors in survey accuracy.

With the current emphasis on "big data" for critical decision-making, survey and sampling science are all about accurately measuring a small number of people to understand the attitudes and predict the behavior of an entire group. Accuracy in survey research is the direct result of identifying, eliminating or correcting for *all* types of error or bias that can enter into research. While "sampling error" is the most visible indicator of survey accuracy reported in the media, your success depends on understanding both sampling and nonsampling errors.

SAMPLING ERROR

Sampling error is the statistical estimate of variation that will occur when using a small number of people (a sample) to approximate a result from a much larger population. One way to think of sampling error is the range of results that would occur if you were to repeat your survey hundreds of times. For example, many surveys report a sampling error of plus or minus 3 percent at the 95 percent confidence interval. This simply means that if you were to repeat this study 100 times, 95 percent of the time your results would fall within a range of 6 percentage points.

NONSAMPLING ERROR

Sampling error is inherent in all surveys. We understand it well and can predict it. Other sources of error are more elusive, yet far more important to accuracy and utility of survey results.

Sample frame. Make sure the sample was taken from the group of people that matter. For example, if the survey is about who will be elected president, the sample should come from people who can actually vote for president: registered voters.

Nonresponse error. Several factors influence a respondent's likelihood to respond (e.g., mode effects, interviewer effects and sensitivity effects). Rather than sampling error, I would much prefer to know the response rate for a survey. A low response rate indicates the survey is less likely to reflect the population in question.

Construct validity. Questions can be worded or constructed to generate just about any result desired. Always read the questions that were asked before interpreting the results. Biased wording will produce biased results.

Institutional reputation. Always check to see who conducted the survey and who paid for it. Reputable companies invest significant time and resources to produce objective findings and eliminate nonsampling errors.

Take a lesson from marketing and survey research companies. Instead of worrying about "sampling error," focus on understanding how to reduce nonsampling error through good survey design, questionnaire construction, interviewing execution and data processing and correction.

enter the student center or interviewing people at a grocery store on Saturday afternoon.

There are also two kinds of errors: sampling and nonsampling. Sampling error is inherent because we are surveying a portion of the population and not the entire population. It is the percentage of possible variance in the sample's answers from the population. We decrease sampling error by increasing sample size; the closer we get to surveying the whole population, the smaller the sampling error. Sampling error is unavoidable in survey research (unless we take a census) and is measured as margin of error.

Nonsampling error is all other types of errors introduced into the process. Mistakes made in questionnaire construction, sample selection, survey implementation, data entry and tabulation are all nonsampling errors. Great care must be taken in selecting the sample as well as in designing and implementing the questionnaire. Question-and-answer categories must be designed to avoid the introduction of bias so that answers accurately reflect the information the researcher needs.

Bias can also be introduced in the implementation of the survey. Ensuring strict confidentiality of responses can lessen courtesy bias. Training interviewers to ask questions without injecting value inflection or personal comments, explanation or other bias is also critical. Further, great care must be taken in coding the surveys and entering the data. Data processing converts the observations and responses into statistics for interpretation. Data analysis manipulates the data to make logical inferences. For the inferences to be reliable, the data must be accurately entered and processed.

Finally, the inferences made must be fully supportable by the data set. A few years ago, a ballot measure in Utah proposed a light rail transportation system to be funded by a small tax increase. When the measure was soundly defeated, many analysts concluded it was a vote against light rail. In reality, it was more likely a vote against the funding method, not the light rail system itself. When we deal with statistics and

NONSAMPLING ERROR
Mistakes made in designing and implementing a questionnaire that may include definitional differences, misunderstandings and misrepresentations as well as coding errors and/or a failure to represent all populations.

make inferences from data, we must be very careful that the data support the conclusions. Otherwise, we have established a faulty foundation for decision-making.

In addition to the types of survey research discussed above, other variations have specific purposes and benefits. The following short descriptions will provide a basis upon which to investigate the techniques for any given research situation.

PURPOSIVE SAMPLING
Identifying and surveying opinion leaders to determine attitudes and behaviors.

Purposive sampling. Based on Katz and Lazarsfeld's two-step flow theory, purposive sampling identifies and surveys opinion leaders to determine attitudes and behaviors. The researcher must devise a procedure that selects the target publics' influentials (or causes them to self-select), and then surveys opinion and behavior. It is also helpful to know a little bit about opinion leaders, such as where they get their information about certain issues. Understanding opinion leaders helps us understand how they will influence others. The Edelman Trust Barometer is an example of purposive sampling.

STRATIFIED SAMPLING
Selecting the sample to ensure proportionate representation of segments within the universe.

Stratified sampling. Truly random sampling should yield a cross section of the population representative of the characteristics within the population (i.e., proportionate numbers of women and men and so on). Whenever we skew the randomness of the sample by using techniques that make it easier for us to complete the research, like surveying every "nth" number in the local telephone directory, we risk jeopardizing the representativeness of our sample. If obtaining a truly proportionate representation is critical, the research sample should be stratified so that it includes appropriate proportions of the key segments of the overall population.

Internet surveys. A growing area of survey research is conducting surveys over the Internet and through social media. While there is inherent bias because of the nature of accessible respondents, this data can be extremely valuable if the purpose is consistent with the population sample. Increasingly, organizations use this method to survey their members, employees or customers. Commercial firms with access to email lists may further facilitate this method. The low-cost nature, ease of conducting and rapid feedback of Internet surveys have fueled their popularity.

Personal interviews. Very sensitive issues and research that requires deep probing for attitudes and behaviors are best addressed through personal interviews. The personal interview ensures greater control over the sample and the data. But not only is this method costly, it requires a lot of time and well-trained interviewers. Nevertheless, in certain circumstances, it is the only viable method to secure reliable and useful information.

Benchmark surveys. This type of survey is simply a periodic reexamination of attitudes and opinions within the population. An initial survey is done to set a benchmark against which subsequent survey results are compared. Benchmark surveys are good tools for measuring change as well as for evaluating the success of a program.

PANEL STUDY
Respondents who have agreed to be surveyed repeatedly to track opinion and attitude change over time.

Panel studies. Sometimes you will want to study attitudes and opinions on a variety of issues over a period of time. Panel studies select respondents who will be available for follow-up surveys at least once and often several times. For example, a newspaper will select individuals from its readership to follow a specific issue or election and respond to queries at specific points in the campaign. Behavioral studies are also sometimes conducted by a panel to assess whether a change in behavior is temporary and what motivates permanent change.

Omnibus surveys. One of the easiest and least expensive methods of obtaining survey data is to add a few questions to an omnibus survey being prepared by a professional research company. These surveys, sometimes called tag-on surveys, usually have multiple research clients that share the costs and the common demographic data collected. Specific data gathered from the questions each client adds remains proprietary. The advantages are the cost saving shared by multiple clients and the currency of the data because the surveys are ongoing and conducted regularly. In addition, the reliability of the data is high as the sample size is usually large.

OMNIBUS SURVEY
An ongoing, open survey to which a company or organization may add a few proprietary questions at a reasonable cost.

Summary

Our environment has changed. CEOs require "big data" to make decisions, and they expect your recommendations to be logically based on reliable information. To secure a constant flow of the kind of information you need to make decisions, meet challenges and plan strategic action, you must find the right combination of continuous research techniques. The purpose of the research and the kind of information desired drive the selection of methodology. Otherwise your research will be useless because it is inaccurate or because it doesn't provide the information you need to design persuasive campaigns.

Exercises

1. Volunteer to conduct focus groups for a nonprofit organization. Subsequently, design and implement a short survey to gather opinions, attitudes and demographics on some of its key publics.

2. Visit the local library and talk with the reference librarian to discover the range of resources, databases, search engines and other references available. Search through some of the material to discover the kinds of information accessible, not just online, but in the library itself.

3. Look up the most recent U.S. Census and write down at least a dozen categories of information available through this rich resource.

4. Compile a list of "go to" sources to quickly find continually updated information on issues, publics and communication channels.

References and additional readings

Babbie, E. (1992). *The practice of social research* (6th ed.). Belmont, CA: Wadsworth Publishing Company.

Fink, A. (2002). *The survey kit* (2nd ed.). Newbury Park, CA: Sage Publications.

Greenbaum, T. L. (1997). *The handbook for focus group research*. Newbury Park, CA: Sage Publications.

Paine, K. D. (2011). *Measure what matters: Online tools for understanding customers, social media, engagement, and key relationships*. Durham, NH: Paine Publishing.

Paine, K. D. (2007). *Measuring public relationships: The data-driven communicator's guide to success*. Durham, NH: Paine Publishing.

Stacks, D. W. (2010). *Primer of public relations research* (2nd ed.). New York: Guilford Publications, Inc.

Stacks, D. W., & Michaelson, D. (2010). *A practitioner's guide to public relations research, measurement and evaluation*. New York: Business Expert Press.

think. That means growth for Green Valley as people move into town to support the new prison, and employment for people in Green Valley who have been without work because of the recent recession.

The client: The state prison system keeps a low profile, and has been able to do so because of virtually no incidents threatening public safety in the last couple of decades. The system is efficiently managed, and employees are competent. Its reputation is unsullied.

The service: The service provided by the taxpayer-funded state penal system is necessary. In this conservative area, the justice system is supported, and the concept of prisons is understood and accepted. There is little, if any, opposition to the idea of a prison; there was simply concern that it would be located here. The issue of safety is the primary concern in the minds of citizens, and the exposure of children to the idea of violent crime in society is a close secondary concern. In a small town like this, children and families would see the prison facility daily, a constant reminder of their vulnerability and the criminal element in society.

Promotions: Research shows that other states that have faced this challenge have been most successful when they have invited the community's voice in the process. Providing full information on location, plans, timelines, construction and operation along with inviting public discussion and comment have typically allowed communities to weigh the pros and cons and come to a decision of support. Economic benefits, safety procedures and safety records of other state facilities have all been powerful messages. When communities have a voice in the process, are assured of the safety of their families, recognize the economic benefits and see the meticulous planning for the least disruption of their lives, they tend to be supportive of a prison in their community. A pervasive public information effort, the support of local opinion leaders and community forums have been the most effective tools to engage publics and gain support.

Competition: The only competition is the publics' perceptions, attitudes and values. Fear for safety and fear for a loss of innocence present opposition. Those can be overcome with accurate information and recognition of the benefits. There is also a potential for legal opposition for a project like this.

Resources: Opinion leaders will be critical resources in this public information and persuasion campaign, particularly local officials, school administrators and local media. The community's need for economic growth and stability, as well as jobs, can be considered a resource. City hall, the high school and the local recreation center are established community meeting places that can be used for community forums. A weekly newspaper and a local radio station will also be resources for information dissemination.

(Continued)

Research background, situation analysis and core problem/opportunity (*continued*)

SWOT analysis:

STRENGTHS	WEAKNESSES
1. Economic benefits 2. Penal system safety record 3. Support of local leaders	1. Construction inconvenience 2. Daily visibility of negative element
OPPORTUNITIES	**THREATS**
1. Jobs 2. Local media	1. Safety 2. Family values 3. Legal opposition

Market research: This requires a full demographic breakdown of the area in terms of ages, income, employment and other characteristics. It also requires psychographic data on attitudes, values and beliefs for political, social and economic issues, as well as for the prison specifically. The psychographic breakdown would include lifestyles, recreation and other similar data. It would also include identification of opinion leaders, self-interests, information sources and preferred media channels.

SITUATION ANALYSIS

The announcement that the state is planning to construct a new prison facility in Green Valley has been met with initial resistance. While residents are generally supportive of the state's penal system, which has an excellence record of safety and competence, they fear the introduction of the criminal element into their peaceful community. Safety has been the overriding concern of residents, overshadowing the economic benefits that would come from the construction and maintenance of this facility. This project would bring in several million dollars annually and 750 jobs to this economically struggling community. It would boost the business and professional communities, improve medical facilities, strengthen funding of education and provide an economic injection that would significantly improve the quality of life for the vast majority of area residents. A solid 80 percent of residents have expressed concerns over safety, but only 35 percent could name a potential economic benefit. Fewer than 20 percent thought the new facility would improve other local services like education and health care. Nearly three-quarters of residents have a favorable opinion of the state corrections department, but only one-quarter indicate that they would be fully supportive of a prison in Green Valley. While only 30 percent are outright opposed to locating the prison here, 45 percent have significant concerns. Should those concerns not be alleviated, the opposition could potentially mobilize a legal challenge to the project.

The primary challenge seems to be public awareness and education. Other efforts have shown that giving the community a voice in the process and being completely transparent and open about plans and operation have improved community support, especially given the economic benefits. Safety will always be an issue, but the reputation and safety record of the department of corrections as well as procedures in place to ensure safety can assure the community that there is low risk associated with housing a prison in the community. Local opinion leaders and local media are well-informed on relevant issues and are supportive. But if opposition can't be converted to support, Green Valley will likely lose the opportunity to improve the standard of living for residents by locating the prison there.

CORE PROBLEM/OPPORTUNITY

Raise public awareness of safety and the benefits of the new prison to gain public support and neutralize opposition so that the Green Valley prison project can go forward without costly delay or legal opposition.

This chapter is designed to help you pull together information and analysis into a succinct document focused on a specific purpose. That purpose might be a complete strategic plan, a budget request for a new communications effort, a solution to a problem or challenge, a response to a perceived threat or a proposal to take advantage of an emergent opportunity. For our purposes here, we call this part of a plan or proposal the research section to facilitate parallelism with the Research, Action Planning, Communication and Evaluation (RACE) model. As depicted in the Strategic Communications Planning Matrix and Matrix Applied example, the research section consists of the background, situation analysis and core problem/opportunity.

Background

The background is a summary of pertinent facts and information drawn from primary and secondary research. It must be comprehensive, but written concisely. It does not contain everything you discovered in research, only the information necessary to establish credibility with your client or manager and build the foundation for your plan. A good background will often depict data and more detailed information in the form of figures and graphs. Data is more easily understood in graphic form. The checklist in Figure 4.1 represents the development of content that may be appropriate for the background. At the very least, it represents how comprehensive your understanding of organizations, issues and publics should be.

The background sets the stage for understanding the situation at hand. It contains information about the industry and the client specifically: past efforts and events affecting organizational success and where the client currently stands in the marketplace or in relationship to the issue. Remember that it selects and highlights only those bits of information that build the foundation for the solution or plan you will propose. Although you have not yet fully defined the problem or begun the planning process, some obvious alternatives will emerge as your team gathers and evaluates the research. The background should organize the information and present it in a way that will demonstrate to your client or manager the wisdom of the solutions you propose.

SWOT analysis

As you have organized and synthesized your data and information according to the first eight categories of the checklist in Figure 4.1, you have probably begun to make some inferences and drawn some conclusions relative to the issue or opportunity you are addressing. At this point, take some time to do a **SWOT analysis** — strengths, weaknesses, opportunities, threats. According to Stacy Collett, a SWOT analysis is:

> A way to analyze a company's or a department's position in the market in relation to its competitors. The goal is to identify all the major factors affecting competitiveness before crafting a business strategy.

Although typically designed to support development of marketing strategy, a SWOT analysis is useful in supporting all the relationships of the organization, not just those developed with customers. It is equally valuable to analyze the internal and external factors affecting issues and the entire environment within which the organization exists. When conducting a SWOT analysis, remember that your organization's relationships with key publics as well as the key publics' opinions and values can also be considered strengths or weaknesses.

This analysis is a great way to sum up your research and focus your knowledge on the opportunity you face and the barriers to be overcome. The process takes pages of information and focuses them into a few key words that will help shape a successful campaign.

Market research

The last step on the checklist is to use market research as a foundation to understand public segments. Remember that you cannot select *key* publics at this point because you have not set objectives. You have to decide what you need to do to meet the challenge/opportunity (objectives) before you decide who (publics) you need to reach and motivate to act. Nevertheless, this research will be invaluable to you as you proceed to plan. With good market research, you will be armed with the knowledge and understanding you need to select the best combination of key publics when the time comes.

SWOT ANALYSIS
A structured analysis tool set up in a 2-by-2 table that examines strengths, weaknesses, opportunities and threats.

The market research should contain both demographic and psychographic information (gained through primary and secondary research), as well as any information that will help you reach publics (like media preferences and habits). It includes attitudes, values, opinions, behaviors, lifestyles, purchasing preferences, recreation habits, media usage and much more. Some of the information is hard data such as census or opinion research. Other information may be from focus groups, secondary research, personal observation and informed stereotypes.

Identifying self-interests

Your research helps you determine motivating **self-interests** in connection with the issue at hand as well as with opinion leaders. This will be important in designing messages that will motivate key publics. Remember that people don't do what you want them to do just because you want them to do it. They act in their own

SELF-INTEREST
The fundamental motivation for an individual's behavior.

TIPS FROM THE PROS

Discovering self-interest

Cathy Chamberlain, a market research expert and president and CEO of CTC, Inc., tips you off on getting to what is personally relevant.

Does a mother pay an extra $75 to buy her teenage daughter a pair of name-brand jeans because they are more durable and double stitched? Obviously not. What she's really attempting to do is buy her daughter self-esteem. In-depth research that allows you to probe into a person's subconscious mind and tap into emotions and values can be the key to understanding self-interests and creating messages that change behavior. Here are five tips to help you understand what makes people tick.

Look beyond just numbers. Numbers alone often don't tell the whole story.

Understand your key audience. What really matters to them in their everyday lives? Ask yourself, "How does this issue affect them?" Look for ways to tie the issue or opportunity to your target audience's self-interests.

Ask a few open-ended questions. "What do you worry about when you can't sleep at night?" When looking at a specific issue, ask: "What are the benefits or consequences? How does it make you feel? Why is it so important to you?"

Find the themes that show up over and over. People will describe things differently, but look for commonalities that can be used to group responses into themes.

Pick two or three dominant themes. Develop your key messages around the most salient themes that emerge. Don't try to cover every point.

self-interest, and unless you can plainly identify those self-interests and appeal to them, publics will not do what you want them to do. But don't confuse self-interest with selfishness. People are often motivated to act from intrinsic values like care and concern, community improvement, quality of life, welfare of family and friends and because it is the "right thing to do."

Clearly, it is in our self-interest to feel good about ourselves, to take care of our families and friends and to improve the quality of our community and living situation. That doesn't mean money and power are not motivators, but relying upon them as the primary or overriding self-interests for our publics will probably limit our success. Refer back to the discussion in Chapter 1 about the critical values underlying trust and relationships. Your market research should help you understand publics at this deeper level, and you will be more successful as a result.

As you will see in the following chapters, appealing to the self-interest of a public is necessary at two levels. You already know you must use a self-interest appeal to move a public to action. But with the clutter of messages and information bombarding everyone today, we must also appeal to self-interest just to get a public to pay attention to our message. People choose to perceive a message only when they believe it is in their self-interest to do so, otherwise they just tune out. Regardless of the channels used, you have to get over the perception hurdle before you can complete your primary task of informing or motivating.

Identifying opinion leaders

The market research should also tell you who influences different publics. Who are the opinion leaders regarding the particular issue or challenge to be addressed? As discussed in Chapter 2, a public's opinion leaders are individuals (either by personal acquaintance or reputation) who have the credibility to effectively give advice, affect opinion or call for action. They are typically heavy consumers of media and possess significant information and expertise. Most importantly, they are trusted.

How do you identify who a public's opinion leaders are? Formal opinion leaders are relatively easy to determine. We see them every day (e.g., political officials) or know who they are by the issue or influence involved (e.g., religious leaders). Nevertheless, just because someone may hold a position of authority does not mean he/she can actually sway the opinion of our public. Identifying informal opinion leaders can be tricky. So how do we find out who actually influences a public? The answer is deceptively simple: We ask them. Part of research is asking people whose advice they trust when making decisions. Focus groups and surveys are particularly useful in this process. We can also observe behaviors — watching how people react when they receive messages from different sources.

Opinion leaders are best used to persuade and motivate. Nevertheless, their credibility is based upon our assessment of their character and judgment. Opinion leaders lose influence if they are perceived to be manipulated or manipulative. Using them in that manner is unethical and will ultimately lead to a decline in their influence.

Assessing relationships

It is also important to use the market research to assess the current state of the relationship your client has with its publics. This assessment may use a formal methodology like establishing a scale of strength indicators of the relationship — or the assessment may be more informal. Research has shown the key factors or dimensions to be considered in a relationship include levels of: 1) loyalty, 2) trust, 3) openness, 4) involvement, 5) community investment and 6) commitment (Ledingham and Bruning).

Significant research has been conducted within the relationship-building and the relationship-management schools of thought in public relations. While those disciplines have been advocating a relationship-building approach to dealing with all organizational publics since the mid-1980s, it is only recently that research has led to the methodology to measure the strength of those relationships. The six factors identified above are those most often used and measured. Loyalty and trust are arguably two-way factors, the strength of which is measured both from the perspectives of the organization and the publics. The other four primarily measure the public's perception of the organization's performance. The openness, involvement, community investment and commitment of the organization to publics and issues are typically seen as responsibilities of the organization.

The purpose of your communication, particularly long term, is to strengthen relationships with publics and move them to mutually beneficial action. Communication that highlights the organization's performance on these six factors will help you do that.

Without market research, you won't be able to make sound decisions about key publics when the time comes. It is equally important to have market research about intervening publics. You gain their cooperation in the same way you motivate action in key publics: by making it in their self-interest. For this reason, you need to know about them, understand their self-interests as they relate to your problem, know who influences them and understand the status of your relationship with them.

© Andresr/Shutterstock.com

Situation analysis

Although the problem or challenge was identified for us initially as we began the research process, it is important to redefine the situation after we have synthesized all available and pertinent information. The client's initial perception of the problem or opportunity may be quite unlike the actual situation. You may have initially believed people didn't donate to a cause because they didn't see the need. Research may have discovered the real reason was that they didn't know how. Remember the before-mentioned plan put before voters to expand metro rail. When it was voted down, the county assumed voters were against expansion when they were actually voting against the proposed funding method: an increase in sales tax.

Come out and stay with Hilton

MINI CASE

HILTON

BACKSTORY

From being the first coast-to-coast hotel chain in America to opening the first airport hotel, Hilton has prided itself on being a hospitality innovator. After closely following trends and gathering appropriate research, the company has recently taken major steps in marketing to the lesbian, gay, bisexual and transgender community worldwide — a demographic that generates significant revenue within the travel and tourism industry each year. Hilton's most influential campaign targeting this group — "Stay Hilton. Go Out." — was launched in March 2012 and offered holiday packages and promotions specifically aimed at LGBT travelers.

KEY FACTS

- Average household income among LGBTs is $81,500, or about 80 percent higher than typical U.S. households.
- U.S. LGBT travelers alone generate $65 billion of the $1.3 trillion produced from travel and tourism annually.
- A study by Greenfield Research & Kinsey Report showed that 94 percent of LGBT travelers will go out of their way to purchase products and services marketed directly to them.
- Special LGBT packages offered by Hilton included 10 percent off best available rates, free one-year subscription to the world's most-read gay magazine, OUT, and entry into sweepstakes for tickets to LGBT events.

How would you choose to target the LGBT segment?

HILTON'S STRATEGY

Hilton knew that demand for LGBT travel in California would skyrocket as Proposition 8 was overturned. In an effort to position Hilton as the top-of-mind hotel choice for same-sex couples, the company decided to host the wedding of Paul Katami and Jeff Zarrillo — co-plaintiffs in the Supreme Court case — at the iconic Beverly Hilton in Beverly Hills.

Wanting to further capitalize on the high disposable income of the LGBT community, Hilton expanded its outreach in an attempt to seize a greater market share within the demographic. With ample secondary research to back up its decision-making, the hotel chain sponsored a number of high-profile gay rights events around the world including the Advocate's 45th anniversary party, Gay Days Orlando, WorldPride London, Atlanta Pride and OUT100. Hilton also chose

© Tupungato/Shutterstock.com

Hilton hotel on 6th Avenue in New York City.

to triple the number of hotels that would offer "Stay Hilton. Go Out." campaign perks.

RESULTS

- The positive media coverage Hilton garnered during the campaign was instrumental in winning the loyalty of LGBT travelers worldwide.
- In a survey conducted by Community Marketing Inc., Hilton was voted the hotel chain with best outreach to the LGBT community in 2012.
- While still growing, Hilton's campaign efforts to date have contributed to more than 3,600 new HHonors members and 3,400 "opt-ins" to the company's LGBT email database.

Because Hilton was able to successfully convert its research findings into effective messages, strategies and tactics, it established brand loyalty among the LGBT community and seized greater market share.

WORKS CITED:

Community Marketing Inc. (2009, December 28). CMI's 14th annual gay & lesbian tourism study. Retrieved from http://www.gayadnetwork.com/files/tourismstudy.pdf

Community Marketing Inc. (2011). CMI's 16th annual gay & lesbian tourism report. Retrieved from http://www.gayadnetwork.com/files/CMItourismstudy2011.pdf

Public Relations Society of America. (2013). Stay Hilton Go Out - Hilton targets LGBT travelers with pride. Retrieved from http://kallibeanportfolio.files.wordpress.com/2014/03/stay-hilton.pdf

Hilton Worldwide. (2014, June 9). Hilton Hotels & Resorts invites travelers to celebrate national LGBT pride month. Retrieved from http://news.hilton.com/index.cfm/newsroom/detail/26957?tl=fr

Based on the background, assess and describe in one paragraph the situation as it appears after the data has been organized and analyzed. This paragraph should include those most pertinent pieces of data that will become benchmarks upon which to later base your objectives. That means your analysis of the data should yield numerical markers that must be improved to resolve your problem or meet the challenge.

In describing a problem, you might know that 75 percent of public opinion is that your organization doesn't care about the community. Obviously that is a statistic that must be improved to meet your challenge. Those are the critical pieces of data that must be included in the situation analysis. If you can explain research data in terms of measures, then writing measurable objectives to meet the challenge is easy. Further, using actual data — numbers — to summarize the attitudes, opinions and behaviors that must be changed will inspire confidence in your superiors that you have a realistic grasp of the problem and understand how to overcome it.

So don't just say your publics don't trust the organization; identify what the specific trust levels are among which publics. Don't just conclude people lack information; find the statistics to describe which publics lack which specific understandings or pieces of information. Find the critical data that not only describe publics, attitudes, opinions and behaviors but also provide the benchmarks to measure success.

In a second paragraph, identify any related issues, problems or difficulties. Honestly assess potential barriers to success that must be overcome, but use your research as a confidence builder so your client or manager will be certain that the difficulties can be overcome. Identifying difficulties and then suggesting reasonable ways to neutralize them may be the best approach.

Core problem or opportunity

Based on the synthesis of research in the background, you have narrowed the issue or challenge to a short assessment of the situation and any related difficulties. Now cut to the heart of the problem or opportunity in one sentence. For example, "Because key publics are not getting adequate and timely information about mobile blood drives, blood donations have declined, threatening the local hospital's immediate access to needed lifesaving units." The statement gets right to the central core of the problem and translates it to a tangible consequence if the problem is not solved. Be careful not to mistake symptoms of a problem for the problem itself. Like an onion, problems are made up of many layers. The layers surrounding the problem often take the form of symptoms and effects. In order to identify the core problem you need to peel back the symptoms and effects to find out what is really causing the difficulty.

Summary

Organizing background research according to the research checklist helps lay the foundation for decision-making. The background, SWOT analysis and market research help to focus everything we know into a solution or plan. It funnels research into the problem-solving and planning process because it has driven us to think analytically, to evaluate what is known and to identify how that will assist in the selection of publics and resources to solve the problem.

The situation analysis likely identifies some key factors not known when the challenge or opportunity was first discovered. Using data to describe the real situation after we have completed our background analysis helps us focus more clearly on the core challenge/opportunity and to marshal all knowledge, information, skills and resources to succeed.

Exercises

1. Identify an organization with a communications and/or marketing problem. List everything you know about the organization, its environment, the problem and the market. Then list everything you need to know to define the real problem and devise a solution. What research tools and information sources would you use to get the additional information you need?

2. Choose a public you are familiar with such as university students. Gather existing market research to describe that public's values, attitudes, opinions, lifestyles and media use. Identify their motivating self-interests, opinion leaders and the best channels to reach them.

3. Find a nonprofit organization with a communications challenge that you are familiar with. Write two paragraphs that will be your situation analysis for the organization. Then summarize this information into one core problem/opportunity statement.

References and additional readings

Bruning, S., & Ledingham, J. (1999). Relationships between organizations and publics: Development of a multi-dimensional organization-public relationship scale. *Public Relations Review*, 25(2), 157-170.

Bruning, S., & Ledingham, J. (2000). Organization and key public relationships: Testing the influence of the relationship dimensions in a business-to-business context. In Ledingham and Bruning (Eds.), *Public relations as relationship management: A relational approach to the study and practice of public relations.* Mahwah, NJ: Lawrence Erlbaum Associates.

Collett, S. (1999, July 19). SWOT analysis: Quickstudy. *Computerworld.*

Ledingham, J., & Bruning, S. (1998). Relationship management and public relations: Dimensions of an organization-public relationship. *Public Relations Review*, 24, 55-65.

Paine, K. D. (2011). *Measure what matters: Online tools for understanding customers, social media, engagement, and key relationships.* Durham, NH: Paine Publishing.

Paine, K. D. (2007). *Measuring public relationships: The data-driven communicator's guide to success.* Durham, NH: Paine Publishing.

Stacks, D. W. (2002). *Primer of public relations research.* New York: Guilford Publications, Inc.

CHAPTER 5

SETTING GOALS AND OBJECTIVES

"If you fail to plan, you are planning to fail!"

—Benjamin Franklin
AUTHOR, INVENTOR, SCIENTIST AND STATESMAN

LEARNING IMPERATIVES

- To be able to turn a problem/opportunity statement into a goal.

- To understand the characteristics of good objectives.

- To learn how to write objectives to support the accomplishment of a goal.

PLANNING
The process of using research to chart the step-by-step course to solve a problem, take advantage of an opportunity or meet a challenge.

GOAL
The result or desired outcome that solves a problem, takes advantage of an opportunity or meets a challenge.

The second step of the RACE model is action planning. **Planning** and the programming it generates is how we get from here to there. "Here" is where we are now. It is our current situation as we have described it after synthesizing our research and redefining the challenge or opportunity we face. "There" is where we want to be; it's our **goal.** Planning helps us to look ahead, to chart our course to ensure we get there. Like sailing a boat, planning must be flexible and open to course correction as we receive feedback or obtain new information. Nevertheless, unless we know where we are going and have some idea of an appropriate course to get there, our arrival at the destination will be left to chance. The more complete our planning — based on good research — the better our chances of arriving at our destination.

The matrix approach to planning

The heart of the Strategic Communications Planning Matrix is the action planning section. The research process — including the collection, organization and analysis of information and honing it into a situation analysis and core problem/opportunity — lays the foundation for the action planning process. Broom and Sha (2013) call this a "searching look backward," a "wide look around," a "deep look inside" and a "long look ahead."

The matrix addresses each of the remaining three steps — action planning, communication and evaluation — as discrete functions. Nevertheless, this is a planning matrix; the emphasis is on planning each step before implementing. Thus, the resulting plan, although dynamic, should drive both the communication and evaluation steps in the process.

Planning occurs at two distinct levels within any organization. First, long-term planning looks at the entirety of the organization and its mission. It identifies goals,

STRATEGIC PLANNING MATRIX

ACTION PLANNING

4. GOAL AND OBJECTIVES

Goal   The goal is a one-sentence statement of the overall result needed to solve the problem or seize the opportunity. The goal does not have to be quantified.

Objectives   Objectives are numbered or bulleted statements of specific results that will lead to the achievement of the goal. Objectives must be specific, written, measurable, attainable, time-bound, cost-conscious, efficient and mission-driven. If objectives are clear, key publics become obvious.

objectives, publics and messages that address the long-term accomplishment of the organization's mission.

Second, short-term planning is designed to target more immediate needs such as managing a crisis, launching a new product line and repairing a damaged reputation. Effective high-level planning should, nonetheless, inform planning for more specific short-term campaigns. Although they are focused on a more specific challenge, short-term communications efforts should always reinforce the key messages, goals and objectives of the long-term plan. Nevertheless, by their nature, they may also address publics that may not be long-term key publics to the organization but that are crucial to the accomplishment of the short-term effort.

Research helps us define the challenge and the current environment within which the opportunity has occurred or will occur. As shown in the complete matrix in chapter one, planning identifies what specifically needs to be accomplished (goal and objectives) to overcome the challenge, who (key publics) we need to reach and/or motivate to accomplish the goal and objectives, what we need to convey (messages) to those publics to stimulate action and help us achieve our objectives, and how (strategies and tactics) to get those messages to those publics so they both receive and act upon them. This latest edition of the matrix has the big idea concept to better tie together the who, what and how of a campaign under a creative unifying theme.

The process is analytical, with the decisions made and actions planned in each step driving the decisions made and actions planned in each subsequent step. Further, each step must be taken in turn. For example, the key publics for a particular problem-solving effort cannot be selected until we have determined the goal and the objectives necessary to achieve that goal. Only then can we select the publics that are needed to accomplish our objectives. Similarly, we can only design effective messages after we have selected key publics, know what we need them to do and determined their self-interests. The decisions we make about the information a public needs, what will motivate the public to act and who should deliver the message to the public are prerequisite to designing messages that result in action that accomplishes objectives.

Effective informational and motivational messages cannot be designed for a given public without a thorough analysis of its research profile, examination of the status of the current relationship with that public and knowledge of its self-interests as they pertain to the problem at hand and related issues. Strategies and tactics appropriate to send the designed messages to the selected publics cannot be determined until we know what those messages are. Quite simply, the matrix approach requires us to decide what we want to do, who we need to reach to do it, what messages we need to send to obtain cooperation and how we can most effectively send those messages. The steps must be taken in order or our planning is left to chance and will most likely be flawed and offtrack.

We have all seen campaigns that had good research but somehow misconnected in the planning process. One poignant example is Salt Lake City's campaign to win the bid for the 1998, and subsequently the 2002, Winter Olympics. Previously, the Denver organizing committee had to withdraw its candidacy as the U.S. representative in a previous Olympic Games bid because of opposing public opinion in the

OBJECTIVE
Specific, measurable statement of what needs to be accomplished to reach the goal.

Denver area. Consequently, the Salt Lake City organizers decided it was important to have a public referendum on the issue to demonstrate to the U.S. Olympic Committee and the International Olympic Committee that Utah was fully supportive of Salt Lake's candidacy. With support running high in the state (upwards of 80 percent), the organizing committee expected the referendum would send a strong message that Utah residents were squarely behind the effort. Nevertheless, its own polling showed there was weak support and even opposition among senior citizens, environmentalists and ultra-conservative segments of the population. While these groups actually comprised only a small percentage of the Utah population, the organizing committee worried that, in an off-year election, those three publics were the most likely to vote. Given that information, the goal and objectives were to get out the supportive vote.

The strategy was to air clever, creative and visually appealing TV spots (tactics) that gave people a good feeling about Utah hosting the Olympic Games. The end of the spots showed a box with a checkmark in it to indicate a vote supportive of the Olympic bid. But the ads were essentially still seeking intrinsic public support of the games. The ads didn't ask people to get out of their chairs and go vote. The bid already had a high public approval rating. What the committee really needed was to motivate those who approved to get to the polls and cast their supportive vote. But the committee — through its ads — never actually asked the approving publics to go vote. So they didn't. The referendum passed by only a very slim margin. The organizing committee was plagued with explaining the low margin of public support to the IOC in almost every subsequent interaction.

Once the city won the opportunity to host the 2002 Winter Olympics, the organizing committee no longer had to address the issue of citizen support to the IOC. Nevertheless, the low voter support of the referendum was continual fodder for the active (albeit minority) opposition to the games in Utah. No public opinion poll could ever entirely dispel the results of the actual vote.

The Salt Lake Olympic Committee had good research data and analysis. It knew what it had to do: get out the supportive publics who don't typically vote in an off-year election. The committee knew the profiles of the publics it had to reach. Yet the committee designed a message that did not specifically ask those publics to do what needed to be done. The committee also sent the message in a broadly targeted tactic through a mass medium ill-suited to the purpose at hand — reaching and motivating highly segmented publics.

Each step of the matrix planning process must build on the previous step. The logic must flow consistently and coherently. Disregarding the information accumulated, the decisions made and the actions planned in one step will almost always ensure that the decisions made and actions planned in the subsequent step are off target and headed for failure.

With this important lesson in mind, the next few chapters address the action planning steps of the Strategic Communications Planning Matrix. This chapter begins that discussion with identifying what needs to be done to meet the challenge or to seize the opportunity at hand.

Establishing goals

Once the core problem or opportunity is accurately established, setting the goal is a simple task. The goal is actually a positive restatement of the core problem. If your challenge is declining confidence among investors leading to a decline in stock price, your goal is to reestablish confidence and boost your stock price. If your problem is a lack of accurate information regarding the process of organ donation, thereby causing a shortage of available organs for transplant, your goal is to increase the number of organs donated by overcoming misperceptions about the process. The goal should be broader and more general than the objectives that follow. A goal also does not have to be specifically measurable. The measured achievement of strategic objectives should ensure that the overall goal is reached.

Nevertheless, determining the goal may not be as simple as it appears. Too often, organizational communications and marketing personnel act unilaterally to set goals. But those are not isolated functions within an organization; they should be integral parts of the overall management approach. Setting campaign goals in isolation, or without consideration of the organization's overall goals, is dangerous and can lead to a lack of internal support.

Two precautions can aid you in avoiding this problem. First, be sure you closely align campaign goals with the organization's mission. Doing so will also align campaign goals and objectives with the organization's long-term purpose. A campaign goal is not as broad as a mission statement, but should be seen as a significant step toward achieving the organization's mission.

Second, verify that the campaign goal does not conflict with existing goals and objectives. Does my campaign goal mesh with what marketing, advertising, sales and public relations are already trying to accomplish? Will the campaign be cooperating with or competing against existing initiatives?

It is typically not enough to "not conflict" with the goals of other entities. Truly sound and defensible goals and objectives will enhance and support the overall organizational mission and goals. Figure 5.1 identifies some examples of possible organizational

Figure 5.1 _____
Examples of organizational goals

Business sector
- Maintain profitability.
- Maintain and gradually improve stock rating.
- Achieve a positive trust ranking.
- Maintain an operating environment with minimal government regulation.

Public sector
- Increase use of funded social programs.
- Cut overhead and increase flow of funds to programs.
- Decrease fraudulent use of social programs.
- Improve citizen access to and use of information.
- Increase government funding.

Nonprofit sector
- Expand research efforts.
- Expand program reach.
- Secure private financial support of programs.
- Provide for the safety of the community.

goals. Remember that effective communication with key publics is necessary to create the environment in which the organization can reach its goals. Any single campaign — whether designed to solve a problem or to proactively position the organization — must be planned within the framework of the organization's goals.

Identifying objectives

Once the goal is set, the challenge is to break down what you want to accomplish into smaller, more specific tasks. If your company's goal is to expand a research program, your communications campaign may need to set objectives that involve securing public approval, generating funding, attracting personnel and building community support for the renovation of facilities. Objectives are specific, measurable statements of what needs to be accomplished for the goal to be reached. Whereas a goal may be somewhat ambiguous (e.g., not defining how much is enough funding or profit), objectives must be absolutely precise.

We strongly recommend that objectives meet the following eight criteria that have been carefully refined by communications and business professionals. Keep in mind that precision is important in not only being able to carry out but also to effectively measure your objectives.

Specific. Objectives should be free from ambiguity. What you are hoping to accomplish should be specific and clearly articulated. Each objective should address only one outcome. You shouldn't write an objective to increase awareness and improve sales. Similarly, achieving general awareness may not be enough. Be specific about what kind of awareness you are seeking. Do you want to increase awareness of an organization's existence or of a specific product line? Are you targeting HIV awareness or, more specifically, the effect of its transmission to newborns? And what levels of awareness are you seeking based on current levels of public knowledge? Having specific objectives helps you more clearly understand what publics you need to reach and what you need each public to do. Your approach to achieving these outcomes and the associated tasks will become the strategies and tactics used to reach key publics later in the planning process.

Written. Objectives must be written down and published (at least shared with the communications and marketing team). This may seem obvious, but too often organizations assume everyone knows about and understands the campaign's purpose and objectives. Unless they are written and shared, they have probably not been well thought out, and there may be differing perceptions of what the objectives really are. One member of the team may be working toward something entirely different than the other members because his/her perception of the desired outcome is different than the rest of the team's. Putting your objectives in writing helps to solidify and refine the plan while avoiding confusion over what you are trying to accomplish.

Further, written objectives serve as reference points throughout the planning process. When you come to a point of disagreement on any element of the planning process or when you run out of ideas somewhere in the process, it often helps to go back and review exactly what it is you are trying to accomplish. Finally, written objectives serve as tangible guides for evaluation. They allow you to demonstrate how far you've come — not only in a campaign but also as a professional.

Measurable. Objectives must be improvement-oriented and quantifiable. Anything measurable must have a number tied to it. Numbers can be represented in percentages or simple figures. Examples of percentage-based objectives are: a 20 percent increase in sales, a 50 percent jump in donations and a 60 percent decline in the number of high school students who have experimented with drugs before graduation. Examples of simple figure objectives are: raising $200,000 for the women's shelter, getting 3,000 participants in a 5K and engaging 6,000 people on an issue through social media.

To be improvement-oriented, objectives must work together in order to achieve your overall goal. Rarely will one objective suffice. Plan to have a number of objectives that all measure progress toward the goal. If your goal is to open a new food bank, objectives could focus on fundraising, citizen support, government support and determining the best location.

When working with percentages, remember to carefully state the percent increase or decrease and use clarifying phrases. Otherwise, you might set yourself up to disappoint management's expectations created by your own objectives. If you want to increase the percentage of elementary school kids brushing their teeth at least twice a day, you should follow up that number by specifically stating the benchmark or starting point. You might write an objective like this: to increase the number of elementary school children in Arizona who brush their teeth at least twice a day from 25 percent to 75 percent by May 1, 2015. Make sure you know the difference between a *50 percent* increase and a *50 percentage-point* increase. The first is dependent on the starting point to calculate the actual increase. Fifty percent of 25 is 12.5, which would make your target 37.5 percent of school children brushing their teeth. A 50 percentage point-increase takes you from 25 percent to 75 percent of school children brushing — two very different results. Similarly, a 20 percent increase in participation among a total population of 100 is not 20 people. The percent increase depends on the current level of participation, not the total population. If 50 of 100 people are currently participating, a 20 percent increase would be 10 people (20 percent of 50), from 50 to 60 participants, or a 10 percentage-point improvement. Be very precise when planning and writing your objectives.

Sometimes statistics on opinion, awareness and action are not readily available. If you are certain the level of knowledge or participation is minimal, you can reasonably state the level it needs to rise to in order to accomplish the goal. If you don't have statistical measures for something, find another way to count the improvement.

Attainable. Objectives need to be realistic if they are to be attainable. Keeping objectives specific and clear will help you set realistic targets. But you still need to set your sights on significant improvement. Management will scorn objectives that don't cause the organization to stretch and are too easily achieved. Executives have little respect for employees and managers who are unwilling to reach a bit, to take some risks and to challenge themselves. Nevertheless, if you shoot for the moon and just hit the stars, you may be branded as having fallen short, even if the stars were all you really needed to reach.

Writing goals and objectives

The local oil refinery has a good record of community involvement and an approval rating among local publics of 75 percent. Nevertheless, it continually faces scrutiny and even opposition from environmental activists. Recently, one of the pipelines sprung a leak. Before the leak was found and fixed, the equivalent of 100 barrels of oil seeped out into a small creek that runs through a residential neighborhood. The company immediately mobilized teams of experts, employees and local volunteers to clean up the small spill and restore the area (as much as possible) to its original pristine condition.

GOAL

To restore the company's approval rating and neutralize regulatory threats.

OBJECTIVES

1. Raise awareness to 80 percent of the company's efforts to respond responsibly to the spill within three weeks.
2. Raise awareness to 80 percent of the company's local contribution to the community and economy within six months.
3. Restore public approval to its previous 75 percent level within six months.
4. Ensure no new state or local regulations (resulting from the spill) are enacted within the next three years.

Time-bound. Objectives need to have a deadline. They should clearly outline when you expect to achieve a specific outcome. Setting objectives in time also determines when you will measure your success or failure. The duration of a campaign will be determined by the problem or opportunity being addressed. Some campaigns may require short, quick efforts (a few days, weeks or months) while others may necessitate long-range efforts. Some campaigns have built-in deadlines (e.g., attendance at a special event for a product launch). Others are designed to change perceptions and attitudes, which happens slowly.

Every objective, however, must include a target date. In some cases, interim measures may be helpful in measuring progress along the way and keeping you on track to reach the objective. For example, you might have a fundraising objective to raise $30 million for the construction of a new community theatre. Benchmarking the objective to raise $10 million in the first six months may be necessary to give the project the momentum it needs to succeed.

© Tukkata Moji/Shutterstock.com

Cost-conscious. Objectives must take into consideration the available budget. It goes without saying that you should choose the most cost-effective ways to achieve the desired outcomes in any campaign. There will always be organizational pressure to accomplish more with less. Smart strategists look for low-cost options first.

Although you won't always know what budget will be available for a specific program when you are at this preliminary stage of planning, be sensitive to the organization's internal climate. A recession, slow sales or downsizing may necessitate objectives that create more modest expectations. They may also force greater creativity in your planning. So keep perspective when crafting your objectives. It is not feasible, for example, to spend 50 percent of a campaign budget on opinion research. You will need money to develop and deliver your messages and motivate action.

While you must set objectives to solve the problem and reach the goal, the objectives you set also shape the organization's expectations of you and your communications and marketing team.

Efficient. Objectives should also look for the easiest way to reach the goal. There are indeed many roads that lead to Rome. Whenever possible, pick the most direct route. As you write your objectives, it is helpful to spend some time thinking about how you will measure them. Determining exactly how you will evaluate whether you reached your desired outcome will help you keep objectives simple and efficient.

Trying to measure the percent of students on a university campus distracted by electronics after 10 p.m. will not be easy and will be even more difficult to validate. By contrast, measuring the reported number of hours students sleep per night is much more straightforward. Similarly, measuring interest in a new product is more difficult than tracking sales of the product.

Mission-driven. As previously discussed, objectives must be in line with and support the organizational mission and goals. Objectives are required to address issues, problems, opportunities or improvements that management perceives as valuable.

Keep in mind why the company is in business or why the organization exists. What are the key factors that have and are contributing to its success? Then ask yourself if your objectives will contribute to or detract from the organization's main purpose. Always doing this makes you strategic — of value to your organization because you help it accomplish its mission.

Informational versus motivational objectives

In addition to the characteristics of good objectives, it is important to recognize there are two basic kinds of objectives: informational and motivational. Each serves a different purpose, but both are integral to the overall accomplishment of any campaign.

TIPS FROM THE PROS

Differentiating between goals and objectives

J. Michael Neumeier, APR, principal and co-founder of Arketi Group, an integrated public relations and marketing consultancy, tips you off on how to tell a goal from an objective.

All too often, the terms *goal* and *objective* are used as interchangeable ways of saying the same thing. Plainly put, they are not — and the resulting lack of precision can be problematic.

GOALS

A goal is a "statement of being" for the plan. Often, one goal is enough. PR and marketing goals should always be consistent with management goals, and they should be carefully crafted with the end result in mind.

A communications plan goal might be "to increase the level of government funding" or "to expand our industry leadership."

While the completion of the goal signifies the end of your plan, the objectives, strategies and tactics are the means to that end.

OBJECTIVES

Compared to the goal, objectives are more focused and specific. The best-formulated objectives express results as measurable outcomes. Think in terms of the awareness, attitude or action that you hope to invoke. Often there are multiple objectives in support of a single goal. Meaningful objectives start with action verbs and have three parts. They state a measurable outcome, set an attainment level and set a time-frame.

Examples of objectives are "to secure 20 percent more media coverage in trade publications in fiscal year 2014" or "to increase news flow from the company by 25 percent during the calendar year."

When writing objectives, keep these tips in mind:

Seek input from management. Output measurements, such as daily blog posts, are sometimes very important to executives. Objectives that are easy to measure are as important as objectives that require complex and expensive metrics.

Don't force yourself into long time frames like a year. You will likely craft a stronger objective if you can tightly define a time frame to even a month or two.

Get a second opinion. The best second opinions come from other PR professionals that are not working directly on the plan.

Audiences do not have to be limited to external targets. Many times getting internal stakeholders to understand and embrace a campaign can be a very worthy objective.

If you know you cannot measure it, don't build it into an objective.

Informational objectives lay a foundation of understanding and awareness necessary for any kind of persuasive effort. They address the dissemination of information and an increase in awareness among key publics. This is a necessary step in order for publics to develop attitudes that will drive the behavior we are seeking.

Informational objectives are usually easy to accomplish because you are just spreading information, not attempting to change anything. In fact, much of today's corporate communications practice is heavily engaged in information dissemination and awareness- or consciousness-raising. Nevertheless, Wilcox, Cameron and Reber (2014) contend that it is difficult to measure the accomplishment of such an objective because you are trying to measure a cognitive function (increase in information or understanding) on a sliding scale (how much information or understanding). In other words, have you simply achieved name recognition, or does your public have an understanding of what you do?

Although informational objectives are necessary to lay a foundation to persuade people to act, they are never enough by themselves. It is recommended that at least half of your objectives focus on motivating action.

Motivational objectives are directly tied to behavior. As a result, they are usually easier to measure and harder to achieve according to Wilcox, et al. (2014). It is a relatively simple matter to measure a desired behavior. People voted for your candidate or they didn't; consumers bought the product or they didn't; children were inoculated or they weren't. Nevertheless, changing attitudes and opinions and creating the triggering event to move the public from awareness to action is much more difficult than just disseminating information and raising awareness of an issue or problem.

Use informational objectives to lay the foundation for persuasive efforts and motivational objectives to get publics to act. People can't vote the way you want them to on an issue if they are not aware of the issue and its effect on their lives. Consumers cannot buy a new product that will make life easier or more pleasant if they are not aware of its existence and benefits. Create awareness and information objectives, with all the characteristics of good objectives, to lay the foundation to accomplish your motivational objectives.

Keep in mind that disseminating information is easy, but motivating behavior is more difficult. You will typically be able to reach a far higher level of awareness than you will behavior. You may be able to inform upwards of 90 percent of your target population on a particular issue. Nevertheless, 90 percent awareness does not translate to motivating 90 percent of a public to act. The achievable percentage of behavior will always lag behind the level of awareness. On some issues it may be only slightly lower; on other issues there may be a dramatic difference.

Summary

The Strategic Communications Planning Matrix guides the planning process in communication and problem solving. It is the analytical tool that ensures research data and information are applied to solving the problem or seizing the opportunity. This matrix requires that good information, sound reasoning and clear logic drive decisions regarding the objectives needed in a campaign, what publics you need to reach, what messages you need to send to motivate those publics to act, and what communication tools (tactics) will ensure key publics select and act on your messages.

The matrix transforms each step of the RACE model into strategic functions. It ensures that the communication process is not just a succession of steps to be completed, but that it is an interactive, integrated methodology for finding the best and most timely solution for the lowest cost. The process must be guided by specific, written, measurable, attainable, time-bound, cost-conscious, efficient and mission-driven objectives that lead to the accomplishment of a clearly articulated goal. Remember that a campaign goal is a positive restatement of the core problem identified in the research section of the matrix.

Objectives lay the foundation for the selection of a campaign big idea and the key publics you must reach. They also help determine the messages, strategies and tactics necessary to inform and motivate publics to act.

Exercises

1. Based on your research, create goals and objectives for the nonprofit organization you identified in the previous chapter's exercises. Make sure you set a goal that overcomes the problem you identified, and set objectives to attain the goal that follow the eight characteristics of good objectives.

2. Select a local company, and request a copy of its mission statement and goals. Then brainstorm the objectives necessary to reach the goals. Make sure your objectives meet all the criteria of good objectives.

References and additional readings

Cutlip, S., Center, A., & Broom, G. (2013). *Effective public relations* (11th ed.). Englewood Cliffs, NJ: Prentice-Hall, Inc.

Drucker, P. (1974). *Management tasks, responsibilities, practices.* New York: Harper and Row.

Hainsworth, B. E., & Wilson, L. J. (1992). Strategic program planning. *Public Relations Review*, 18(1), 9-15.

Koestler, F. A. (1977). *Planning and setting objectives*. New York: Foundation for Public Relations Research and Education.

Newsom, D., Turk J. V. & Kruckeberg D. (2004). *This is PR: The realities of public relations* (8th ed.). Belmont, CA.: Wadsworth Publishing Company.

Norris, J. S. (1984). *Public relations*. Englewood Cliffs, NJ: Prentice-Hall, Inc.

Wilcox, D. L., Cameron, G. T., & Reber, B. H. (2014). *Public relations: Strategies and tactics* (11th ed.). Upper Saddle River, NJ: Pearson Education.

CHAPTER 6

CREATIVITY AND BIG IDEAS

"It's kind of fun to do the impossible."

— Walter Elias Disney

ANIMATOR, FILMMAKER AND BUSINESS MAGNATE

It took roughly 100 men and women five years — including a lot of holidays, weekends and late nights — to create the first feature-length film fully animated on a computer. But when "Toy Story" debuted Thanksgiving weekend in 1995, it forever changed the landscape for animated films.

Disney executives had advised the upstarts at Pixar to fill the movie with songs, but the company resisted. "Despite being novice filmmakers at a fledgling studio in dire financial straits, we had put our faith in a simple idea: If we made something that *we* wanted to see, others would want to see it, too," says Ed Catmull, president of Pixar. "For so long, it felt like we had been pushing that rock uphill, trying to do the impossible...Now, we were suddenly being held up as an example of what could happen when artists trusted their guts."

"Toy Story" became the biggest grossing movie of the year, earning $358 million worldwide. The name Pixar has become synonymous with **creativity** and innovation. The company has won an incredible 12 academy awards for its animated films including "Toy Story," "Monster's Inc.," "Finding Nemo," "The Incredibles," "Ratatouille," "WALL-E," "Up," "Toy Story 3" and "Brave."

CREATIVITY

The process of looking outside ourselves and our routine to discover new ideas and innovative solutions.

Creativity

Creativity is, in many ways, really another word for experimenting — taking existing ideas and adding something to them or putting them together in new ways. The 80-minute experiment we know as "Toy Story" was really the answer to a question. Can we make an animated film using only computers? The answer launched a company and a new industry of computer graphic animation or CGI that is now used across many disciplines including communications, medicine, education and engineering.

Creativity in the planning process

Creativity is an essential part of any good strategy. Step five in the matrix requires high levels of creativity to come up with a big idea as well as strategies and tactics that break through all the information and persuasion clutter with which your publics are bombarded. You must design creative strategies and tactics that will cause the target public to *choose* to perceive your messages, *choose* to retain them and *choose* to act upon them. The matrix process provides the framework or strategic structure to focus your creativity, ensuring it is on target in terms of meeting your challenge.

You'll first use creative tools to help you develop a big idea. The elements that make up a big idea are discussed later in the chapter. Once you have a big idea and have settled on your key publics, you'll want to see how you can experiment with different approaches

Buzz Lightyear from Pixar's "Toy Story."

© Featureflash/Shutterstock.com

STRATEGIC PLANNING MATRIX

ACTION PLANNING

5. BIG IDEA, KEY PUBLICS, MESSAGES, STRATEGIES AND TACTICS

Big Idea   A "big idea" is a creative, overarching strategy and message that appeals to all publics you will target. Describe your big idea in one sentence. Then include a bullet for each of these three components: Big idea strategy, message and visual representation of the idea. An optional fourth bullet could be a slogan that encapsulates the big idea message and strategy.

and channels to deliver your messages to your publics. Then, let your creativity loose again, **brainstorming** the tactics to accomplish each strategy.

Marrying creativity and strategy

Only by channeling your creativity within the analytical process will you avoid a common mistake: allowing a creative tactic to drive your campaign. Just because you have a great opportunity to use a celebrity in a campaign doesn't mean that approach will serve your public, purpose and message. Creative ideas not founded in logical reasoning and analysis of publics, purposes and messages result in lots of money wasted on campaigns that accomplish nothing. BlackBerry's 2014 Super Bowl campaign is a prime example. The company spent $4 million in airtime alone to bring the brand back and launch its new Z10 handset. Instead, the money and opportunity were wasted. The highly creative campaign was fun to watch, but it failed miserably because it didn't target the right publics and motivate them to act.

If you get a creative idea that doesn't work for a specific purpose, public and message, put it on the shelf to be adapted and used in a later communication effort. No good idea is wasted in the long run. You'll be surprised how it will surface again and how you'll be able to modify it for future use in another campaign.

Breaking habits

French naturalist Jean-Henri Fabre writes of the processionary caterpillar. Processionary caterpillars feed on pine needles as they move through the forest in a long procession, with one head fitted snugly against the behind of the caterpillar before. In his experiments, Fabre enticed a group of these caterpillars onto the rim of a flower pot where he got the first one connected with the last so they were moving in an unending procession around the top of the pot.

> **BRAINSTORMING**
> A structured group creative exercise to generate as many ideas as possible in a specified amount of time.

Caterpillars following one another in a procession.

Fabre expected the caterpillars would catch on to their useless march and move off in a new direction, especially since he had placed food nearby. Not so. The force of habit caused them to continue moving in their unending circle, round and round the rim of the flower pot. Even though food was visible nearby, the caterpillars continued their march for seven days and nights, and probably would have continued longer had they not collapsed from sheer exhaustion and ultimate starvation. The food was outside the range of the circle, off the beaten path. They followed instinct, habit, custom, tradition, precedent and past experience. They confused activity with accomplishment. They were in constant motion, but they made no progress.

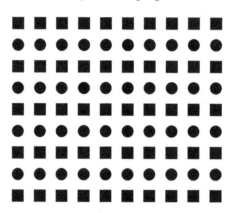

Take a look at the square and circle diagram. Most people see this pattern as rows of squares and circles. Some might see a large square composed of smaller squares and circles. Few, however, see it as columns of alternating squares and circles. Once this is pointed out, it's very easy to see columns of alternating shapes. One creativity expert, Michael Michalko, explains it this way, "We have become habituated to passively organize similar items together in our minds. Geniuses, on the other hand, subvert habituation by actively looking for alternative ways to look at and think about things."

Creativity is the process of looking outside ourselves, our habit, our custom and our tradition to find new solutions and innovative ideas. The strategic program planning process is designed to analytically drive our planning and decisions. But it should not limit our creativity in searching for solutions.

In fact, unless we develop creative big ideas, strategies and tactics, our publics are not likely to perceive the messages we have designed to motivate them.

Brainstorming and ideation

Many people think that creativity is inborn — you either have it or you don't. But the greatest scientific discoveries and inventions came out of years of experimentation, trial and error. The Royal Bank of Canada tells its employees that innovation is like playing hockey: The best players miss more shots than they make. But they also try more often. The more you shoot, the more you score. That's why one of the rules of brainstorming (see Figure 6.1) is not to evaluate or criticize while in the brainstorming process. The object is to get as many ideas on the table as possible, no matter how ridiculous they might initially appear. Those ridiculous ideas, reevaluated, rearranged and combined, frequently become the innovative solutions that are praised, awarded and used as examples of phenomenal creativity.

⬡ Figure 6.1
Rules for brainstorming

1. **Assemble a diverse group of people (at least three).**

2. **Set a time limit for the brainstorming session.** Plan no fewer than five minutes but no more than 20-30 minutes to ensure urgency and, hence, a rapid flow of ideas.

3. **Record the session for later transcription.**

4. **Do not evaluate ideas while in the session.** Even laughter can be an act of evaluation that may stifle the flow of ideas (although in a truly free-flowing session, it is difficult not to laugh).

5. **Engage in freewheeling.** Verbalize any idea that comes into your mind. Otherwise you are silently evaluating your own ideas and perhaps censuring those that are most creative.

6. **Reserve the details for the post-session evaluation.** Use your time to generate as many ideas as possible, not to explain your ideas in any detail.

7. **Piggyback on ideas.** For example, if someone mentions a tactic like bumper stickers, try to spiral off with similar transportation-related ideas like bus boards or sun visor wraparounds.

8. **Take some time as a group after the session to evaluate each idea for its merits.** Try to find ways that each might work. Try modifying, combining and rearranging before discarding an idea.

Various types of brainstorming or **ideation** are used to generate campaign ideas as well as specific strategies and tactics. One of the difficulties with most brainstorming techniques is that participants are put on the spot to come up with fresh, creative ideas. Rarely do the best ideas emerge on command in the 45 to 60 minutes allocated for a brainstorming session. Most research suggests it's best to prime brainstorming events several days in advance. Give the group a topic and the vision of where you'd like to end up so that ideas can be percolating before the session begins. Creativity is spawned through observation and association. Give your group a topic and direction so they can spend some time observing and associating long before you gather together to brainstorm.

Another helpful technique is to introduce a brainstorming topic and draft a series of questions related to the topic. The questions are then each written across the top of a separate poster-sized piece of paper and posted around the perimeter of the room. After a brief orientation to the topic and ultimate goal, participants are given a stack of sticky notes and asked to write down an idea for each question. This process of posting ideas under each question is repeated four or five times as individuals rotate around the room. This ideation method puts everyone participating on the same footing and values input equally. It also encourages subordinates and shy participants to share their ideas. With each idea on a sticky note, grouping related ideas together and analyzing the results becomes much easier.

IDEATION
The formation of new ideas.

Miracle at Calgary International

BACKSTORY

The mission of Canadian air carrier, WestJet, is to provide its customers with safe, affordable and friendly air travel. Its core values include being fun, caring, positive and passionate in everything it does. Combining all these values into one big idea, WestJet created one of the greatest Christmas stunts ever attempted: the "Christmas Miracle" campaign. The campaign was not only fun and memorable, but became a viral hit on YouTube because of its creativity, unexpectedness and flawless execution.

In late November 2013, while passengers waited to board flights to Calgary from Toronto Pearson and John C. Munro Hamilton airports, they were greeted by a virtual Santa booth. After scanning their boarding passes, Santa asked passengers what they wanted for Christmas over live video chat.

While both flights were en route, WestJet employees in Calgary began dashing around the city purchasing gifts customers had asked for from Santa. As passengers awaited their baggage, fake snow began to fall and Christmas music played over the speakers as customers' asked-for presents suddenly started to fill up the carousel. WestJet surprised 250 unsuspecting passengers with 357 personally wrapped gifts that included a 50-inch TV, cameras, smartphones, tablets, toys for the kids and even some socks and underwear.

KEY FACTS

- Flight time from Hamilton and Toronto airports to Calgary is roughly four hours.
- WestJet captured the event on 19 hidden cameras placed in the airport terminals, onboard one of the aircraft and at the baggage claim area.
- Filming took place on Nov. 21, 2013. WestJet then posted the video on YouTube Dec. 8, 2013.
- WestJet hired Studio M to create the campaign's YouTube video, Globacore handled the design and fabrication of the virtual Santa booth, and Mosaic was responsible for the PR efforts.
- Promotion of the campaign's video cost WestJet less than it would have cost to rent billboard space in Toronto for three months.

How would you create a memorable event for airline passengers?

WESTJET'S STRATEGY

In order to keep within budget, WestJet decided to approach several companies to participate in the campaign in return for positive exposure in the video.

© Leonard Zhukovsky/Shutterstock.com

The airline also wanted to involve its own employees in the execution of the "Christmas Miracle" campaign — reinforcing the fun and passionate ideals of the company.

Finally, WestJet understood the majority of its key publics are active in social media. WestJet intended to appeal to these groups by reaching out to several influential bloggers who would then share the video, generating greater exposure for the company.

RESULTS

- In the two weeks following the release of the video, traffic to WestJet's website increased 100 percent, bookings increased 77 percent and revenue rose 86 percent.
- The YouTube video, "WestJet Christmas Miracle: real-time giving," went viral, receiving 27 million views in one week. It became the number one trending topic globally as well as the most shared viral ad in Canada during 2013.
- The video generated more than 1 billion impressions on Twitter in one month.
- The story has been covered more than 1,600 times by media outlets globally.

LINKS

https://www.youtube.com/watch?v=zIElvi2MuEk

http://simpliflying.com/2013/westjet-christmas-miracle-statistics/

WORKS CITED

Androich, A. (2013, December 9). WestJet gives shocked travelers gifts in real-time. *Marketing Magazine.* Retrieved from http://www.marketingmag.ca/news/marketer-news/westjet-gives-shocked-travellers-gifts-in-real-time-96106

Anonymous. (2014, February 13). WestJet's social Christmas campaign: 'nothing short of astounding.' *EyeforTravel.* Retrieved from http://www.eyefortravel.com/social-media-and-marketing/westjet's-social-christmas-campaign-'nothing-short-astounding'

Anonymous. (2014, February 22). WestJet's Christmas miracle — statistics from social media. *WordPress.* Retrieved from http://westjetcase.wordpress.com/author/rmithanoisscc/

Kuchinskas, S. (2013, December 13). Inside WestJet's Christmas marketing miracle. *Clickz.* Retrieved from http://www.clickz.com/clickz/news/2319134/story-behind-westjets-christmas-marketing-miracle

Mudd, J. What made WestJet's "Christmas miracle" PR stunt so great. *Axia Public Relations.* Retrieved from http://www.axiapr.com/blog/thepublicrelationsblog/made-westjets-christmas-miracle-pr-stunt-great

Prendergast, C. (2014, May 8). More from EMS 2014: WestJet's Christmas miracle. *AgencyEA.* Retrieved from http://www.agencyea.com/news/blog/more-from-ems-2014-westjets-christmas-miracle/

Shorty Awards. (2014, February 12). WestJet Christmas miracle: Real-time giving. *Shorty Awards.* Retrieved from http://industry.shortyawards.com/category/6th_annual/travel/iK/westjet-christmas-miracle-real-time-giving

WestJet. (2013, December 9). WestJet Christmas miracle: real-time giving. *WestJet.* Retrieved from http://blog.westjet.com/westjet-christmas-miracle-video-real-time-giving/

WestJet. *About WestJet.* Retrieved from https://www.westjet.com/guest/en/about/

Hilton hotels, which completed the largest initial public offering for a hospitality company on Dec. 12, 2013, brainstormed how to generate media interest and investor momentum for its IPO. The communications team came up with the idea of turning the New York Stock Exchange into a hotel for the day. The company, which has 11 brands and more than 300,000 employees worldwide, used its own people — putting a doorman at every door of the exchange, serving food and having team members on the platform. Company executives also donned hotel bathrobes for the occasion. The money shot seen around the world and shared through social media was of the Hilton CEO wearing a bathrobe on the floor of the NYSE. Creative approaches like this often come from the most unexpected places. Make sure you invite new people — those from outside your work group or department — to help with each brainstorming session.

Observing and seizing opportunities

In 2006, a newly hired marketing and communications director at Blendtec, a manufacturer of commercial blenders for the food service industry, walked by the research and development suite and noticed wood shavings on the floor. Inquiries led to the discovery that one of the R&D guys liked to play around blending odd things to test the sturdiness of Blendtec's heavy-duty blenders. The marketing director got a video camera and began shooting as they blended rakes, iPods, golf balls and everything else imaginable. He posted the videos on YouTube to launch the new line of home blenders. The "Will It Blend?" series went viral. Sales of the blenders doubled in a month. Eight years later, the company's YouTube channel boasts more than 100 million views. Blendtec has also engaged with thousands of customers responding to suggestions on what it should blend next. The Blendtec viral campaign cost less than $100 to initiate. A savvy marketing and communications director saw an opportunity and took a chance. With a supportive CEO, it paid off handsomely.

The Blendtec campaign is the result of looking at a blender differently. It wasn't designed to pulverize a 2-by-4 piece of lumber, a Bic lighter or a "human" skeleton for Halloween, but it certainly can. This leads us to the big idea. Blendtec blenders

are so tough they can take on just about anything — leaving no question they can crush the ice in your next fruit smoothie. Big ideas like this are born of curiosity, observation and adaptation or experimentation.

Thomas Edison said that creativity is "10 percent inspiration and 90 percent perspiration." It may well begin when you realize that there is no particular benefit in doing things as they have always been done. It also does not require complete originality. Creativity often means borrowing and adapting ideas. Modify and rearrange, make them bigger or smaller. Brainstorm ways to change and adapt an idea. In fact, practice brainstorming on a topic just to see how many different ideas you can come up with. Try free association. Piggyback on ideas. Practice saying whatever idea comes into your head.

Giving yourself permission

These are all good exercises, but to be creative, you must first allow that you can be. Break the barriers to creative thinking identified in Figure 6.2. Explore your imagination. Think. Create fantasies and play with ideas. And then cultivate the habit. The more you challenge yourself to think creatively, the better you will become.

© wavebreakmedia/Shutterstock.com

Figure 6.2
Roger von Oech's mental locks to creativity

Be practical
Don't disregard impossible suggestions, rather use them as stepping stones to workable solutions.

That's not my area
Specializing causes us to miss out on a lot. Interdisciplinary answers are better solutions.

Don't be foolish
Poking fun at proposals provides feedback that prevents group think.

I'm not creative
Self-fulfilling prophecy. Allow yourself to be creative.

To err is wrong
Get over the stigma that being wrong is all bad. Use mistakes to learn.

The right answer
Looking for the one right answer keeps us from realizing that there may be many possibilities.

Follow the rules
Creativity is often enhanced by breaking the rules, going outside the normal parameters.

That's not logical
Don't disregard thinking outside the boundaries because it doesn't fit the analytical approach.

Play is frivolous
Fun environments are productive, creative environments.

Avoid ambiguity
Introducing ambiguity into a creative session can help generate answers. Also use humor and paradoxes.

In her book, "Teaching Creative Behavior," Doris Shallcross (1981) provides a number of exercises that require you to challenge the parameters of your thinking. For example, how many squares do you see in the illustration below? The expected answer would be 16, but count all the squares.

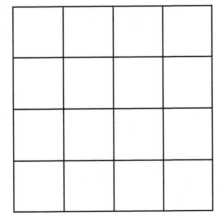

TIPS FROM THE PROS

Stoking creativity for award-winning ideas

Grace Leong, APR, managing partner of Hunter Public Relations, who leads a team that services the nation's top consumer products companies, tips you off on coming up with "big ideas."

Be an everyday student of creativity. Build a database of great ideas. The best brainstormers are those who read, see and retain good ideas daily. Keep a file of "great ideas" that catch your eye: a new product launch that used an innovative strategy or a clever idea for a media kit or website. Your personal library of ideas will serve you well when you are asked to be creative "on the spot."

Never respond to the question: "What's the Big Idea?" To get to the big idea in a brainstorm, you need to put people's minds at ease: Play creative games, ask seemingly unrelated questions, make the environment fun. When minds are stimulated in a creative atmosphere, ideas flow and a big idea will emerge naturally.

Strive for singles and doubles, and you will hit more home runs. Hank Aaron was the home run king of baseball, but he also ranks high on the all-time strike-out list. Allow yourself hundreds of strikes, singles and doubles for every home run. People who are not afraid of striking out are more likely to hit the ball out of the park.

Create an environment that inspires your creativity. At Hunter PR, we assembled a team of people with diverse backgrounds and outlooks on life, and we inspire each other to look at opportunities from multiple perspectives. We are a culture that regularly permits people to slay the sacred cow. No idea is a bad idea even if it goes against convention. If you do not live in a culture like this, fix that first, and then watch the creativity flow.

Assuming this diagram is on a flat plane, there are 30 of them, all different sizes. One is the outside square. You will also see 2-by-2 squares and 3-by-3 squares. A door is opened to our creative brain when we obtain permission — indeed are given direction — to look outside the traditional boundaries and expected perception!

The next test from Shallcross is one you may have seen before, but it powerfully illustrates the need to go outside the boundaries we set for ourselves. Connect all nine dots with four straight lines. Go through each dot only once and do not lift your pen from the page. Take a few minutes to take the test on the next page before reading on. (The solution is located at the end of the chapter.)

This test is specifically designed to show us that we set our own artificial boundaries. There was no instruction indicating the connecting lines had to be kept within the invisible boundary set by the dots in the diagram. Yet we are accustomed to setting those boundaries ourselves. One of the greatest marketing ploys of all time was to print a margin line an inch in from the edge of notebook paper and on legal pads. Most of us automatically observe that margin and leave the space on the left side of the line blank. Most notepaper and pads are used for taking notes no one else will ever see. What does it matter if we observe the margin? But much more notepaper is sold to students and companies each year because the artificial boundary restricts what fits on the page.

It is interesting to note how powerfully ingrained these artificial boundaries are. In using the Shallcross dots test each semester over two decades, we have found that most students have seen it before and have been shown that the solution is to go outside the artificial boundary. But the vast majority of those can't remember the principle and revert to trying to connect the dots inside the perceived, but actually nonexistent, boundary. They are too acculturated to staying within perceived limitations, even when no limitations actually exist.

Where did we learn to set these kinds of invisible boundaries? Remember when you began coloring? What are some of the first lessons — or rules — you were taught? One was to always color inside the lines. That rule was so ingrained that we even traced the lines with the crayon before coloring to make sure we didn't accidentally breach the boundary. We were also taught to choose the appropriate colors. Frogs are green, not purple or blue. So we always had to choose the right color for the item pictured, so much so that fights erupted in grade school over color crayons. Now grade school kids buy their own set of crayons so they don't have to fight with anyone to get the green crayon for their frog. But in a graphic design, wouldn't a purple frog get more second glances than a green one? Or better yet, one wearing a beanie or winking?

Creative ideas and solutions are, by nature, out of our typical range of experience. Problems with obvious, traditional solutions seldom require much time. To find truly innovative solutions to challenges we face, we must reach outside our comfort zone and the artificial boundaries we have created for ourselves.

Overcoming fear

Fear is probably the single greatest barrier to creative behavior. Author John Holt has said that the real test of intelligence is "not how much we know how to do, but how we behave when we don't know what to do." What do we fear? We fear failure and rejection. No one likes their ideas to be rejected, laughed at or ridiculed. We often fail to contribute our ideas for fear we will look silly or stupid. We think that people who fail do not get promoted. They do not get raises. But if we never take a risk we will also never succeed.

Remember the hockey player, and work to create an environment friendly to creativity. Accept that shots will be missed and mistakes will be made, but praise the courage and effort to seek new ideas and solutions, even if you frequently miss the mark. Companies that foster this kind of environment are typically known for their creative products and solutions. Some even give annual awards for the most spectacular failure because management recognizes that if employees are afraid to be creative, the company will lose its competitive edge in the marketplace. Make your workplace safe for creativity. Praise the creative effort even if the ideas don't or won't work. Celebrate new ideas and ways of doing things. Color a few frogs purple.

Creative environments and people

While you may not be working for an organization that openly rewards failure, you can still create an environment that stimulates ideation and innovation. Not all business environments work for all people, but there is strong consensus among creativity and innovation experts that surroundings affect performance. One of the most important considerations in planning workspace is an organization's culture. Does the work environment support the culture? The company HubSpot, for example, values an open culture and the free exchange of information and ideas. To facilitate this, no one in the company has an office. They all rotate desks on a regular basis and assign seats by pulling names out of a hat.

© Marriott International, 2014.

Photo of "The Underground" at Marriott Headquarters in Bethesda, Md.

GEN X

Generation born between the early 1960s and 1980s.

GEN Y

Generation born between the early 1980s and 2000s, also called millenials.

BIG IDEA

A creative, overriding strategy and message that provides direction to a campaign.

Max Chopovsky, founder of Chicago Creative Space, says that even traditional companies need to think about how environment reflects on their corporate culture. "Baby boomers are retiring and millennials have a different perspective of what a work environment should be," he says. "It all comes down to two trends: technology and demographics. Literally, my phone can be my office," Chopovsky says. "If I have a laptop and all other tech available, I literally never have to come into the office. I come in because of ideas, collaboration. That's where creativity happens."

Marriott International has given new focus to innovation in recent years to reinvigorate its brands and appeal to a growing number of **Gen X** and **Gen Y** travelers. The basement of its corporate headquarters in Bethesda, Md., was turned into a giant lab called, "The Underground." The space is used to test new room concepts and other projects that come from ideation sessions held with Marriott associates around the globe.

Many companies, like Disney, encourage employees to decorate their workspace. Others, particularly tech companies, build creative spaces to support their culture, like Groupon's enchanted forest. The important thing is to make sure there are places for people to gather, talk, exchange information and ideate. In the end it's about people. The culture will be the most important factor in attracting employees with fresh ideas and perspectives.

Big ideas

The concept of the **"Big Idea"** comes from advertising. In the 1960s advertising genius David Ogilvy coined the term, which had an immediate impact in the field of advertising. It later spread to marketing and public relations.

According to Ogilvy, "You will never win fame and fortune unless you also invent big ideas. It takes a big idea to attract the attention of consumers and get them to buy your product. Unless your advertising contains a big idea, it will pass like a ship in the night."

Ogilvy believed that such ideas sprang from the unconscious mind. "Your unconscious has to be well-informed, or your idea will be irrelevant," he said. "Stuff your conscious mind with information; then unhook your rational thought process."

Researchers and communications experts believe there are ways to stimulate the unconscious mind to draw out creativity. A few of the tools and concepts used to do this were discussed earlier. We refer you to the references and additional readings for more tools and examples.

What is a big idea?

A big idea is more than a unique selling point used by advertisers and marketers to sell a product. It's more than the articulation of a competitive advantage. A big idea is a creative strategy and overriding message that appeals to all key publics and ties a campaign together. You might think about it as an umbrella. All other strategies and messages fit under it and as a result stay nice and dry.

David Ogilvy, widely hailed as "The Father of Advertising."

Big ideas shouldn't be complicated and shouldn't require much explanation. They should pretty much stand on their own. There will often be a tangible way to represent a big idea in a campaign — this could be the most creative part.

The hardest part about building a campaign around a big idea may very well be learning how to recognize one. Ogilvy suggested asking these five questions:

1. Did it make me gasp when I first saw it?
2. Do I wish I had thought of it myself?
3. Is it unique?
4. Does it fit the strategy of the product?
5. Could it be used for 30 years?

Long-lasting, he believed, was one of the most important concepts behind big ideas. A good example of a big idea with staying power is Dove soap. For more than 60 years, Dove advertisements have made the claim in one way or another that "Dove doesn't dry your skin the way soap can." More recently the brand message is, "Dove is one-quarter moisturizing cream."

Big ideas in PR

While these questions and the Dove soap example may belong more to advertising than public relations and marketing, they help describe the origins and thinking behind big ideas: to serve as a unifying theme.

In 2013, American Express celebrated the 50th anniversary of the "Member Since" date being added to the card. Amex created the notion of membership, which cardmembers have come to view as a badge of honor. This big idea is both a creative strategy and a message.

The strategy is the approach: to create an initiation date for each new cardmember, the tangible representation of which is stamping every card with the date an individual joined. This personalizes the card experience and adds a sense of pride with each year of membership. The message is that you are joining an elite club and you are special. There is a sense of exclusivity with American Express that has allowed the company to charge higher fees than competitors Visa, MasterCard and Discover. The cost of this big idea was almost zero, yet it's a concept that continues to yield dividends.

To celebrate the 50-year milestone of the "member since" idea, Amex launched a special members since app available through its Facebook page. The company asked users to select the year they became Amex cardmembers. Then, it presented a tidbit from American Express history for that year, along with the opportunity to post the result on users' Facebook timelines and subsequently via Twitter. One 81-year-old man who's been a cardmember since 1958 tweeted that he was one of the original charter members alongside Elvis Presley. Another woman jokingly shared that she got her card when she was planning her wedding 10 years ago. She still has the card, but not the husband.

Crafting your big idea

The big idea is strategically placed after goals and objectives and before key publics, messages, strategies and tactics in the action planning section of the matrix. This is done because it is at the heart of the campaign. Although you will be thinking of potential publics, the big idea comes before the identification of key publics because of its appeal across all key publics and its direct tie to the accomplishment of the objectives.

The big idea is a campaign's master strategy and overriding message. If a key public is selected that doesn't seem to fit with the big idea, you either chose the wrong key public or came up with a bad big idea. They must all fit tightly together.

The best way to write down your big idea is to start with a sentence or two that succinctly describes your big idea. You can then identify four components:

1. The big idea strategy.
2. The big idea message.
3. The tangible representation of the big idea.
4. An optional slogan that encapsulates the big idea strategy and message.

Here's an example from the Marriott School of Management at Brigham Young University that may be useful. October 2013 marked the 25th anniversary of the school being named for Marriott Hotel founders J. Willard and Alice S. Marriott. The school's external relations team came up with a big idea to drive its year-long celebration.

The big idea was to tie the school's anniversary to the Marriott company's "Spirit to Serve" initiative and log 25,000 hours of service during the year. This would help business students overcome a common misperception that they care only about money.

1. Big idea strategy: Motivate individuals to serve by showcasing service opportunities and visually tracking progress in a creative way.
2. Big idea message: We have a great name and legacy to live up to — join the celebration by serving.

Big idea

A couple of years ago, a handful of engineering and business students at Brigham Young University and Utah Valley University got together with the idea to use their technical skills to help others in the world. Most had spent time abroad in developing countries. One of the things they had seen was leg amputees with only makeshift prostheses. But after some research they learned that a single below-the-knee prosthesis can cost thousands of dollars. How could they help hundreds to walk and run again?

Using their training, the students developed a simple, flexible prosthetic leg made mostly of PVC material (i.e., common sprinkler pipe). It was a revolutionary design. But perhaps most importantly, it could be made locally in places like Tonga. After some refinements, the team was able to start producing custom PVC prosthetics for about $25 of materials each. They, fittingly, named their organization, 2ft Prosthetics. Their challenge going forward was to raise money, secure supplies and get volunteers to help them expand their work into target areas such as Micronesia.

The following is a combination of what students did and what could be done to begin building a campaign around a big idea.

BIG IDEA

Because of 2ft Prosthetics, it actually costs VERY little to help someone get a new leg. The big idea is to focus on how low the cost is to help people in developing countries run and walk again.

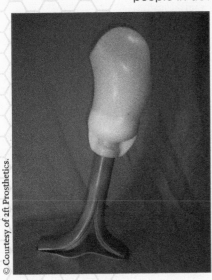

© Courtesy of 2ft Prosthetics.

1. *Big idea strategy:* Motivate individuals to get involved by tapping into emotions. This can be done by showing how easy it is to make a big difference in the lives of amputees around the world.
2. *Big idea message:* It takes only $25 — about the cost of dinner and a movie — to help an amputee walk again.
3. *Tangible representation:* Build several prototype legs that can be used in fundraising and volunteer recruiting. Also film recipients telling their stories and show the recipients walking and running again.
4. *Optional slogan:* How far would you go to help someone walk again?

3. Tangible representation: Build a giant Lucite "M" in the school's atrium and let students add a blue tennis ball for every hour of service.
4. Optional slogan: Marriott School 25 Spirit to Serve (website: marriott25. byu.edu)

The school's 25th anniversary campaign had a lot of other components — including creating ways to involve alumni living across the country who could log their service hours online at marriott25.byu.edu — all tying back to the big idea.

Slogans and taglines

Not every big idea has to have a **slogan**. But slogans and taglines are good ways of reducing your strategy and overriding message to a few words. We recommend experimenting with slogans to see how much information you can convey in a phrase. Slogans should be short, compelling and attention-getting. They should be general enough to relate to all of the publics you will target, and strong enough to appeal to some of their shared self-interests. Some examples of pervasive slogans with high retention value include the "Just Say No" anti-drug slogan and Nike's "Just Do It." Another successful slogan was developed in 1992 for the American Plastics Council, "Plastics Make it Possible." The campaign built around this theme redefined the debate about plastics. The big idea of the campaign, summarized in the tagline, focused key publics on the positive associations they have with plastic such as keeping food fresh, keeping people safe and making possible many of today's lifesaving medical technologies. Instead of directly taking on the environmental concerns people have about plastic, the campaign worked to generate appreciation for the material's unique properties. "Plastics Make it Possible" has been so successful that the American Plastics Council continues to use the tagline today.

Notwithstanding their utility in summarizing key messages, slogans and advertising taglines cannot stand alone as messages to your publics. They are useful in creating synergy among all publics in a campaign and can dramatically affect recall of public-specific messages sent in other channels. A slogan like "Working Toward a More Healthy Community" will bring to mind public-specific messages regarding economic well-being to a business public, messages of physical and mental health to the health care public, and messages of combating drug and alcohol abuse to a parental public. The slogan in and of itself is not an effective message. It is only as good as the public-specific messages that support it.

A big idea at HP

Hewlett-Packard used a big idea to help turn around the company's reputation by rethinking employee communications. In 2011, HP hired Meg Whitman, the sixth CEO of the company in as many years. HP's reputation was at an all-time low. It had been blasted by the media as one of the worst-run companies in the world. Analysts had called for it to be broken up and sold off. Headlines such as "Is HP's Autonomy the worst place to work on the planet?", "Why a Bad CEO is a company killer — sell Hewlett-Packard" and "How Hewlett-Packard Lost Its Way" were not uncommon. HP employees were, understandably, depressed, frustrated and, in some cases, downright angry. The company was in crisis. But the new CEO was committed to keeping the company together. Whitman believed the company had great products and a powerful global workforce of 330,000 employees. But it had to change. And the change had to start from within.

Whitman believed the company could draw upon the power of HP employees as an engine to drive internal change. The company selected Stacey MacNeil, an experienced communications and news practitioner, as a new VP of employee communications to help restore faith in the future of the company and trust in its leadership. The internal communications team came up with a big idea: to give employees permission and encouragement to generate, produce and share company news. Employee communications needed a huge shot of credibility. So MacNeil and her team turned their focus to organic storytelling within the company. "We needed to connect with employees and absolutely build trust," MacNeil says. "We had to activate the employee voice in our communications."

The slogan, "We make it matter," was adapted from HP's "Make it matter" mantra. The overriding message being shared was that HP employees matter in big ways — that they believe in the company and that they are a force for innovation and good that generates thousands of products used throughout the world.

The tangible representation of the big idea at HP was the introduction of HP News Now, an online source for employees posted securely outside the company's firewall. This was done so employees could access it anywhere, including on their mobile devices. HP News Now focuses on transparency: sharing the good and the bad. "We want to talk about where things have gone wrong. We call these 'Teachable Moments.'

HP employee signs wall at "Make it Matter" event in India.

These are sometimes tough stories that are not easily consumed by all employees," MacNeil explains. "We are on a mission to change behavior of the company. Meg asked for us to do this. It's a vibrant conversation."

Another tangible tactic for HPs big idea was to erect giant walls at different company locations where employees could write comments expressing their support for and commitment to the future of the company. Surprisingly, despite the problems HP had faced, the vast majority of comments were positive. The comment walls were put up in advance of Whitman's visits to HP locations around the world. The walls were so successful in engaging employees in conversation that some were left up and preserved as photo backdrops.

Summary

Creativity is more important than ever in building successful campaigns. It's also a skill that can be learned and honed over time. Creativity shows up in several places in the Strategic Planning Matrix — namely under big ideas, messages, strategies and tactics. Use good brainstorming techniques such as priming to help generate fresh ideas. And give yourself permission to be creative. Once you have license to ideate, you can overcome your fears and begin to train yourself to be curious, to observe, to adapt and to experiment by joining concepts together in new ways.

Big ideas are useful in tying an overall campaign strategy and message together. Use brainstorming and other creativity exercises to come up with a tangible representation of your big idea. Then try to encapsulate the idea into a succinct slogan that will appeal across many target publics.

Exercises

1. Brainstorm different themes and activities you could have for a local company's summer employee party. Write at least four questions that you'd like to brainstorm and post them about the room. Hand out pads of sticky notes and ask participants to share at least five ideas per question.

2. Develop a big idea for the employee party. Include the strategy and message. Then add a tangible representation of the big idea. Finally, try your hand at writing a slogan for the activity.

3. Take a week and practice good observation skills. Take pictures of and jot down some notes about at least three creative visuals, messages, slogans or tactics you see each day. Create a best public relations ideas hashtag (#bestprideas) and share your findings through Twitter or Instagram.

Solution to Shallcross test

How easy the answer appears when we give ourselves the permission to breach the perceived boundaries.

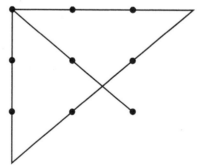

References and additional readings

Blendtec. (2014). "Will It Blend?" Retrieved from http://www.youtube.com/user/Blendtec

Catmull, E., & Wallace, A. (2014). Creativity, Inc.: Overcoming the unseen forces that stand in the way of true inspiration. New York: Random House.

Edelman Worldwide. (2014, May 3). 2014 Edelman Trust Barometer. Retrieved from
http://techli.com/2014/02/chicago-creative-space-sheds-new-light-on-office-culture

Financial Services Team. (2013, November 12). Amex's "Member Since" Legacy Goes Social.
Retrieved from http://www.business2community.com/social-business/amexs-member-
since-legacy-goes-social-0679822#!9Bweg

Irwin, T. (2013, November 26). American Express celebrates "member since," Retrieved from
http://www.mediapost.com/publications/article/214065/american-express-celebrates-
member-since.html

Michalko, M. (2001). Cracking creativity: The secrets of creative genius. Berkeley, CA:
Ten Speed Press.

Ogilvy, D. (1983). Ogilvy on advertising. New York: Vintage Books.

Posternatsky, O. (2014). 10 Steps to establishing a marketing 'big idea' that sells. Retrieved
from http://www.japkin.com/websites/blog/10-steps-to-establishing-a-marketing-big-
idea-that-sells/

Shallcross, D. J. (1981). Teaching creative behavior. Englewood Cliffs, N.J.:Prentice-Hall, Inc.

Tomer, C. (2014). Chicago Creative Space sheds new light on office culture. Retrieved from
http://techli.com/2014/02/chicago-creative-space-sheds-new-light-on-office-culture/

von Oech, R. (1990). A whack on the side of the head: How to be creative. New York:
Warner Books.

von Oech, R. (1983). A whack on the side of the head: How to unlock your mind for
innovation. New York: Warner Books.

Warren, C. (2013, February 4), BlackBerry Super Bowl ad fails to bring the brand back.
[Mashable Op-Ed piece]. Retrieved from http://mashable.com/2013/02/04/blackberry-
super-bowl-oped/

CHAPTER 7

KEY PUBLICS

"An audience is not a demographic. Demographics are the boundaries, psychographics fill in the boundaries."

—Linda Hadley
DIRECTOR OF MARKETING AT METHODIST HOSPITALS

LEARNING IMPERATIVES

- To learn how to effectively select key publics.

- To learn how to use research to profile and analyze publics to discover motivating self-interests, current relationship and opinion leaders.

- To discover the best channels to reach each public so messages are received and result in desired behaviors.

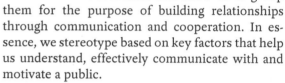

KEY PUBLIC

Segmented group of people whose support and cooperation is essential to the long-term survival of an organization or the short-term accomplishment of specific objectives.

I n Chapter 5, we discussed setting the objectives to be accomplished to meet the challenge of the core problem. Having done so, we can identify the **key publics** whose cooperation will be essential to the success of our big idea and achieving our objectives. In the next chapter, we will discuss designing and delivering the messages that will motivate those publics to act, or to allow the organization to act.

Public versus audience

We use the term "public" to describe a multidimensional active and interactive group of individuals with a few common characteristics that allow us to group them for the purpose of building relationships through communication and cooperation. In essence, we stereotype based on key factors that help us understand, effectively communicate with and motivate a public.

In public relations, we tend to avoid referring to target groups as audiences. Audiences are often defined as spectators or listeners at an event and are therefore more passive than a public. Publics are groups we want to engage with through dynamic two-way symmetrical communication. Thinking about publics as groups to have a conversation with — a certain give and take — will help you identify those you need to work with to accomplish your objectives and goal.

Objective-focused

For some communicators, it has become habit to select key publics before setting objectives. As a result, objectives are determined by who you want to reach rather than what you need to accomplish. Every organization should have identified publics who are key to its long-term success. And the organization should systematically work to build relationships with those publics. But when a problem or challenge emerges, assuming this same set of publics is all that's required to solve it is a prescription for failure. You may be successful at reaching the organization's existing key publics, but you risk missing other publics who are key to seizing the opportunity at hand.

Think about it: If there is a problem, then either your communication is failing, or you've missed some key publics. Either way, the problem won't be corrected until you've analyzed it and set objectives to overcome it. Only when you know what you need to do can you identify the publics needed to help you do it.

Don't waste time and money informing and motivating publics that won't necessarily help you accomplish your goal. First identify the outcomes (objectives) you need to accomplish, and then select those publics that you need to reach and motivate to achieve those outcomes. Your strategies (approach) for a public then become the specific tasks (tactics) you must accomplish with that public to achieve your objectives.

STRATEGIC PLANNING MATRIX

5. BIG IDEA, **KEY PUBLICS,** MESSAGES, STRATEGIES AND TACTICS

Key Publics   Key publics include a description of each group that must be reached to achieve the goal and objectives. Identify:

- Objectives accomplished by key publics
- Demographics and psychographics
- Relationship with organization or issue

- Opinion leaders
- Motivating self-interests
- Viable communication channels

Plan specific messages, strategies and tactics for one public before moving to the next public.

Determining key publics

By this time in your study and practice of marketing communications and public relations, you should be well aware that there is no "general public." Targeting a general public is useless because people won't pay attention to a message that isn't tailored to their self-interests and received through a channel they use. Yet as communicators, our use of so-called mass media seems to perpetuate our tendency to generalize publics. In fact, communicators will often segment publics and then devise a single message to reach all of their segmented publics through the mass media. The segmentation was a waste of time and resources, and the message sent even more of a waste. Remember that just because a medium is designated mass does not mean that the publics consuming the information provided therein are mass.

Think for a moment about how you get your news. Do you read every story in your newsfeed? How about every word in the stories you choose? Probably not. When you read a news story, you choose what you read based on headlines and pictures. Then you continue to read a story only as long as it is of personal interest. The same perceptual behavior applies to new and social media tactics like websites, blogs, Instagram and email. You look at a photo, headline or subject line. If that draws you in by appealing to your self-interests, you continue to read. But the minute it loses its appeal to you personally, you delete it or move on. No matter the channel or tactic, people choose to perceive our messages only when we design them specifically to appeal to their interests. It is clear that for a message to be selected, perceived and retained by our publics from any kind of medium, it must be carefully and specifically targeted to a segmented public included within the viewership, readership, followership or listenership of that medium. If its appeal is general, no public will consider it for perception and retention. It may get sent, but if it doesn't obviously address the self-interests of specific target publics, it will be ignored.

TIPS FROM THE PROS

Breaking through in B2B PR

Kristie Heins Fox, a senior vice president at Edelman, is a 15-year PR veteran who has worked with a variety of business-to-business companies ranging from startups to Fortune 100 corporations. She tips you off on the best practices in B2B PR.

Become an expert. If there is one best practice that I always reinforce with entry-level professionals looking to build a career in B2B public relations, it's to become an expert in the subject matter. That's not to say you specialize out of the gate, but rather put in the time, energy and effort to know your clients' businesses better than they do. Share breaking industry news bubbling up in social media and bring them ideas based on research you've done.

Know your stakeholders. One of the first steps in building out a campaign is understanding the key publics. What works for a general consumer public won't work for electrical engineers, manufacturers or any other B2B customer. And it's not just what you say, but how you say it and the channels you use to communicate. For example, many B2B brands are just testing the waters in social media, so before investing heavily, do your research to determine if your customers are even using social media. In addition, PR is no longer a one-way street, so you must become comfortable communicating with multiple audiences and stakeholder groups in order to drive your clients' messages.

Understand the ecosystem. When working on behalf of a B2B company, it's imperative that you understand not only the company and its customers but also the broad ecosystem of players affecting the company's business. As an example, if you're representing a wireless infrastructure company, the global ecosystem encompasses device/hardware manufacturers, service providers, software and application providers, content providers, semiconductor manufacturers and services/billing providers. All of those must be addressed in your communication.

Identify and get to know key influencers, or opinion leaders. One of the nice things about B2B is that the universe of influencers, or opinion leaders, is well-defined. That said, the growth of social media has turned a lot of enthusiasts into influencers. Some top-line research will help you quickly determine the influencers in a given industry. Edelman launched two tools called TweetLevel and BlogLevel, which are free tools for identifying influencers on Twitter and blogs. Reach out to key opinion leaders, get to know them and provide them with insight and information that helps them do their jobs better while simultaneously building relationships.

Be mindful of ROI. This is always the million-dollar question in every PR program — how do we measure success? The key is establishing clear objectives upfront to set a baseline against which you can measure at regular intervals. The more specific your objectives, the easier it will be to both measure a program's success and, if necessary, adjust your strategy.

Segmenting publics

There are lots of ways to segment publics. The way you choose to segment publics for a particular campaign depends on the issue and your purpose. If you are addressing the quality of education in the community, public segmentation would include parents, teachers, administrators and future employers. If the issue is zoning regulations within that very same community, your segmentation would recategorize the community members as nonproperty owners, residential property owners, commercial property owners or business people and civic and government leaders. In both campaigns, they are the very same people but how you group people together and describe them for the purpose of reaching and motivating them is based upon the issue at hand and the self-interests tied to that issue.

In the background step of the research section, you access market research to understand audience segments using both demographic and psychographic data. The primary and secondary data gathered on publics includes their opinions, attitudes, values, beliefs and lifestyles. The market research tells you their media habits and the best channels to use in communicating with them. Your research describes their current relationships with the issue and organization as well as identifies self-interests and opinion leaders. Because you have gathered and studied that market research, you have a deeper understanding of the potential publics needed to meet your current challenge. Now, review your objectives and determine which public segments are essential in helping you achieve those objectives. Remember that more than one public may need to be reached to accomplish each objective and that a key public may help you achieve more than one objective.

Bear in mind that there may be several different combinations of key publics that can help you accomplish the objectives. As described in Figure 7.1, your task is to discover the combination that: first, does the best job of combining to solve the problem; second, is most logical in terms of ongoing organizational efforts to build relationships; and third, provides the most benefit for the lowest cost in terms of resources (time, money and effort).

Consider, for example, a presidential election campaign. Political campaigns are probably one of the best examples of using thorough research to guide decision-making. The research consultant to a presidential candidate has access to thousands of pieces of information from a variety of research techniques including, at a minimum, focus groups, panel studies and opinion polls. The consultant has divided the voting population into dozens of different segments and has an in-depth, research-based profile of each. The research profiles the attitudes, behaviors and voting preferences of every demographically segmented public by age, income, education, gender, religion, geography, occupation and any other descriptor you can imagine. Further, the consultant has included in the profiles their lifestyles, consumer preferences, habits and other psychographic and value-based characteristics.

Selecting key publics

Arizona's State Department of Health has verified that bubonic plague has been discovered in rats in rural areas of the state, with one confirmed human case. Research shows that while 60 percent of Arizonans know plague is carried by fleas, only 40 percent are aware that rodents in Arizona may be infected. Only 40 percent could identify symptoms of plague, although 45 percent could identify preventive behaviors. Only 35 percent identified antibiotics as the cure. Without treatment, the bubonic plague kills about two out of three infected humans within four days. Because symptoms mimic the flu, treatment is often delayed.

Bubonic plague is generally believed to be the cause of the Black Death that swept through Europe in the 14th century and killed an estimated 25 million people.

Today, the plague occurs mostly in rural areas, so rural residents are at risk. Outdoor recreationalists are at risk, as are farmers, ranchers, pets and pet owners. Those most commonly affected are men ages 20 to 45.

KEY PUBLICS

1. **Outdoor recreationalists.** This public includes all those who participate in outdoor recreation in Arizona's rural areas. Their activities include hunting, fishing, hiking, camping, biking, boating, rock climbing, ATV riding or any other type of outdoor recreation. While they range in age from children to seniors, those most commonly at risk are middle- to upper-class men ages 20 to 45. Most in this group tend to feel invulnerable to risk.

Self-interests:	Enjoying nature and outdoor fun, health and safety.
Relationship:	Informed about plague and prevention. Unaware of current outbreak.
Opinion leaders:	Peers, family, outdoor activity bloggers, personal medical professionals.
Channels:	Recreational venues, recreation retailers, blogs and social media, particularly sites featuring opinion leaders with news, information and tips on outdoor recreation and venues. Targeted cable television programming.

2. **Rural residents.** This public includes residents of small towns as well as farmers and ranchers. They are typically middle-class individuals and families whose roots go back for generations in close-knit communities throughout rural Arizona. They live in the midst of the

recreation venues that draw enthusiasts from all the Western states. They participate in recreation activities as well as provide services to visitors who come for that purpose.

Self-interests:	Health and safety and sustaining lifestyle and community while enjoying the outdoors.
Relationship:	Informed on plague outbreak, preventive behaviors, symptoms and treatment. They are opinion leaders and information sources for outdoor recreationalists.
Opinion leaders:	Peers, family, respected local public servants such as sheriffs.
Channels:	Local community media, word-of-mouth and opinion leaders.

3. **Pet owners.** Because plague is carried by fleas and fleas are attracted to animals, pet owners are important to preventing the spread of disease. A significant portion of the population own at least one pet, many two or more, typically cats or dogs. Demographics of this public are diverse, encompassing all ages and income ranges. Many owners are vigilant in the care of their animals involving grooming and veterinary professionals, but just as many do not invest in such services. Nevertheless, all pet owners purchase pet food and supplies.

Self-interests:	Their health and the health of their animals.
Relationship:	Little awareness of plague in Arizona or the recent outbreak. Little knowledge of symptoms, treatment or prevention.
Opinion leaders:	Neighbors, family, friends, co-workers and pet care providers.
Channels:	Mass media, social media, opinion leaders. Also pet-related retailers and service providers.

4. **Medical professionals.** This public includes all medical professionals whether in private practices, clinics, instacares or hospitals. These are upper-middle-class to upper-class, well-educated individuals. They are opinion leaders to other publics.

Self-interests:	Welfare of patients and their professional reputations.
Relationship:	Familiar with plague routinely occurring in rural areas, unaware of recent outbreak.
Opinion leaders:	Employers, patients, state and county health officials.
Channels:	State and county health departments, employers and local mass media news.

TV anchor Anderson Cooper shakes hands with Debbie Gibson at the 39th Annual Daytime Emmy Awards in Beverly Hills, Calif.

INTERVENING PUBLIC

An influential individual or small group of people used to carry a message to a key public.

With all those segments, there are literally hundreds of combinations of publics that could accomplish the task of election of the candidate for president. A strategist might, for example, choose a combination that includes, among others, 24- to 32-year-olds, Catholics, blue-collar workers and Northeastern voters. The job of the strategist in a political campaign is to select, from the dozens of profiled segments, the combination of voter publics that will best assure victory in the election (priority one in Figure 7.1). In selecting publics to bring victory, the strategist should also consider those publics whose cooperation will be most crucial to the long-term success of the newly elected president (priority two). Finally, the strategist should consider the combination of publics that will bring the most benefit for the least cost (priority three).

Too often in the past, business has operated with that third priority as the first consideration. Leading our decisions with only cost considerations has landed us in the current crisis of trust among those publics that are most essential to survival of organizations in our society. The key publics selected to meet any challenge we face should be those best combined to facilitate proper resolution and long-term success. If cost considerations become a concern, they should be addressed in more creative use of resources rather than jeopardizing the long-term health of the organization.

Intervening publics

An **intervening public** is one that carries our message to the publics we ultimately need to reach and influence. Media and opinion leaders are intervening publics that are often used in communications and persuasion. Teachers or PTA volunteers in school are sometimes good channels to get a message to a parental public. Health care workers are good intervening publics on health issues. Intervening publics are not typically designated as key publics unless you need to persuade them to help you. If you need to develop or strengthen a relationship with an intervening public to ensure its cooperation, you might designate it as a key public. For example, if you've had a problem with media being hostile, unresponsive or inaccurate, you may need to identify them as a key public and develop strategies and tactics that will improve your relationship with them. Otherwise, media are typically an intervening public or channel we often use to reach our key publics.

Figure 7.1 _____
Priorities in selecting the best combination of key publics

1. Which publics working together will produce the best overall solution?

2. Which publics make the most sense for long-term organizational relationships?

3. Which combination of publics will get the desired result for the least amount of additional time, money and other resources?

Is Tylenol making you sick?

MINI CASE

**JOHNSON &
JOHNSON**

BACKSTORY

In November 2009, Johnson & Johnson issued a recall of five lots of Tylenol because of consumer complaints about a mold-like odor and reports that it caused nausea, stomach pain, vomiting and diarrhea. As complaints piled up, the company reluctantly opened an investigation into the problem. After investigating the situation for several months, Johnson & Johnson discovered that the odor was coming from chemically treated wooden pallets used to store and transport the affected medicines.

Upon discovering the probable cause of the contamination, as well as problems with additional products, the health care giant was forced to recall more than 54 million over-the-counter medicines.

While the tainted products were removed from circulation, J&J now faced the challenge of how to regain market share lost in the recall to generic competitors and how to restore confidence in the company's brands.

KEY FACTS

- 100-count Tylenol caplets sell in stores for more than $10, whereas generic brands, such as Equate, sell for only $3.
- McNeil Consumer Healthcare — a subsidiary of Johnson & Johnson — was responsible for the production and recall of the medicines in question.
- Recalled products included not only Tylenol but also Rolaids, St. Joseph Aspirin, Simply Sleep, Benadryl and several Motrin products.
- The FDA reported at least 70 people who exhibited gastrointestinal problems associated with the medicines.
- The Tylenol recall was one of 13 issued by the company in a year.

Spencer Platt/Getty Images News/Getty Images

How would you execute a major product recall?

JOHNSON & JOHNSON'S STRATEGY

J&J was aware of contamination issues as early as May 2008. Knowing that an investigation could potentially harm the company's reputation and shrink sales, J&J chose to lay low and avoid the issue for several months. As more and more complaints were voiced, the company reluctantly opened an investigation in order to appease disgruntled customers. It was quietly initiated and quickly abandoned, labeling the illnesses as "isolated incidents."

In an attempt to maintain its image, J&J constantly downplayed the seriousness of the contamination and failed to provide

(continued)

transparent communications to its key publics — taking more than a year to finally release a statement on the issue.

Finally, hoping that the recall would make the issue go away, J&J continued to downplay the incident and released very little information to its customers. In the week following the recall, apart from a press release, Johnson & Johnson only added a couple of posts to its blog and directed customers to the McNeil website, which contained only scant information about the contamination and recall.

RESULTS

- A YouGov BrandIndex survey that measured media attention named J&J's Tylenol one of the biggest decliners in positive brand perception during 2010.
- A study of consumer satisfaction conducted by 24/7 Wall St., ranked J&J as the 11th most-hated company in America during 2010.
- In the three quarters following the recall, sales of J&J's over-the-counter brands in the U.S. declined 31.1 percent from $2.1 billion to $1.5 billion as concerned customers' loyalty shifted to generic and store brands, which cost significantly less.
- Because J&J tried to hide its problems and acted slowly, customers lost confidence in the company and the efficacy of its products — refusing to pay the premiums J&J once commanded.

WORKS CITED

Anonymous. (2011, November 1). Subway tops BrandIndex buzz chart 2010. Retrieved from http://www.com/marketing/item/27704-subway-tops-brandindex-buzz

Belsie, L. (2010, January 15). With Tylenol recall 2010, a corporate icon stumbles. Retrieved from http://www.csmonitor.com/Business/new-economy/2010/0115/With-Tylenol-recall-2010-a-corporate-icon-stumbles/(page)./3

CBSNews. (2010, October 18). Tylenol recalled for moldy smell. Retrieved from http://www.cbsnews.com/news/tylenol-recalled-for-moldy-smell/

Edwards, J. (2010, October 19). Magic number: Tylenol recall cost J&J $665M in lost sales. Retrieved from http://www.cbsnews.com/news/magic-number-tylenol-recall-cost-jj-665m-in-lost-sales/

Johnson & Johnson. (2010, January 18). Retrieved from http://www.blogjnj.com/?s=recall

King Rogers, L. (2010, April 1). Wood pallets cited as cause for McNeil's Tylenol recall. Retrieved from http://www.mmh.com/article/wood_pallets_cited_as_cause_for_mcneils_tylenol_recall/

Seaman, M. (2010, January 16). Tylenol recall: Johnson & Johnson issues massive recall. Retrieved from http://www.huffingtonpost.com/2010/01/16/tylenol-recall-johnson-jo_n_425754.html

The 10 most hated companies in America. Retrieved from http://www.rankingthebrands.com/The-Brand-Rankings.aspx?rankingID=102&year=256

Turley, J. (2010, January 15). Moldrin: Johnson & Johnson recalls over-the-counter drugs over possible contamination. Retrieved from http://jonathanturley.org/2010/01/15/moldrin-johnson-and-johnson-recalls-over-the-counter-drugs-over-possible-contamination/

U.S. Food and Drug Administration. (2010). Retrieved from http://www.fda.gov/downloads/AboutFDA/CentersOffices/ORA/ORAElectronicReadingRoom/UCM197539.pdf

Plan each public separately

A key public will usually be helpful in accomplishing more than one of your objectives. Strategies for those publics should be planned with a complete view of all you need to accomplish with them. Otherwise strategies for separate objectives will be isolated from each other and may not tie to your big idea. They may also result in tactics that don't integrate well into the overall campaign plan, and in some cases even conflict with each other. Separating publics and strategies by specific outcomes or objectives tends to fragment your efforts and lose the advantage of overlapping reinforcement.

David Beckham launches Home Depot Soccer Academy in Carson, Calif.

When drafting your plan, focus on one public at a time. Write all of the messages, strategies and tactics for that public before moving on to the next public. This approach will help you maximize the whole of their contribution and create synergy among your strategies and tactics. Use your market research to help you make decisions about messages, strategies and tactics that will yield results.

That research will tell you where you stand in terms of your current relationship with each public and give you a baseline to know what you need to do and how to design your messages and strategies. The research also identifies self-interests, which are crucial in designing messages that publics will pay attention to and act on. Further, the research identifies the opinion leaders that may act as intervening publics to provide a personal appeal or challenge to act.

Summary

Once objectives are set, we can select the most effective combination of publics to accomplish them. To be holistic in accomplishing the goal, we need to remember that more than one key public may be needed to reach an objective and that a key public may help satisfy multiple objectives. At this point, we may also select intervening publics to help us get our messages to the key publics.

To design and send effective messages for each of our key publics, we rely on market research. Our selection and incisive analysis of publics is essential to our success. We cannot design and effectively convey messages that will result in the behavior that accomplishes our objectives unless we thoroughly understand each public. Our understanding must include the publics' overriding self-interests regarding the issue, the opinion leaders who influence them on the issue and our current relationship with each public.

Exercises

1. Review the Matrix Applied case in this chapter. Suggest at least two different combinations of publics that could alternatively be used to accomplish the goal and objectives.

2. Select a local small business and do a brief analysis of its function and the issues routinely faced. Then identify the organization's key publics, the key publics' self-interests and opinion leaders and the organization's current relationship with each key public.

3. Conduct some focus groups to discover the formal and informal opinion leaders of a couple of segmented publics on an issue of your choosing.

4. Identify a nonprofit organization and analyze the messages it sends to different publics. Do those messages show evidence of a thorough understanding of each public's self-interests, opinion leaders and preferred communication channels?

References and additional readings

Broom, G. M., & Sha, B. (2013). *Cutlip and Center's effective public relations* (11th ed.). Upper Saddle River, NJ: Pearson Education.

Newsom, D., Turk, J. V., & Kruckeberg, D. (2013). *This is PR: The realities of public relations* (11th ed.). Cengage Learning.

Stern and Company. (2007). Targeting key publics and message definition. Retrieved from asternglance.com/sternco-essays-2/targeting-key-public-and-message-definition

Wilcox, D. L., Cameron, G. T., & Reber, B. H. (2014). *Public relations: Strategies and tactics* (11th ed.). Upper Saddle River, NJ: Pearson Education.

CHAPTER 8

MESSAGES, STRATEGIES AND TACTICS

"Strategy without tactics is the slowest route to victory. Tactics without strategy is the noise before defeat."

—Sun Tzu

CHINESE MILITARY GENERAL, STRATEGIST AND PHILOSOPHER

LEARNING IMPERATIVES

- To be able to design effective messages for each key public that incorporate relevant self-interests.

- To be able to design strategies that reach a public with a message to motivate a desired behavior.

- To understand how to select the best channels to deliver messages to key publics.

- To be able to design creative tactics delivered through specific channels.

- To understand how to use strategy briefs to develop effective tactics.

Now that you know what you need to do to resolve your problem and who you need to reach to accomplish that, you are ready to design and deliver the messages to motivate your key publics to do what you want them to do. Remember that messages are public-specific. You cannot successfully incorporate a public's self-interest into a message generalized to all publics. Each public will need a different appeal based on its particular self-interests.

Message design

Messages are written in two parts: primary and secondary. Primary messages are the leading drivers in the campaign, and secondary messages are more specific details that fill out the primary messages and make them believable.

PRIMARY MESSAGES
Sound-bite statements that encompass what you need the public to do and an appeal to the public's self-interest to act.

Primary messages

Primary messages are the main categories of information for each public. They often resemble sound bites that might be given during a media interview. The primary messages encompass what you want the public to understand, believe or do. They also include a short self-interest appeal (see the Matrix Applied box in this chapter). A campaign to reduce obesity among children, for example, will have a number of primary messages. For parents of children 12 and under, a primary message in this campaign might be, "Healthy adults come from healthy kids — ensure your child's future with a healthy diet today." You want parents to take a more proactive role in looking after the nutrition of their children, and parents want their children to grow into healthy, successful adults.

© Monkey Business Images/Shutterstock.com

As you begin developing primary messages for each key public, remember that all messages should, at least loosely, support the big idea strategy and message of the campaign.

The number of primary messages for a key public will depend upon the breadth and duration of the campaign. This is best determined by the objectives (measurable outcomes) you have set. If you need a particular public's help and support for only one outcome, you may need only one primary message. Several different outcomes or desired actions may require more primary messages. Typically, a key public will have two to four primary messages.

SECONDARY MESSAGES
Bulleted details that include facts, testimonials, examples and all other information or persuasive arguments that support a public's primary message.

Secondary messages

Secondary messages contain the meat, or evidence, that validates the primary messages. There are usually far more secondary messages than primary messages. The secondary messages contain all the facts, statistics, case studies, anecdotes, testimonials and other details that support a primary message. In the above campaign to

STRATEGIC PLANNING MATRIX

ACTION PLANNING

5. BIG IDEA, KEY PUBLICS, **MESSAGES, STRATEGIES AND TACTICS**

Messages Message design is public-specific and focuses on self-interests. Create a small number of primary and a larger number of secondary messages for each public.

Primary messages are short summary statements similar to sound bites. They identify a category of information and/or communicate what action you want a public to take. They also tie the desired action to a public's self-interest(s).

Secondary messages are bulleted statements that give credibility to the primary message with facts, testimonials, examples and stories. They provide the ethos, pathos and logos of persuasion.

Strategies Strategies identify what a public must do to fulfill an objective and the channel(s) through which messages will be sent to motivate that action. Multiple strategies may be required for each public.

Tactics Tactics are the creative elements and tools used to deliver messages through specific channels. A number of tactics are required to support each strategy. Examples are story placements, YouTube videos, Twitter posts, special events, infographics, websites or blogs.

combat obesity in children, secondary messages to support the primary message to parents with young children might be:

- Obesity among children has increased 23 percent during the last decade.
- Most eating and exercise habits among adults form before the teenage years.
- The FDA recently updated its nutrition recommendations for children under the age of 13.
- Ninety percent of obese children have self-esteem issues.

Remember that strong motivational messages always tap into a public's self-interests. Never forget that people don't do what you want them to just because you ask them. They must first become informed and then motivated. Richard Wirthlin, a world-renowned market researcher and founder of Wirthlin Worldwide, advised communicators to "persuade through reason and motivate through emotion." In order to do so, your message must contain rational information (logos), be delivered by someone the key public trusts (ethos) and contain an emotional appeal (pathos) to a public's self-interest.

At the heart of the planning process are the decisions we make about the messages we want to send to our key publics and the best way to get those messages to

Massaging your message

Trevor C. Hale, director of corporate communications, Asia Pacific and Africa at Ford Motor Company, tips you off on how to craft a message that's crisp, cool, clean and contains no transfat.

Joseph Pulitzer gave some famous advice about writing: "Put it before them briefly so they will read it, clearly so they will appreciate it, picturesquely so they will remember it and, above all, accurately so they will be guided by its light."

One of my mentors, University of Alabama at Birmingham's John W. Wittig, said, "A good speech should be like a skirt or a kilt: long enough to cover the subject, but short enough to be interesting." Whether drafting a news release, tweeting a corporate update, trying to make your boss seem funny in a dinner speech or choosing the best hashtag for your Instagram photo, your message should be crisp, customized and memorable and have purpose.

Where's the beef? Garnish is nice, but messages need meat to be newsworthy. Don't make a journalist on deadline or blogger wade through filler to find something digestible. Yuck!

Tough crowd! Know thy audience. Using ancient words like "cool" or "hip" with teenagers in order to appear cool and hip will most assuredly be seen as neither cool nor hip. Can you D-I-G I-T? And if you ever find yourself addressing the Communist leadership of the People's Republic of China at an important state luncheon, don't welcome them as the Republic of China (also known as Taiwan, China's "renegade" province).

There is no B-3 bomber. While not to be used lightly or frequently, according to the famous Chinese military strategist Sun Tzu, misdirection and ambiguity can be very useful in warfare.

It's cliché to avoid clichés. But avoid them like the plague or you'll sound like a broken record. Listen to your heart. Follow your instinct. Stick a fork in me — I'm done.

those publics. It is in this central part of the process that we need most to be guided by our research. Yet, we are most tempted to rely on instinct alone. Not that instinct is necessarily bad. It is often a subconscious process of integrating bits and pieces of knowledge and information and charting an appropriate course given the data. But, it can also be an unwillingness to believe information and data because it conflicts with limited personal observation. In the latter case, instinct usually leads us to follow courses that fail to solve — and often exacerbate — the problem. To avoid that error, we would be wise to always test our instinct against the information and data gathered through research.

If you learn through your research that a particular target public is motivated on a given issue by its self-interest in quality of life for their children, your message must convey the importance of that result. Parents concerned about their children's safety from gang violence are motivated by messages and arguments that promise a safer environment, not by arguments of taxpayer cost. ("Can we place a monetary value on a child's life?") On the other hand, if your target public is more concerned about higher taxes and the government's growing demands on their income to solve social problems, they will be more motivated by messages that focus on perceived low-cost solutions. ("Lock them up; we can't keep spending money on expensive programs for the socially deviant!")

Essential factors

How you **segment publics** to achieve your objectives and the self-interests you identify dictate the messages to be sent. Your message strategy should contain two essential factors: 1) Your purpose — what you need to accomplish, and 2) Your appeal to a key public's self-interest — what will motivate them to act favorably to accomplish your objectives. Messages will essentially be both informational and motivational.

Designing primary and secondary messages in this way provides you with an array of messages that can be combined for use in channels that allow for in-depth coverage such as magazines and brochures, or used individually and in small combinations in social media channels such as Twitter, Facebook and Instagram.

This structure of a few primary messages and a number of more specific, fact-driven secondary messages is also perfect for media training. Top executives and other spokesmen and women can be trained on what the primary messages are for a media interview. But having a wealth of secondary messages that support the small number of primary messages will give them more tools and added depth in responding to inquiries. A CEO might explain that the company is being forced to relocate part of its manufacturing to Asia in order to remain competitive. She/he could then support this assertion (primary message) with a number of secondary messages that contain facts and examples of how the move will enable the company to be more competitive and continue employing most of its existing workforce.

SEGMENTATION
Defining and separating publics by demographics and psychographics to ensure more effective communication.

Delivering messages

Once messages have been carefully crafted, you can now design **strategies** and **tactics** to carry your messages to their intended publics. Strategies and tactics are public-specific — they are designed with one public in mind. They are the best way to give a key public its own message to motivate desired behavior.

We can draw a simple analogy to military strategy. In an overall challenge to win a battle, one objective might be to secure a certain piece of ground or a particular town. A strategy would be devised on how to approach this objective. The strategy may be to weaken the town's defenses and attack through a particularly vulnerable spot in the wall. The tactics supporting the strategy may be an artillery barrage, aerial bombing, a Special Forces patrol to plant explosives to create a breech and a ground assault through the wall into the town. The strategy provides the overall approach to a particular objective answering what and, very generally, how it will be accomplished. Tactics are the specific step-by-step activities necessary to achieve the strategy.

STRATEGIES
Public-specific approaches specifying the channel to send the messages to achieve objectives.

TACTICS
Strategy-specific communication products that carry the message to key publics.

Figure 8.1 _____
Formula for writing an effective strategy

A strategy is an approach, not a list of tasks. Strategies are public-specific and identify a channel or group of related channels you will use to reach a target public to accomplish an objective by appealing to the public's self-interests.

Formula: *Action verb* the *target public* through *communications channel(s)* that *the objective* will satisfy the *target public's self-interests*.

Example: *Convince* the *Orange County Commissioners* through *in-person meetings with company officials and engineers* that *approving the new plant* will have *a significant positive economic impact on the community*.

_____

In communicating with an organization's publics, the strategies are the approaches to reaching a designated public for a particular purpose with the message that will inform or motivate that public. There are many different ways to craft a strategy. Figure 8.1 provides a proven formula for writing an effective strategy.

The tactics that support each strategy identify in greater detail the specific tasks required to send your messages (e.g., blog posts, tweets, employee meetings, newsletter articles, payroll envelope stuffers, special events and emails from the company president). Tactics are strategy-specific because they support a single strategy targeted at a particular public.

Strategies

As we said earlier, your strategy for message delivery is public-specific. In other words, you don't determine how you are going to send a message until you know who you are trying to reach and what you are trying to tell them. The strategy inherently identifies the public, and then addresses what you are trying to do in support of your objectives and the **channel** you propose to use to send the appeal.

CHANNEL
The conduit or medium through which messages are sent to a specific public to accomplish a specific purpose.

Informational versus motivational strategies

Strategies directly support the objectives by identifying what action or behavior is desired. The action part of a strategy may be informational or motivational. Informational strategies (also known as awareness or educational strategies) lay a significant foundation of information for the motivational strategies that ask the key public to act in some way.

As with objectives, it may not be necessary to have a separate informational strategy. If a public is already sufficiently educated and is latently ready to act, necessary information can be carried by the motivational strategy to avoid the risk of fragmenting your strategies and messages. All motivational strategies will contain some information messages either in separate tactics or within each tactic. A tactic that appeals for a citizen's vote will almost always include some information to justify the action. Your job is to determine whether a separate informational strategy is necessary for that public. If there is a significant lack of knowledge and understanding, you probably need an informational strategy to lay a foundation before you can implement strategies to motivate behavior. If the information is already pervasive and people just need to be reminded, the informational tactics within a motivational strategy will be sufficient.

For example, many people still do not understand that many mental illnesses — like depression — have a physiological cause that must be addressed with medication. Any effort to motivate people with mental illness to see a doctor would require creating a better informed public environment. But to motivate people to give blood, you may only need to tell them where and when to show up. Virtually everyone understands the need and the process.

As you know, objectives always require a metric of some kind. Each objective must specify improvement that can be measured. The action identified in a public-specific strategy may also be stated in measurable terms. While not all strategies will detail the action this specifically, it may be necessary for some to do so. If a campaign supporting a local municipal bond requires 55 percent of the vote to pass, public-specific strategies may break that overall percentage down into manageable pieces for each public. A 55 percent overall vote may translate to 85 percent of business leaders, 65 percent of white-collar workers, 45 percent of blue-collar workers and 58 percent of stay-at-home parents. The strategies for each public may include these specific measurements to support the overall objective.

Choosing strategic channels

Determining the right channel or group of channels to send the message in a strategy is dependent upon both the message itself and the public being targeted. Take a look around. Some marketing and communications strategies have become so pervasive in our society that we don't give them a second thought. What has become the almost exclusive strategy to market beer to an age-segmented male audience? The primary strategy is to use humor and celebrity athletes, and the channel is to use sporting events to deliver beer-drinking messages to that target public. This channel has literally hundreds of potential tactics to carry the message. What is the predominant fundraising strategy of your local United Way? It is an annual campaign that leverages workplace peer pressure. The main channel is work-

NASCAR driver Kasey Kahne *watches cars practice at the Food City 500 race in Bristol, Tenn.*

place communication from which you can select specific tactics such as personal invitations from management, department competitions, posters and personalized emails. United Way annual campaign messages are focused at a specific public with the ability to give using tactics that overlap and reinforce one another to accomplish the purpose.

Another example is an objective to double participation in educational programs for disabled children. Parents of disabled children would be a key public. They would require an informational strategy to inform them of the resources available and a motivational strategy to persuade them to tap into these resources.

Message design, strategies and tactics

Once the Arizona State Department of Health has identified which key publics need to be motivated to meet the challenge faced by the recent outbreak of bubonic plague in rural areas, the state must develop effective message design and delivery for each public. This example will cover message design, strategies and tactics for outdoor recreationalists.

OUTDOOR RECREATIONALISTS' MESSAGE DESIGN

Primary message one: You can have many more seasons of outdoor fun by practicing smart plague prevention.

Secondary messages:
- Bubonic plague is a deadly disease transmitted by fleas that are often carried by animals and rodents in rural areas. This plague is believed to be the cause of the Black Death that swept through Europe in the 14th century.
- The plague has been found in rodents living in rural areas of the state.
- To stay healthy and safe, always use insect repellent containing DEET applied to both skin and clothing when in the outdoors. Stay away from debris and other areas where rodents may hide. Never touch or handle wild animals or rodents. Wear protective clothing as appropriate.
- Tell your friends about the outbreak, and encourage them to prevent the spread of the plague.
- Go to www.AZfightsplague.org for more information.

Primary message two: Know the symptoms of plague infection and seek immediate medical attention if you have any symptoms. Your life depends upon it.

Secondary messages:
- Plague manifests itself with flu-like symptoms such as aches, fever and chills.
- The most obvious symptom of bubonic plague is an infection of the lymph glands, which become swollen and painful.
- Without treatment, bubonic plague kills about two out of three infected humans.
- People potentially infected with the plague need immediate treatment and should be given antibiotics within 24 hours of the first symptoms to prevent death.
- Plague can be successfully treated with antibiotics if caught early.
- Tell your friends and encourage them to immediately see a doctor if they have symptoms.
- Go to www.AZfightsplague.org for more information.

OUTDOOR RECREATIONALISTS' MESSAGE DELIVERY

Strategy one: Raise awareness among outdoor recreationalists of the bubonic plague threat and prevention through retailers of recreation products and rental equipment outlets.

Tactics:
1. Letter from state health director and governor explaining threat and asking for their cooperation and participation in an awareness and prevention campaign.
2. Follow-up calls to retailers and rental outlets to encourage participation in the AZ Fights Plague campaign.
3. Information kits containing:
   a. Posters to be displayed in stores.
   b. Flyers to be distributed as bag stuffers with each purchase.
   c. Fact sheet for employees with suggested preventive measures and a list of suggested products.
4. Links to participating retailers on the www.AZfightsplague.org website and Facebook page.

Strategy two: Raise awareness among outdoor recreationalists of the risk of plague in certain areas through targeted recreational venues.

Tactics:
1. Signs prominently placed at trailheads, campsites and other recreational venues with QR code link to AZ Fights Plague website.
2. Posters at fee stations and information booths.
3. Flyers distributed by park rangers and venue employees at fee stations, information booths and park shops and restaurants.
4. Information and AZ Fights Plague links on official BLM, Forest Service and state and National Park Services reservation and permit websites as part of the purchase process.

Strategy three: Use social media to motivate outdoor recreationalists to employ plague prevention behaviors and seek immediate medical treatment when necessary.

Tactics:
1. Launch official Arizona Fights Plague website at www. AZfightsplague.org, which includes:
   a. Fact sheet about bubonic plague.
   b. Map showing areas where plague has been confirmed.
   c. Preventive measures checklist.
   d. Bubonic plague infection warning signs.
   e. Medical treatment options.

(Continued)

Message design, strategies and tactics (*continued*)

      f. Link to YouTube AZ Fights Plague video.

      g. Infographic about plague risks, prevention and how to identify symptoms.

      h. FAQs.

      i. Participating retailer links with downloadable posters and flyers.

      j. Links to recreationalists' blog posts.

2. Set up Facebook page featuring news and information (similar to website) on plague and plague prevention linking to participating retailers and rental outlets.

3. Smart media release to recreational bloggers and local TV/cable recreational shows on plague, symptoms, treatment and prevention.

4. Links to Facebook page and official plague website on state and county venue sites, as well as on websites of groups, clubs and associations organized around outdoor recreational activities such as four-wheeling, rock climbing, hiking and mountain biking.

5. YouTube video about plague prevention and warning signs, which can be shared through social media channels.

6. Infographic about plague risks, prevention and how to identify symptoms.

An informational strategy for this public would be to increase awareness of the resources available to parents of disabled children through a health fair sponsored by the state that showcases the services available to them. Tactics would probably include things like printed materials, videos, websites, Facebook groups and other tactics available at or publicized by the fair.

A motivational strategy would be to persuade parents of disabled children to sign up for one or more of the state's free health services through one-on-one consultations with health care professionals. Tactics for this strategy might include email invitations to meet, referrals from health care professionals and an in-home consultation sign-up at the health fair.

As we've already seen, opinion leader influence is best exerted by people the parents perceive to be operating credibly in a relevant issue environment. In the above example, nurses and other health care providers would have high credibility. Peers — in this case, other parents with disabled children — would also have very high credibility. Volunteer PTA leaders may also wield significant influence with this key public. Design strategies and tactics so that you can use opinion leaders to both inform and motivate your key publics.

The channel stipulated in a strategy should be the best way to get the message to the public for the outlined purpose (e.g., health fair, workplace communication or opinion leaders). In order to be sufficiently planned, each strategy requires the development of specific tactics within the channel (communication tools like signage and T-shirts at staged events, brochures and personalized emails in the workplace and meetings with printed collateral material or tablet presentations for opinion leaders).

How channels help focus your tactics

The tactics specify the communication tools within the channel more precisely. In the previous example, one of your tactics might be to create an app for parents of disabled children that explains all of the services available to them. Other tactics could be an infographic, video or printed brochure. Perhaps a follow-up tactic would also be helpful, such as an email survey following the fair to see how beneficial it was and what parents learned.

By focusing tactics within a specific channel, you ensure that members of the key public will receive the message at least once, but likely more than once. Such focused overlap makes it more certain the message will be selected to be perceived, retained and acted upon. The latest research suggests that a person must be exposed to a message three or four times before it is remembered.

The point is that you must carefully consider your public in determining the best ways to reach them. How a particular public best receives a certain type of message for a specific purpose is the relevant question. You must also carefully consider the message being sent to ensure the channels and media selected are appropriate for the message.

Declining importance of mass media channels

It is critically important to recognize that the effective and extensive use of the mass media to communicate with target audiences mostly belongs to past decades. While mass media can still be highly effective in generating name recognition, their information-disseminating utility is not as great as before because of the proliferation of options and declining trust.

In the Golin/Harris 2002 Trust Index, the communications business sectors all had negative trust scores (Golin, p. 240). Of them all, public relations had the least of the negative scores (-31), followed by journalism (-38) and then advertising/marketing (-41). The situation isn't much better for the media today. In the 2014 Edelman Trust Barometer, media ranked seventh among eight industry categories on trust. Only banks came in behind the media.

While mass media channels have their place, in an environment where media are not trusted, it is unwise to rely on them too heavily. In fact, with peers or "someone like me" being among the most credible sources of information today, social media has largely overtaken traditional media as the best channel for messages.

We are accustomed to segmenting publics for the purpose of persuasion. We have long recognized that identifying a group of people who share common interests and lifestyles (and who may interact with one another) is the best way to devise an appeal that will motivate them. Now, segmentation is required not just to persuade, but to reach our

© Alexey Mark/Shutterstock.com

desired publics. Readership of traditional newspapers is declining and almost non-existent among Gen-X and Gen-Y publics. But even those who still read a newspaper have increased their selectivity in what they read and how they read. Most broad audience magazines have disappeared. The final edition of Newsweek, a popular weekly current affairs magazine, hit newsstands on Dec. 31, 2012. Some of these broad audience publications are still available online, but many have been replaced by highly segmented special-interest and professional or trade publications.

The explosion in cable and satellite television technology is already creating highly segmented viewership, which will continue to increase. In 2013, NBC Universal launched Esquire Network for communicators and marketers looking to reach men outside of sports. The new network is aiming at the elusive upscale man, metropolitan and educated, or as Esquire magazine President David Granger calls them, "the high-normal American male." Another example of the proliferation of channels is the fact that there has been a channel devoted exclusively to tennis for more than a decade. And radio has long been segmented by listeners' preferences for differing formats and music.

The lesson to be learned is that mass media (which arguably never did reach a mass public) are declining in their ability to reach our publics with the messages we need sent. The good news is that as a medium becomes more specific and segmented, it becomes a better buy in terms of reaching the public segments we need to target. So while our jobs may be a bit more difficult in that we need to exercise a greater range of creativity and expertise in using differentiated communication tools, we are promised higher rates of success because of the emergence of social media and the narrowing of mass media audiences.

New technologies and the Internet

The widespread use of technologies has made the digital production and distribution of communication materials (such as infographics, videos and blogs) relatively easy and inexpensive. The range of diversified and alternative media has, as a result, burgeoned. Mobile phones, tablets and laptop computers have all become ubiquitous devices for viewing, creating and sharing information. Most information is consumed electronically — and mobile devices now provide more news to people than laptops or newspapers. News aggregators like Digg, Google News, Pulse and News360 have fueled the use of mobile devices for information consumption because they reduce the need to navigate by doing the legwork for you. These aggregators pull together syndicated Web content from online newspapers, blogs, podcasts and video blogs or vlogs in one location for easy viewing. The rise of mobile apps has also made it easier to access information of interest to users.

The opportunities provided by the Internet include a growing range of options to creatively communicate messages. As in the early days of radio, sponsors and website owners now create online programming — similar to soaps and sitcoms — to secure vehicles for product promotion. Skype, ooVoo, Google Chat and other services now make online video conferencing and chatting easy. WebEx and other software platforms have proliferated the use of **webinars**. And affinity portals, websites

WEBINAR/WEB CONFERENCE

An online conference or workshop where participants can all see and hear a presentation simultaneously and interact with the presenter and each other.

© Andrey Popov/Shutterstock.com

visited often by a particular group of fans or alumni, are an excellent way to reach some targeted publics.

Online newsrooms are now a standard tool used to provide information not only to journalists, but increasingly to opinion leaders and other information-hungry consumers. Electronic newsletters offer specialized information on virtually any subject — from finance to sports to crossword puzzles. Chat rooms, electronic email lists, online forums and many other Internet features are effective tactics to be considered. Smart use of search engines, QR codes and website links can also provide opportunities to communicate additional messages to publics predisposed to be receptive.

While making it easier, faster and less expensive to send messages to certain publics, the Internet also makes it easier for opposing publics, or just someone with a grudge, to attack your organization or products online. Especially with social media, the backlash can be brutal. It is virtually impossible to block or even monitor everything anyone wants to post regarding your organization. And there is no filter or screen for lies and misrepresentations. No one asks whether the attack is credible — sometimes not even the media whose responsibility it is to ask. It is tremendously difficult to deal with false information that can be published so broadly, freely and anonymously. This dilemma underscores the importance of continual trust-building efforts among all key publics.

Citizen journalism and blogs

The astronomical growth of blogs has created new subject-matter experts and opinion leaders that in many cases have far surpassed the influence of mainstream media. Public relations agencies often give prominent bloggers better media credentials than mainstream journalists to attend conventions, product launches and industry events like fashion week. For example, one 16-year-old male fashion blogger was recently seated in front of professional journalists from papers such as USA Today and Daily News at New York Fashion Week. This is because top bloggers have a bigger following than the mass media outlets among a niche group of consumers that really matter. The bloggers are also more likely to be trusted. A 2013 report showed that 81 percent of U.S. consumers trust advice and information they read on blogs, and 61 percent say they have made a purchase based on a blog post.

As of 2012, there were more than 170 million blogs. In the U.S. alone, there are now more than 31 million bloggers. The rapid rise of citizen journalism has been driven by three factors: open publishing, collaborative editing and distributed content. Blogging is more than a pastime. It has grown, for some, into a lucrative and rewarding career. Learning how to effectively pitch content and work with bloggers is an important part of today's media relations.

Social media and the way we connect

Despite all the advances in technology and the extreme segmentation of entertainment and news sources, social media has had and will increasingly have the biggest

TIPS FROM THE PROS

Building a successful blog

Brittany Watson Jepsen, a professional interior designer and creator of the popular blog, The House that Lars Built, tips you off on how to create a successful blog.

Starting a blog from scratch can feel like a daunting task, but it doesn't have to. One way to find out if you are up to the challenge is to try guest blogging for other sites. This will not only strengthen your writing skills but also help you know if blogging is something you're passionate about. When you know you're ready to dive in, follow these five tips to improve the likelihood of your blog taking off.

1. *Find a niche.* Choose a topic that you really enjoy as well as something that you know a lot about or are willing to learn about.
   - Become a subject-matter expert.
   - Do some market research to discover what's already out there and to see what's missing.
   - Leverage your background and training.
2. *Create a unique and cohesive brand.* Decide on an overall theme that you want to carry through long-term.
   - Develop a look and feel with colors, pictures, fonts, logo, tagline and design elements that support your theme.
   - Write your bio in a way that emphasizes the theme and your special expertise.
   - Think about your theme every time you post. If something isn't relevant to your brand, don't write about it.
3. *Keep to a schedule.* Give your readers information about what to expect at different times.
   - Create an editorial calendar for the year that includes your vision of what main events and topics you'd like to cover.
   - Build short-range calendars that have daily, weekly and monthly topics and scheduled posts.
   - Stick to your editorial schedule so your readers know what's coming.
4. *Know your audience.* Have a good idea of the type of person you're writing to.
   - Use analytics to pull together your audience demographics: gender, age, location and income level.
   - Ask questions of your readers, conduct occasional surveys on your blog and regularly read your comments to learn what your readers' goals are, what excites them and how to best cater your content to them.
5. *Use social media to amplify your reach.* Strategic promotion of your blog is crucial to your success.
   - Pick the right mix of social media channels such as Twitter, Pinterest, Instagram, Facebook and others to get the word out.
   - Strategically time your posts to maximize exposure among your social media users and demographics. Experiment with different times to get the best reach.
   - Use appropriate hashtags including those that are currently trending or tied to your brand.

impact on how we interact and communicate. A writer at Pollock Communications, an independent agency specializing in health and wellness, summed up the impact of social media this way:

> "Social media has become an integral part of our everyday lives. We find and share our new favorite clothing and food brands on blogs; we meet people with similar interests on Facebook; we get our news in one sentence on Twitter; we share a picture of that awesome eggs benedict we had for brunch on Instagram and we can even find our future husband or wife on dating sites. We have an amazing ability to be connected, stay in-the-know and share our own interests, ideas and opinions on just about everything."[1]

As public relations and marketing practitioners, it's important to understand how social media is evolving. We need to grasp how people are connecting with each other, how information is passed among individuals and groups, how things go viral and how trust is built and maintained between people who may never meet in person. Much of the information we considered private only a few years ago is now broadly shared. Most people spend a significant portion of their week on social media "working" to stay connected. It almost feels like keeping up with at least a few social media channels is a daily chore. The proliferation of and accessibility of personal information through social media has changed so many things that it may be hard to remember a world without it. One of the changes that may have gone unnoticed is the higher premium that is now placed on honesty and truthfulness. We leave a pretty visible trail across social media that includes our beliefs, interests and behaviors. We are now all, in some sense, public figures.

We'll explore how to effectively use social media for message delivery in Chapter 9. But suffice it to say, social media should be considered an important and dynamic channel with untapped opportunities to explore creative and innovative tactics. This is particularly the case when your strategy involves constructing grass-roots and word-of-mouth campaigns.

Tactics

The first thing that students and many practitioners do when presented with a challenge is jump to tactics. It is what communicators and marketers do the best — and the worst. We're pretty good at developing catchy slogans, social media contests, fun special events and attention-grabbing visuals. The problem is not a lack of ideas for interesting tactics; it is rather not enough careful calculation to ensure the tactics will accomplish your strategies and objectives. Tactics, or communication tools, always need to be approached in the context of your research and the problem/opportunity you're tackling. Following the matrix approach and developing tactics only after your objectives, publics, messages and strategies have been determined will ensure they are aligned to help you accomplish your goal. The creativity required of good tactics must be carefully channeled to ensure strategic alignment of your campaign.

---

[1] Pollock Communications. How Social Media Has Changed the Way We Communicate. *PR Buzz*, May 17, 2014: http://www.lpollockpr.com/2014/05/17/social-media-changed-way-communicate/

Tactics as strategic tools

Tactics are the tools — the hammer, nails, lumber and paint — you need to build a successful campaign. You can also think of them as the tasks you must perform in your campaign. The activities you undertake to implement your campaign are all tactics. Everything that costs money, aside from research and measurement, is a tactic. This is why the items that show up on your calendar and in your budget are all tactics. So regardless of how well you have planned your strategy, the success of your campaign will ultimately rest on the implementation of your tactics. The majority of business strategies fail not because they were ill-conceived, but because there was a breakdown in implementation. Their tactics either did not support the strategies or they were poorly executed. To avoid this scenario, we strongly recommend you use strategy briefs for all of your tactics (see Figure 8.2). **Strategy briefs** are concise design tools that help you plan each tactic around your strategy. We'll explain more about them later in this chapter.

STRATEGY BRIEF
An analytical tool that infuses strategic planning into the creation of effective tactics.

Difference between strategies and tactics

One of the hardest things to work through when learning the matrix is the difference between strategies and tactics. It's simple, really, when you think about it this way: A strategy is an approach, and a tactic is a task. You need many tasks to accomplish a strategy. A helpful question to ask is, "Can the tool be broken down any more?" If the answer is no, it's a tactic. Mass media, for example, can be broken down into many different tactics — news release, radio actuality, public service announcement, op-ed piece — so it's a channel within a strategy. A brochure, on the other hand, can't be broken down any further so it's a tactic. A special event is trickier. It can be either a strategy or a tactic. If it's a large event with many elements to it such as a conference or the FIFA World Cup, it's probably a strategy. If your special event is more straightforward and simple, like an employee awards ceremony, it's probably best treated as a tactic.

Diversity of tactics

In addition to not always tying tactics to strategy, another problem has been the tendency to rely on the same tactics or communication tools over and over. Although there is nothing wrong with reusing tactics that work well with particular publics, communicators should be careful not to fall into the routine of the processionary caterpillars described earlier. Using a tactic repeatedly sometimes causes us to select that tactic without thinking about its appropriateness to get a particular message to a particular public for a particular purpose. We fall into a pattern of selecting tactics because we've always used them, or because the tactic worked before.

Remember to review the analytical process to select communication tools each time you design messages and strategies for publics. Change is one of the only constants in business and marketing. Publics change, circumstances change, purposes change, messages change and communication channels change. If communicators stay with the same plan for the same publics without recognizing the constantly changing environment, communication efforts will miss their targets. A practitioner will be left (possibly without a job) wondering why it didn't work this time since it had always worked before.

Figure 8.2
Strategy brief — news release

Key public (brief profile including motivating self-interests):

Secondary publics (if any):

Action desired from public(s):

Proposed headline:

Proposed lead:

News hook:

SEO terms (10-20 key words or phrases):

Primary messages (two-five short statements, similar to sound bites)

Secondary messages (bulleted supporting data, facts, examples, stories, testimonials, etc.)

1. Primary:

   Secondary
   -
   -
   -

2. Primary:

   Secondary:
   -
   -
   -

3. Primary:

   Secondary:
   -
   -
   -

Opinion leaders and how they will be used (testimonials, quotes, etc.):

Photos/charts/graphics (if any):

Where and when distributed:

Additional uses after publication:

Timeline/deadline:

Tip: Use the strategy brief for an email news pitch to send your news release to targeted reporters, bloggers, etc.

The other inherent danger in using the same tools continually is stifling creativity. Communicators may ignore new creative and innovative ways to get messages to publics. But in a society flooded with messages in the typical media channels, creative and innovative delivery of messages is necessary to cut through the message clutter to reach our targets. Remember the challenge is twofold: You must motivate the members of your key public to choose to perceive the message (and retain it), and to choose to act upon it. Both require an appeal to the public's self-interests, but self-interest appeals alone will not get you over the perception hurdle. You may not find a solution to your specific need in textbooks that teach how to design communication tactics. You must be able to create innovative delivery systems and then follow the principles of persuasive communication theory to send your messages in creative ways that command attention.

The diversity of tactics available is limited only by the imagination. Nevertheless, there are abundant numbers of books, articles and other references that identify a variety of some of the standard communication tools and their appropriate uses. We refer you to a broad range of easily available resources (some of which are identified in this chapter's references and additional readings) that suggest dozens of tactics and instructions on their preparation and use. Because of the vast resources which give specific direction on preparing and using communication tools, it is not our purpose here to review specific tactics. Rather, it is more important to provide a process to assist communication professionals in determining how to select the tactics most appropriate for a specific public, purpose and message.

Most popular introductory textbooks in communication segment tools and tactics into written, spoken and visual categories. But today's communication professionals focused on key publics and messages recognize that, in the radically changed communication environment, such divisions are artificial, especially considering that the most effective tactics combine at least two, and often all three, of those senses. Further, that type of categorization puts undue emphasis on the medium or channel, with less thought of the purpose, the target audience and the message itself. Such categorization may be partially responsible for communications practice that is excessively tactic-driven rather than strategic.

It might be more sensible to address tactics in a grid (see Figure 8.3) with one axis ranging from personal communication to mass-produced messages, and the other measuring the level of interaction (two-way communication) from highly interactive to noninteractive. The grid visually depicts how we design tactics for a specific public. When we need a highly interactive approach, we also make the tactic highly personal — increasing the likelihood of selection and retention. The other end of the grid forms a megaphone that depicts a wide distribution of a message with little or no **interactivity**. For example, if the public and the specific message to be delivered requires a personal or peer influence, the tactics will be designed to invoke personal interaction and may include phone calls, Facebook posts or handwritten notes. If, however, a breadth of coverage rather than personal influence is needed, a medium with a broader reach to publics may be more appropriate, including tactics such as radio public service announcements, podcasts or news releases. In the middle of the grid would be highly segmented media like special interest magazines, tweets to followers and blog posts.

Identifying communication tactics in this fashion helps us select the best communication tools for the public, purpose and message. Otherwise, the medium

INTERACTIVITY
The degree to which the tactic provides interaction between the sender of the message and the receiver.

Figure 8.3
Interactivity grid of communication tactics

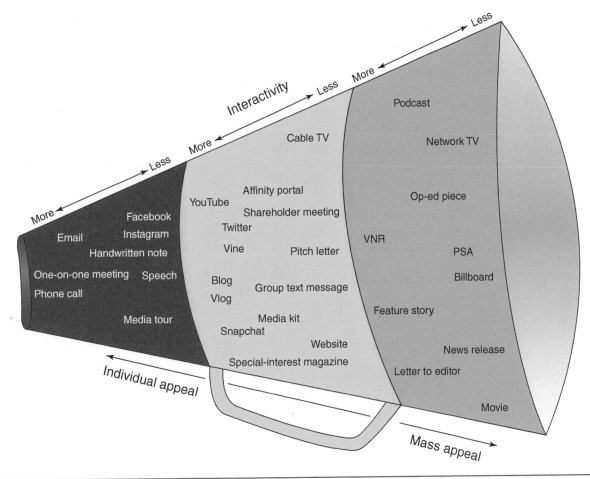

(print/broadcast/Internet/social media) and budget tend to determine what tactics we use rather than which tool would best accomplish our purpose. Using the grid, tactics fall into three categories: highly personal and interactive, segmented and moderately interactive and mass-produced mass media.

Highly personal and interactive

The basis of the relational or cooperative community approach to public relations is the overwhelming power of personal and interactive communication. The personal influence of opinion leaders and peers is particularly important in a persuasion campaign. It is in this area of tactics that creativity and innovation are most needed. This type of tactic is very specifically tailored to the public (usually made up of identifiable individuals) and personalized in its delivery. It is has typically been direct human-to-human communication, often handwritten, spoken one-on-one and/or delivered in person by an influential. However, social media now makes this

What's in your taco?

BACKSTORY

Taco Bell's dominance of the fast food market — as the sixth largest chain in the U.S. and holding 52 percent of the Mexican fast food market — came into question when a class-action lawsuit claimed its meat wasn't beef. Its stock price, sales and reputation dipped as the claims received national media attention, requiring a rapid and aggressive response.

KEY FACTS

- Beasley Allen, an Alabama law firm, filed suit in January 2011 alleging Taco Bell meat contained less than 35 percent ground beef.
- Following the lawsuit, stocks fell approximately $1.80 per share — an $82.8 million decline in shareholder value.
- Taco Bell's YouGov BrandIndex score — which measures reputation — dropped from 25.2 to 11.7 the week following the lawsuit. The national BrandIndex average was 12.2.

How would you respond?

TACO BELL'S STRATEGY

Taco Bell, knowing the claim was inaccurate, responded aggressively by attacking the accuser. The company demanded an apology from the lawyers and threatened legal action for the false claims. It stood firmly behind its products, even revealing its taco meat recipe: 88 percent USDA-inspected quality beef; 3 percent to 5 percent water; 3 percent to 5 percent spices; and 3 percent to 5 percent other ingredients, such as oats for texture and taste.

Taco Bell immediately took out full-page advertisements in national papers such as The New York Times, USA Today and the Wall Street Journal, as well as in regional papers including The Boston Globe and Chicago Tribune. It spent $3 million to $4 million in ads to tell the truth about its product. Taco Bell President Greg Creed was a fixture on major TV media outlets defending Taco Bell's reputation and product quality.

Creed also appeared in YouTube videos addressing the suit. One video was viewed 170,000 times by mid-February. Coupons for free tacos were distributed via Facebook and Twitter, allowing consumers to test the meat themselves. Taco Bell engaged in search engine optimization efforts and purchased sponsored Web links to control

the online story. It also created a website containing the campaign's ads, press releases, YouTube videos and detailed ingredient information.

RESULTS
- Within a few weeks, the stock price had fully recovered, and six months later the stock was up $9 per share.
- After the lawsuit was dropped in April 2011, Taco Bell repeated many of the same tactics to demand a public apology from the firm. Trust increased immediately.
- Taco Bell's BrandIndex score rose to 20.5 by May and continued to rise.

WORKS CITED

Annual Report Owl. (2011). Taco Bell 2011 Annual Report. Retrieved from http://www.annualreportowl.com/Taco%20Bell/2011/Annual%20Report

Barclay, E. (2011, April 19). With lawsuit over, Taco Bell's mystery meat is a mystery no longer. Retrieved from http://www.npr.org/blogs/health/2011/04/22/135539926/with-lawsuit-over-taco-bells-mystery-meat-is-a-mystery-no-longer

Beasley Allen Law Firm. (2011, January 21). Beasley Allen files lawsuit against Taco Bell on behalf of all consumers [Press release]. Retrieved from http://www.prnewswire.com/news-releases/beasley-allen-files-lawsuit-against-taco-bell-on-behalf-of-all-consumers-114381074.html

Horovitz, B. (2011, January 29). Taco Bell fights beef charges with 'truth' ads, may countersue. [*USA Today* article]. Retrieved from http://usatoday30.usatoday.com/money/industries/food/2011-01-28-taco-bell-ads_N.htm

Huffington Post. (2001, August 9). America's biggest food chains, ranked. Retrieved from http://www.huffingtonpost.com/2011/08/09/americas-biggest-fast-food-chains_n_922241.html#s325608&title=10_Sonic

Kerley, P. (2011, February 17). What brands can learn from Taco Bell's social media lawsuit defense. [*Mashable* article]. Retrieved from http://mashable.com/2011/02/17/taco-bell-social-media-defense/

Lukovitz, K. (2011, June 7). QSRs: Taco Bell shows (positive) perception uptrends. [*Marketing Daily* article]. Retrieved from http://www.mediapost.com/publications/article/151946/?print#axzz2iQPuYGWt

Macedo, D. (2011, April 26). Taco Bell still has beef with firm that dropped lawsuit. Retrieved from http://www.foxnews.com/us/2011/04/26/taco-bell-threatens-sue-law-firm-brought-beef-suit/

McConnell, A., & Bhasin, K. (2012, July 12). Ranked: The most popular fast food restaurants in America. Retrieved from http://www.businessinsider.com/the-most-popular-fast-food-restaurants-in-america-2012-7?op=1

Neal, R. (2011, May 29). Where's the beef? Taco Bell earnings take a hit. [*KnoxViews* blog]. Retrieved from http://www.knoxviews.com/node/16397

Oches, S. (2011, August). The 2011 QSR 50. [Special report]. Retrieved from http://www.qsrmagazine.com/reports/2011-qsr-50

Taco Bell. (2011, January 27). Taco Bell: Of course we use real beef! [Video file]. Retrieved from http://www.youtube.com/watch?v=ah05FEWcJWM

Taco Bell. (n.d.). About our seasoned beef. Retrieved from http://www.tacobell.com/nutrition/foodfacts/BeefQuality

Wasserman, T. (2011, January 29). Taco Bell uses social media to ward off PR crisis. Mashable. Retrieved from http://mashable.com/2011/01/28/taco-bell-social-media-crisis/

Yahoo! Finance. (n.d.). Yum! Brands, Inc. Historical prices. Retrieved from http://finance.yahoo.com/q/hp?s=YUM&a=00&b=21&c=2011&d=05&e=21&f=2011&g=d&z=66&y=0

Zack's Equity Research. (2011, April 20). Taco Bell lawsuit dissolved. Retrieved from http://www.zacks.com/stock/news/51610/Taco-Bell-Lawsuit-Dissolved

kind of interaction possible, to some degree, digitally, and to a much larger group of "friends."

A personal delivery system engenders interactivity. Interactivity is important in several ways. First, interaction is a basis of strong relationships and cooperation. Second, as discussed in the chapter on persuasion, it is a key to the crystallization of opinion. Third, interactivity provides a personal commitment and stimulus for action. For these reasons, this kind of tactic is highly effective. Nevertheless, it is also time-consuming and often expensive. The advantages must be weighed carefully against the costs (time and money) to determine the best circumstances in which to use personal communication channels and tools. Although not quite as personal, social media channels offer a low-cost way for many opinion leaders to connect with key publics. The ease of sharing through social media makes these tools less labor-intensive and less expensive. The tradeoff for those benefits is that you must largely relinquish control of the message and its distribution.

In some situations, it's possible to create the one-on-one communication hierarchically. A good example is United Way's workplace campaign. Companies that support the United Way in their community by running workplace campaigns identify a company representative who is trained by local volunteers to hold an employee information meeting and to subsequently personally ask each individual in the company to support local community social service efforts through monthly payroll deductions. Often the company provides an endorsement of the campaign by making a corporate, or leadership, donation. In larger organizations, the company representative trains representatives in each department to do the personal asking. This hierarchical system uses opinion leadership, personal influentials and one-on-one communication supported by collateral materials to reach hundreds of thousands of people within a community. Nevertheless, it is highly labor intensive, even though the laborers are volunteers.

Segmented and moderately interactive

© mandritoiu/Shutterstock.com

Tactics in the middle of the grid — segmented and moderately interactive — combine elements of mass and personal as well as interactivity (see Figure 8.3). Although not nearly as personal, this category still provides a highly targeted message to a larger target audience than personal communication typically can. These tactics use, or sometimes establish, a channel that is specifically designed for an already segmented public. Good examples include blogs and special interest magazines that are clearly designed and targeted to meet the needs of a very specific group. Other examples might be a shareholder meeting for all stockholders which, in some companies, can be thousands of people, or mobile phone apps providing a specific kind of service. The segmentation of cable channels also allows for the effective use of this kind of tactic.

These types of tactics are more interactive than the mass media. Because the target audience is an interest group, it tends to be more responsive to surveys, and more active in initiating feedback, phone calls and emails. This environment is perfect for communicators to build in response mechanisms that provide the interactivity necessary for symmetry in communication with the organization's key publics.

Further, because the segmented channel has already identified the needs of its audience, it is a fairly simple matter for the public relations practitioner to tap into and help satisfy those needs. Such channels are often shorter on funding than traditional media channels, and are therefore hungry for material that honestly meets the needs of their audiences. It is to the practitioner's advantage to identify such channels that target the organization's key publics and to include them within the plan to build strong, mutually beneficial relationships.

Most Internet tactics, including websites, typically fall in this moderately interactive and semi-personal category. Websites today are prime real estate for most organizations. They represent the company to its stakeholders. They are as important as a storefront or headquarters building and represent the primary communications hub for many organizations. As a result, websites must be carefully planned and intuitively organized to communicate messages to key publics. One public, journalists, for example, should be able to quickly find an organization's online newsroom. Each element of the website should be mapped out like a separate tactic with particular publics, purposes and messages in mind. From frequently asked questions (FAQs) to corporate histories and product information pages, the needs and self-interests of various key publics should drive the messages for each element and their delivery. Journalists get a specific message aimed at them from the online newsroom. Investors get their own message from the sometimes password-protected elements targeted at them. Consumers get their specific message from product information pages on the website. The various key publics access the website to meet their needs. Their needs are all different and their messages public-specific.

The savvy practitioner will always remember that today's publics differ from publics of the past in that they have much more control over access to information. Past practitioners had the control over channels, messages and their delivery. With the rise of Internet communication and particularly the explosion of social media, our publics now control how, when and where they receive messages, and they are also in a new role as senders of messages. They vacillate between being hungry for information and tuning it out because of overload. And they control the switch. In this environment, public relations has become the content provider, giving rise to the mantra "content is king." Such an environment reinforces the necessity of public-specific messages (or content) delivered by channels and tactics our publics themselves choose to access.

PUMA hosts annual shareholder meeting in Nuremberg, Germany.

Mass-produced mass media

Although we pronounced mass media nearly dead, mass-produced and mass media tactics still have their place in some campaigns. The use of electronic media to broadly disseminate messages will undoubtedly keep this category alive for years to come. The technology facilitates broad coverage of certain publics that probably would not be reached any other way. Nevertheless, it is important to remember the advantages and disadvantages of specific mass media channels and to use them appropriately. Further, just because we use mass media does not mean we are targeting a mass audience. It is just as important to segment publics and design public-specific messages for mass media as it is for segmented media.

Mass media can provide immediacy, credibility and a strong impact. Nevertheless, practitioners often take a passive approach to mass media placement. While we can't directly control news placements, there are communication tools available that help us be more active in building relationships with media. Active corporate Twitter feeds, YouTube channels, satellite media tours, syndicated columns or programs, B-roll accompanying video news releases and other techniques can help get a message used more readily than it might otherwise have been. Such tactics can be quite effective if you remember a few important guidelines:

- Become familiar with your media contacts and work to meet their needs as they meet the needs of their audiences. Be familiar with their past work and what kind of material they prefer. Your job is to help make their jobs easier.
- Know the media market or audiences and adapt your material to meet their needs. Don't expect media to accept copy or programming that is blatantly self-serving. You must provide solid news.
- Localize your material. Whether it is a video news release, a feature story or a public service announcement, unless it specifically targets the local community it will not be used. For special interest media — print, broadcast and online — the community is not geographical, but it is still a community.
- Provide quality media products. Use their writing and editing style, and provide error-free copy well in advance of deadlines. Provide a consistent point of contact and train executives and experts for interviews. Select interviewees who are knowledgeable and personable.
- Don't call a news conference unless you have a story that legitimately requires one. If it can be handled in a news release, statement or interview, do so.

Sponsored content and social responsibility

The digital disruption is not just upending traditional editorial coverage — it is also changing how news and information are funded. The price of digital advertising has declined by 75 percent in the last two years. Media outlets now generate more revenue from circulation than from advertising. And a growing percentage of the content we consume is paid for and produced by public relations and marketing people. This **sponsored content** differs from the advertorial placements of a decade ago in that it is as well-read as regular editorial. Further, brands and companies are increasingly looked upon to address societal needs. A recent example of this occurred when 13 brands disassociated themselves with the Los Angeles Clippers after racist comments were made by owner Donald Sterling. The brands acted on their own and more quickly than the NBA, which eventually banned Sterling from the league. CVS Pharmacy recently announced it would stop selling tobacco products — a highly profitable segment of its business — because the product conflicts with its mission. And Gap recently raised its minimum wage for all employees to $9 per hour with plans to jump to $10 per hour in June 2015. These organizations all moved to put societal needs ahead of money (Edelman, 2014).

SPONSORED CONTENT/NATIVE ADVERTISING
Online editorial content paid for by a company that is designed to feel more like regular editorial content so it is less intrusive.

What's happening now is a convergence of marketing, advertising, digital and public relations into what Richard Edelman called, "communications marketing." This is storytelling through earned, owned and paid media channels. Edelman explained, "The goal of communications is to provide information that moves people to action. I believe that the market is beginning to understand that marketing has things backwards. We believe in communications marketing because it is based on substantive storytelling."

There is little doubt mass media has a role to play in this emerging paradigm. Communicators will continue using mass media extensively for message dissemination. Make sure you establish strong media relationships based on honesty, trust and ethical practice to enhance your ability to use mass media to target key organizational publics.

Pedestrians walk past CVS Pharmacy in New York City, NY.

Other considerations in selecting tactics

Although tactic selection should depend primarily on the public and the best way to reach them to accomplish your purpose, the content of the message will also be a determinant. For example, detailed messages with lots of information usually require a printed or online medium that allows a receiver the luxury of rereading or studying. Similarly, broadcast messages must typically be simple and highly memorable because they cannot be reviewed at will unless they are also posted on the Internet. In both of these cases, the content and length or complexity of the message are factors in media selection.

Further, the practitioner should consider the degree to which he/she controls the medium selected. Heitpas discusses two types of media channels: controlled and uncontrolled. Controlled channels allow the practitioner to dictate the content, timing and placement or distribution. Examples are paid advertising, trade shows and brochures. Such tactics are entirely designed and written by the communicator. No intervening gatekeepers affect the final product and its placement. Nevertheless, that advantage is tempered by a typically higher cost and lower credibility. Publics are well aware that controlled tactics convey exactly what the organization paying for the space wants. There is no doubt in the consumer's mind that when he/she is reading paid advertising, that the advertiser is telling only one side of the story to motivate consumer purchase.

On the other hand, uncontrolled channels are typically more credible because of the intervention of a third party, most often a reporter or blogger. They are usually less costly because much of the work is done by the "objective" third party. But the practitioner is unable to dictate the exact copy or message, placement or timing. The risk that the message may be buried or distorted is the price paid for credibility gained through perceived third-party objectivity.

Finally, you should remember that combinations of tactics are often preferable to tactics used individually or in isolation. If you determine that a critical company

Matthew McConaughey at the 86th Academy Awards at Dolby Theater on March 2, 2014, in Los Angeles.

policy statement included in a press kit may not be fully appreciated by key opinion leaders unless you use a more personally interactive tactic, mail it to them separately with a handwritten note from an organizational executive or some other influential indicating key points that may specifically interest them. If you think your key investors need more personal attention regarding the latest stock jump, email them a copy of the news clipping with an FYI corner notation from the president of the company. There are a number of ways to "personalize" existing mass and segmented media messages.

On the other hand, some personal and interactive messages may be made mass through media coverage, editorial comments or online posting. However, use care when deciding whether to turn a personal message into a mass message. It may not only dilute the appeal, but it may alienate those originally touched by the personal message.

Some communication tools lend themselves to all three categories of tactics. A special event, for example, may be designed to be personal and interactive (like a private dinner for a major donor), segmented and moderately interactive (like a media tour of facilities or an awards ceremony) or mass-produced mass media (like the Democratic or Republican national conventions). Turning a special event into a media event requires that care be taken to stage the event with messaging for the immediate attendees, but it must be packaged in such a way that the messages will also appeal to viewers and listeners. Just remember that even though a special event is organized as a celebration or some other routine commemoration, you've wasted the organization's opportunities and resources if you don't also use it to convey primary messages to key organizational publics.

2012 Republican presidential campaign rally in Henderson, Nev.

Additionally, combining tactics stimulates greater care in assuring they are integrated to support and enhance each other. Using name tags at a staged event can be planned to strategically support other tactics. You might color code the tags to identify separate key publics and prepare separate packets of supporting materials to be distributed based on nametag color. All tactics should be developed to magnify the effect of other tactics. They should be timed to support and enhance each other. The whole of the tactics supporting any strategy should be greater than the sum of the parts. They are like pieces to a puzzle that must interlock and intertwine for the complete picture to appear.

Creating individual tactics

The process of developing communication tactics must employ creativity and innovation. The Strategic Planning Matrix provides the analytical framework necessary to channel creativity in the planning process. But it is also necessary to channel creativity at the tactical level. Otherwise, the creator may lose the proper focus on public, purpose and message.

Strategy briefs

The secret to maintaining focus in the creative process at the tactical level is to employ an analytical tool used to design the content of a tactic before actually producing it. Strategy briefs have been devised for this purpose to supplement and extend the strategic planning process. Take a minute to study Figure 8.2. Strategy briefs are simple outlines uniquely tailored to the development of a specific tactic. They ask questions and contain categories of information for the strategic planner to complete before beginning work on the specific tool or tactic. They ensure that tactics will be consistent with the overall plan and that all important details are included in the copy or visuals. Similar to an outline used to organize and detail a paper or presentation, the strategy brief is an analytical piece that joins the public, purpose and message in a logical, persuasive fashion.

Each strategy brief begins by identifying the key public, which must be one of the publics identified in the campaign plan and the public for which the strategy supported by the specific tactic was designed. If your strategy brief begins by identifying a public who is not in your strategic plan, then you need to reevaluate. Either you neglected an important public in your plan, or you're wasting time and money on an unnecessary tactic. The strategy brief also states the desired action as well as identifies the key public's self-interest as part of the appeal.

The brief then gets specific in terms of details. Keeping in mind the public and purpose identified at the top, it asks, what are the primary and secondary messages that the key public needs to receive to understand and perform the desired action? These become the copy for your tactic and, in effect, the first draft of the communication tool. The messages are pulled from those you previously designed for this public in step five of the matrix and should be stated specifically enough that another member of your campaign team, your firm or your department in an organization can edit and produce the communication tool without much other information. The messages contain each piece of information necessary to inform the public and motivate them to act. That means, for example, that you must be specific and accurate about dates and times of events you are publicizing, provide contact information for individuals to request more information and include statistics when supporting logical arguments.

After identifying the messages to be used in this product or tactic, the strategy brief requires you to list opinion leaders and how they are used either as part of the messages or in distributing the tactic. For example, in a brochure on personal hygiene for low-income parents, you might ask for testimonials or information from a recognized health care provider. You may also ask nurses at free clinics to distribute the brochure. Both methods use third-party influentials or opinion leaders to strengthen the appeal.

Make sure to include specific details in your strategy brief. When the brain is in the analytical mode, you can determine exactly what information must be included to accomplish your purpose. But when the brain shifts to the creative mode, you may fail to include critical information in the process of creating great copy. You must channel your creativity by knowing the public, purpose and message, and then you must check the resultant creation against the strategy brief that your analytical mind created for effectiveness. The most frequently omitted detail in primary and secondary messages (or copy) is the information that provides a way for the public to do what you have asked them to do. Nothing is more frustrating to people than to be persuaded to act but not be given the information necessary to do so. Provide a phone number to call, a website to get more information or specific instructions on what to do.

Next, the strategy brief details your distribution plan. If it is a media product, designate each specific media channel (television or radio station, newspaper or other publication) that will receive the tactic. Indicate the delivery method and if any follow-up is required. If it is a brochure or flyer, indicate how it will be distributed. If it is a blog post, tell how you will direct other social media traffic to your post.

Appendix B contains strategy briefs for 23 different tactics. These include tools like a news release, website, special event, infographic and video. Each strategy brief has been appropriately altered to request the specific information needed for that tactic. Although the strategy briefs provided in this text cover a wide range of communication tools, you can create your own brief for any tool you wish to use. Before designing your own strategy briefs, make sure you understand each communication tool or product well enough to custom design your own briefs.

Remember that the strategy brief is an analytical tool used to guide the development of creative products that will support your strategic plan. Each must contain the specific detail that you determined was necessary to inform, persuade and motivate the public to action.

The use of strategy briefs will save you time and frustration in the development of your tactics. You should spend more time developing your strategy briefs than creating the actual tactics. You will find that, if you plan your strategy briefs carefully and completely, your communication tools will always be on target and will take less time and money to create.

Once a communication product (tactic) is completed, you can use the strategy brief to succinctly explain your product's purpose and use. It will demonstrate the quality of your planning and the strategic thought behind the development of each tactic. It also shows your client or manager that the product was the result of systematic planning and thought. Executives will be more assured of the wisdom of committing resources to production when products have been designed to achieve the purpose identified in your campaign to reach goals and objectives already established.

Summary

Messages are the way we get a public's attention and provide the information and motivation people need to act. Primary messages contain what we want a public to do and appeal to its self-interest in doing that. Secondary messages provide all the detail necessary to support the primary message and facilitate the public's accomplishment of your purpose.

Carefully planned strategies and tactics will ensure not only that your messages reach your target publics but also that they motivate a desired action or behavior. Strategies determine which channels are most appropriate to reach key publics. Tactics detail the creative tools designed to convey your messages and solicit action from your key publics. They are the specific tasks that are the implementation of the campaign. Strategy briefs are used to design communication pieces that are consistent with your overall strategy and plans. They also make sure important written and visual details are included and the desired action from key publics is clearly stated.

Because many practitioners often find themselves choosing and implementing the same strategies and tactics over and over, it is important to remember the need for creativity. Additionally, tactics are best chosen by how much interactivity and personalization is required by the strategy. Don't fall into the trap identified in the quote at the beginning of the chapter that reminds us, "Tactics without strategy is the noise before defeat." Strategic communication requires creative thinking and implementation, particularly in the planning of strategies and tactics.

Exercises

1. Look up the Gap announcement about raising the minimum wage for its workers. Identify the primary and secondary messages the company used.

2. Next, draft a strategy to communicate the company's new wage policy to Gap employees through social media. Select specific tactics that you feel would be most effective.

3. Watch local news to discover an organization running a campaign to solve a problem or meet a challenge. Try to identify all the strategies and tactics being used to send messages to the publics. Evaluate the effectiveness of the strategies and tactics, and think about how you might have designed them differently or sent them through different channels to make them more effective.

References and additional readings

Cutlip, S., Center, A., & Broom, G. (2006). *Effective public relations* (9th ed.). Englewood Cliffs, NJ: Prentice-Hall, Inc.

Edelman Worldwide (2014, May 3). 2014 Edelman Trust Barometer. Retrieved from http://www.edelman.com/insights/intellectual-property/2014-edelman-trust-barometer/trust-around-the-world/

Edleman, R. (2014, June 26). Storytelling@the Speed of Now. 2014 *Academic Summit*. Speech given at DePaul University, Chicago.

Hainsworth, B. E., & Wilson, L. J. (1992). Strategic program planning. *Public Relations Review*, 18(1), 9-15.

Howard, C., & Mathews, W. (2000). *On deadline: Managing media relations* (3rd ed.). Prospect Heights, IL: Waveland Press.

Lenhart, A. et al. (2003). The evershifting Internet population: A new look at Internet access and the digital divide. Retrieved from www.pewinternet.org

Newsom, D., Turk, J. V., & Kruckeberg, D. (2007). *This is PR: The realities of public relations* (9th ed.). Belmont, CA: Wadsworth Publishing Company.

Poggi, J. (2013, Dec. 26). New TV networks scorecard: Eight cable channels to watch in 2014. *Advertising Age*. Retrieved from http://adage.com/article/media/tv-networks-scorecard-channels-watch-2014/245770/

Pollock Communications. (2014, May 17). How social media has changed the way we communicate. (PR Buzz.) Retrieved from http://www.lpollockpr.com/2014/05/17/social-media-changed-way-communicate/

Saba, J., & Lauria, P. (2012, Oct. 8). After 79 years in print, Newsweek goes digital only. Retrieved from http://www.reuters.com/article/2012/10/18/us-newsweek-digital-idUSBRE89H0L020121018

Tucker, K., Derelian, D., & Rouner, D. (1994). *Public relations writing: An issue-driven behavioral approach* (2nd ed.). Englewood Cliffs, NJ: Prentice-Hall, Inc.

Wilcox, D. L., Cameron, G. T., & Reber, B. H. (2014). *Public relations: Strategies and tactics* (11th ed.). Upper Saddle River, NJ: Pearson Education.

CHAPTER 9

USING SOCIAL MEDIA FOR MESSAGE DELIVERY

"A brand is no longer what we tell the consumer it is — it is what consumers tell each other it is."

—Scott Cook
FOUNDER OF INTUIT

LEARNING IMPERATIVES

- To understand the critical role of social media in the establishment and maintenance of a brand.

- To know how to use social media tools to engage with consumers and key publics about issues and products.

- To be able to effectively select the best social media channels to reach target publics.

- To be able to creatively design social media tactics to inform publics and motivate their behavior.

TWEET
A publicly visible, 140-character text message sent through Twitter.

On Sept. 21, 2013, unidentified gunmen attacked the Westgate shopping mall in Nairobi, Kenya. The attack and subsequent hostage situation, which lasted for three days, left 67 dead and more than 175 wounded. Before the standoff had ended, British Prime Minister David Cameron used Twitter to announce to the media and to his country that six British Nationals were among those killed in the terrorist attack. The news of these deaths was broken through a **tweet**. Astoundingly, it took the Independent and Mirror another five days to confirm the prime minister's report. The incident demonstrates the immediacy and power of social media to share information broadly. It also underscores the power of Twitter as a media relations tool — particularly in disseminating news in a crisis.

It appears that even the conservative prime minister who once said, "Too many tweets make a twat" has embraced the use of social media as a powerful communication tool.

Another significant event in 2013 underscored Twitter's power to help build brands. When the lights went out at the Superdome during Super Bowl XLVII at 8:38 p.m., the creative team at 360i and Oreo seized the moment. Within minutes the brand had tweeted a picture with an Oreo cookie under a spotlight along with the phrase, "You can still dunk in the dark" (see Figure 9.1). The tweet lit up Twitter with more than 10,000 retweets, 18,000 likes and 5,000 shares in the first hour. In the end it earned five times as many media impressions as there were people watching the game.

Will Oremus, senior technology writer at Slate, says, "So bowled over by Oreo's display of basic social media competence were the nation's business media that editors around the country raced to be the first to explain to an awestruck nation exactly how the company pulled it off." Headlines appeared in more than 100 countries. Oreo's agency summed it up: One tweet, zero media dollars, 525 million impressions earned.

So how did they do it? Sarah Hofstetter, 360i president, told BuzzFeed, "We had a mission control set up at our office with the brand and 360i, and when the

Investigators gather at the front entrance to the Westgate mall in Nairobi, Kenya, Oct 1, 2013.

blackout happened, the team looked at it as an opportunity. Because the brand team was there, it was easy to get approvals and get it up in minutes. The brand's attempt to engage increased its visibility and showed its relevance.

SOCIAL MEDIA
A collective of online communications channels that enables users to create and share content and participate in community-based input, interaction and collaboration.

What is social media?

In the midst of all the buzz, it might be helpful to pause for just a moment to define what we're talking about. The term **social media** actually appeared in this context for the first time in 2004. Since then, many definitions have been written. We like the

Figure 9.1
Oreo's 2014 Super Bowl tweet

following relatively concise definition: Social media is a collective of online communications channels that enables users to create and share content and participate in community-based input, interaction and collaboration (Wigmore, 2014). Examples of some of the types of social media channels include forums, blogs, **microblogs**, social networking sites, **wikis**, music sites, picture sites, video sites and reviews and rating sites.

As a platform, social media provides important communication advantages that allow brands and organizations to:

- Engage with customers and stakeholders.
- Develop loyalty.
- Increase transparency.
- Manage perceptions.
- Provide real-time feedback and customer service.
- Respond quickly during a crisis.

The unique attributes of social media make it a brilliant platform to use in building and maintaining trust with key publics. It's also a great listening tool to better understand what people are talking about and how they feel about a product or issue. Social media is now used extensively for communication, human resources, branding, community relations, customer service, fundraising, marketing and sales. All of these activities were made possible with the launch of Web 2.0 around 2004

MICROBLOG
A type of blog that lets users post short text updates. Microblogging features are often embedded in social networking sites.

WIKI
A Web app that allows users to add, modify or delete content in collaboration with others.

when technologies began to appear that allowed users to interact and collaborate with each other as creators of content that is shared in a virtual community.

Scope and trends

In 2013, the Pew Research Center found that 73 percent of online adults now use social networking sites of some kind. But perhaps even more interesting is that 42 percent of online adults use multiple sites such as LinkedIn, Pinterest, Twitter and Instagram. Facebook remains the dominant social networking platform even among younger users, although some have started giving more attention to newer technologies such as Twitter, Snapchat and Vine.

Users on Facebook, Instagram and Twitter tend to have the highest level of engagement. For example, 63 percent of Facebook users visit the site at least once a day, and 40 percent visit multiple times a day. The numbers for Instagram are slightly lower and a little lower still for Twitter. But all three platforms have higher engagement than Pinterest and LinkedIn (see Figure 9.2).

Figure 9.2
Frequency of social media site use in the United States

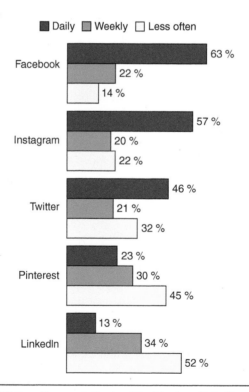

Source: Social Media Update 2013, Pew Research Center, Washington, D.C. (January 8, 2014).
http://www.pewinternet.org/2014/01/08/social-media-update-2013/frequency-of-social-media-site-use

Figure 9.3
News consumption varies widely across social networking sites

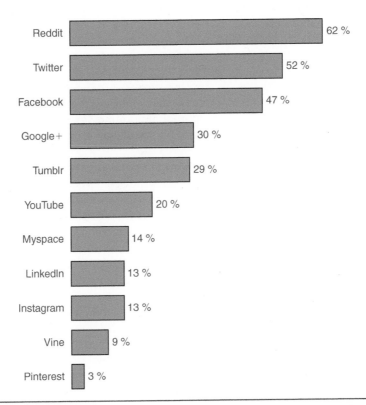

Source: Pew Research Center, *New Use Across Social Media Platforms*, November 14, 2013. http://www.journalism.org/2013/11/14/news-use-across-social-media-platforms/

As you would guess, many social media users also get their news online. Nearly two-thirds say they get news from Reddit. Twitter and Facebook are also prime sources for news among online users while Google+, Tumblr and YouTube play a significant but more minor role in delivering news (see Figure 9.3).

The next big thing in social media is already here. And it's mobile. The trend in social media usage toward mobile devices continues to pick up steam. Phones are bigger and faster and data plans cheaper. And the use of tablets is now widespread. As a result, more and more content is being downloaded to mobile devices. In 2013, 54 percent of U.S. Twitter users said they read news on their mobile device. This has also caused a shift in how news and other social content is designed and delivered. A growing percentage of content is now designed first for mobile devices and second for laptops and other computers. This is important to keep in mind as you select tactics and craft social media messages. Pay careful attention to social media demographic data when deciding which channels and design platforms will best meet the needs of your target public.

TIPS FROM THE PROS

The power of human-to-human marketing

Carlos Garcia, CEO of Nobox, a Miami-based social marketing agency of global brands, tips you off on how to turn consumers into marketers through social media.

There is no doubt that the best marketing is honest, direct and, most importantly, human. That said, connecting directly on a personal level and communicating like real people is merely the tip of the iceberg. The true potential of human-to-human marketing lies beneath the surface, where a massive number of people communicate and share with each other freely.

The power of H2H is turning your consumers into your marketers. What defines many marketers today is the ability to connect at a personal level with messages that are designed to be shared and then scaled. Crafting a message that is designed to be shared is easier said than done. You have to think as a social scientist, constantly studying what people share to understand the psychology behind it. The most common mistake is not asking the basic question, "Will people share this?" and, even worse, rationalizing a negative response. Take travel for example. We share our travel experiences on social media because they elevate our profile. Our friends are, in turn, curious about where we are. Furthermore, when we share our travel experiences, we give our friends the opportunity to comment and elevate their profiles as well. The typical comment is something like, "I was there last year . . . you should try (restaurant). They make the best . . ." As a social scientist/marketer in the travel industry, you have to craft messages that follow this pattern:

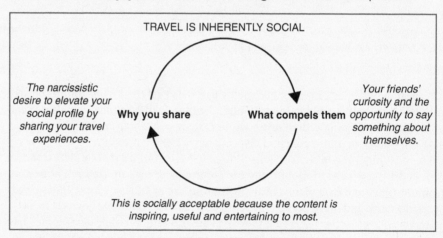

TRAVEL IS INHERENTLY SOCIAL

The narcissistic desire to elevate your social profile by sharing your travel experiences. — **Why you share**

What compels them — *Your friends' curiosity and the opportunity to say something about themselves.*

This is socially acceptable because the content is inspiring, useful and entertaining to most.

My suggestions on how to become an H2H marketer:
1. Research what people share organically, related to your industry.
2. Analyze the context and trends.
3. Hypothesize the reasons (psychological drivers) to share.
4. Focus on the types of content that generate the most engagement. (Keep in mind that sometimes sharing can be selfish, but there are

content/context combinations that are socially acceptable and warrant more engagement.)

5. Craft a branded message that can be shared by real people, and ask whether you and others would share this content. Don't be afraid to adopt the terms that your target audience is using organically.

6. Alternatively, deliver a call-to-action to share content that is similar to what is already shared organically but in the context of your brand. (Perhaps with a branded hashtag.)

7. If you are going to add an incentive to your call-to-action, make sure that it can be extended from the person that shares the content to others. This will enable a chain reaction. For example, you can use sweepstakes mechanics where those who re-share are also participating to win.

8. Finally, leverage social media as a branding lab for H2H marketing. You need to test and optimize continuously to maximize results.

How to choose the best platforms

Are bigger and more popular social media channels better? It depends. Facebook, for example, had 1.28 billion users on April 24, 2014. But that doesn't mean it's the best social media channel for many key publics. Take a situation where you want to communicate in a highly visual way with teenage girls. You may want to choose a more segmented and emerging social media platform such as Snapchat. It is estimated that this relatively new platform, which launched less than three years ago, reached 82 million active users globally in May 2014. But more importantly, the majority of Snapchat's users are female and 71 percent are under 25 years old. The engagement is also very high on this platform. About 40 percent of 18-year-olds in the U.S. say they use Snapchat multiple times a day to communicate with family and friends. Snapchat is only about one-third the size of Instagram, but its strong engagement, demographics and the dazzle and allure of visuals that disappear after a specified period may make it a better choice for communicating with teenage girls.

How do you really decide which platforms are best for each audience and the actions desired? Here are six factors you should carefully consider when weighing your options: users, usage, engagement, compatibility, SEO and potential.

Users. The question of who is using each platform is mostly about demographics. Use social media research and analytics to help you identify at least five key demographics: age, gender, geography, income and education. Additional demographics such as ethnicity, religion and language can also be very helpful in understanding who is using different social media platforms. Most of the platforms provide this basic demographic profile information free-of-charge to advertisers and many publish it on their websites.

Usage. Once we know who is using the social media platforms we're considering, we need to find out how they're using them. What kinds of activities do users

© Twin Design/Shutterstock.com

engage in? Do they treat the platform like a public diary? Do they use it to plan their weekends and parties? Do they share stories? Do they post pictures and videos? Do they look for recipes or decorating ideas? Do they meet new people for dates or hookups? Do they post reviews?

Let's say you were a food company and wanted to promote a recipe with your product as one of the primary ingredients. You'd want to ask yourself which platforms have the most interaction around cooking and recipes. Although you could easily post recipes on Facebook, most users would not turn to Facebook to find an awesome cupcake recipe. However, Pinterest would probably be a platform to consider.

Engagement. Part of knowing how people are using social media is understanding their level of engagement. In social media terms, engagement is how often people visit your site and how long they stay. Tap into each platforms' published analytics to find out this kind of information for different demographic segments. Then determine how much engagement you really need.

A recent report states that engagement on Instagram, for example, is 15 times that on Facebook. Instagram users spend an average of 257 minutes per month on the site that receives 1,000 comments and 8,500 likes per second or 1.2 billion likes per day. But Facebook would still be a better choice for many different types of messages and for organizations that use the platform as a hub for all their social media strategies.

Compatibility. This is a measure of how well-suited a platform is to your purpose. Each social media platform was born because it gave users a new and different way to interact. But being a one-trick pony doesn't usually lead to survival, so these new platforms were either acquired by other social media sites or they grew by adding new functionality.

LinkedIn is a good example. The platform is now a little more than 11 years old. It began as an online address book or Rolodex. But that wasn't enough. Competitors like Facebook offered so much more. So LinkedIn acquired CardMunch, Connected, Rapportive, SlideShare and Pulse to strengthen the ability for users to network on the LinkedIn platform. The company has made it possible for people to manage their contact relationships from the very beginning when a business card is presented to maintaining the friendship by following updates and keeping in touch.

When evaluating the compatibility of social media options, determine the activities at which each platform excels. Then match up the platforms with the needs of your key publics and messages.

SEO. Search engine optimization has become increasingly tied to social media. It usually begins with Web links, which remain one of the important factors in determining the quality of source information. Most links today are achieved through developing original content that is, in turn, shared across social media. Links to your content on Facebook, Twitter, LinkedIn, Google+, YouTube and other social networks help the search engines understand what websites are credible and should be ranked for what keyword phrases.

Other important social media factors affecting SEO rank include: Google author rank; how quickly content gets indexed; how many connections, followers and friends a user has; keyword boosts from posted content; the number of relevant location searches (from networks like Yelp, Foursquare and Urbanspoon); and the social connections and interactions a person has with your brand on sites like Google+ and Facebook.

Potential. The last factor to consider is a platform's potential to grow. As many brands have discovered, being an early adopter of a new social media site can be an unprecedented opportunity for branding, visibility and platform building. It not only ensures that companies and brands stay relevant in a fast-changing communications and marketing landscape but also positions them as leaders among influentials. It's a lot easier to get attention and to build trust with influencers or opinion leaders by connecting with them early before a platform gets crowded with competitors.

The first step to early adoption is to engage with a new platform. You need to understand its nuances before you can determine how to use it. Starbucks was an early adopter of Pinterest. But the brand did little to direct its followers, and its **pinboard** became a target for negative responses. Honda, on the other hand, picked up quickly that Pinterest provided an opportunity for collaboration. "It was a brilliant pivot, and one that would shape the future of marketing on Pinterest," wrote Rosie Scott, a digital content strategist and avid blogger. "Honda launched a campaign called Pintermission, promising $500 to five top pinners to take a break from their pinning habit by taking a spin in a new Honda."

Take the time to begin personally using a new site before deciding if it's a good platform for your organization to engage with. Once you decide to engage, quickly seek out the influencers.

PINBOARD
Pages on Pinterest where users can save individual pins organized by a central topic or theme.

Social media content

In general, social media content must be fresh, concise, visually interesting and highly shareable. This means that writing for social media is slightly different than writing for traditional media. News hooks must be highly relevant and timely. You can't talk about "yesterday's game." Yesterday may as well have been last year. Sentence length should be slightly shorter and varied. Ideas should be communicated crisply. Visuals that were an afterthought in traditional media must be a forethought with social media. Every blog post pretty much needs a picture — and the picture will largely determine how much attention the post gets.

Finally, to make things shareable they must contain a strong self-interest appeal. This appeal could be funny, informative, tragic, celebratory or draw on any number of other emotions. The key to making content shareable is to provide something no one else has. People share things that demonstrate their personalities, show what they're interested in and, perhaps more than anything else, elevate their standing among their peers.

Branded content

In 2012, The Coca-Cola Company overhauled its corporate website for the first time since 2005. The project was really the result of a big idea. The idea was to become a

MINI CASE

UNITED AIRLINES

Why does United Airlines break guitars?

BACKSTORY

Country music singer and songwriter Dave Carroll was stunned to see baggage handlers for United Airlines tossing his band's instruments while unloading the plane in Chicago. His band, Sons of Maxwell, was on its way from Canada to Nebraska for a weeklong concert tour. Carroll says that a woman sitting behind them, who didn't know they were musicians, yelled, "My God, they're throwing guitars out there." Mike, the bass player, looked out the window in time to see his bass guitar being heaved without regard by a baggage handler. Carroll's $3,500 Taylor guitar had already been tossed to the tarmac.

Appeals for help from the flight attendant were referred to the gate agent who referred them to another agent, who referred them to a United employee who said, "But hun, that's why we make you sign the waiver."

The airline had insisted the bandmembers check their instruments, but had not given them a damage waiver. Regardless, Carroll's prized Taylor guitar had been severely damaged. After spending nine months appealing to the airline to pay for the repairs to his guitar, the band leader decided to take matters into his own hands.

KEY FACTS

- United Airlines required Carroll to check his model 710 Taylor guitar, worth $3,500.
- Baggage handlers damaged the guitar during a plane change in Chicago.
- The cost of repairs for Carroll's prized guitar totaled $1,200.
- In the nine months that Carroll spent petitioning the airline to cover repair costs, he spoke with United employees in Canada, India, Chicago and New York.
- United finally denied Carroll's claim and said the matter was closed.

How would you use social media to get reparation?

Dave Carroll performing with his band Sons of Maxwell.

© Matthew Jacques/Shutterstock.com

CARROLL'S STRATEGY

"It occurred to me that I had been fighting a losing battle all this time and that fighting over this at all was a waste of time," Carroll said. "The system is designed to frustrate affected customers into giving up their claims, and United is very good at it. But I realized that as a songwriter and traveling musician I wasn't without options." Carroll decided to leverage his musical talents and the power of social media to rally others to his cause.

In his final reply to United, Carroll told the airline he would be writing three songs about his United experience. He also said he planned to make videos for these songs and post them on his website and on YouTube.

Viewers could vote on which they liked best. His objective was to get one million YouTube views within a year.

RESULTS

- Carroll reached his objective of getting one million views in just four days. United eventually attempted to compensate Carroll, but he refused the offer, suggesting the money be given to someone else whose luggage had been damaged.
- The YouTube video received 3.2 million views and 14,000 comments within 10 days of its release. To date, Carroll's music videos have been watched more than 16 million times.
- In the end, the video cost Carroll about $150. Conversely, the bad publicity severely damaged United's reputation and contributed to a 10 percent drop in stock price — costing United shareholders an estimated $180 million.
- Because United failed to respond publicly even after the videos were posted, the airline's story was never told. Conversely, Carroll's story was picked up and shared with an estimated 100 million people through social media and traditional media, including CNN, The Wall Street Journal, BBC, the CBS Morning Show and many other news outlets.

LINKS

http://www.youtube.com/watch?v=5YGc4zOqozo&feature=related

http://www.youtube.com/watch?v=h-UoERHaSQg&feature=channel

http://www.youtube.com/watch?v=P45E0uGVyeg&feature=channel

http://www.youtube.com/watch?v=n12WFZq2__0&feature=player_embedded

http://www.youtube.com/watch?v=T_X-Qoh__mw&feature=related

WORKS CITED

Carroll, D. (2008). United breaks guitars: Story. Retrieved from http://www.davecarrollmusic.com/music/ubg/story/

Evans, M. (2012, February 13). Broken guitar leads to startup consumer gripe site. Retrieved from http://www.theglobeandmail.com/report-on-business/small-business/starting-out/broken-guitar-leads-to-startup-consumer-gripe-site/article4171528/

Huffington Post. (2009, August 24). 'United breaks guitars': Did it really cost the airline $180 million? Retrieved from http://www.huffingtonpost.com/2009/07/24/united-breaks-guitars-did_n_244357.html

Right side of sight. (2010, August). Submission to Forrester Groundswell Awards: Social impact category. Retrieved from http://www.rightsideofright.com/2010/08/submission-to-forrester-groundswell-awards-social-impact-category/

Roseman, E. (2012, May 18). Dave Carroll is still having problems with airlines: Roseman. Retrieved from http://www.thestar.com/business/2012/05/18/dave_carroll_is_still_having_problems_with_airlines_roseman.html

Scott, D. M. (2011, December 1). Real-time marketing and PR: How to instantly engage your market, connect with customers, and create products that grow your business now. Retrieved from http://books.google.com/books?id=9kn87w8-zRsC&pg=PT25&dq=united+break+guitars&hl=en&sa=X&ei=nxXIU_GQEYnfoASbj4GQAg&ved=0CC0Q6AEwAQ#v=onepage&q=united%20break%20guitars&f=false

Van Grove, J. (2009, July 15). United breaks guitars surpasses 3 million views in 10 days. Retrieved from http://mashable.com/2009/07/15/united-breaks-guitars/

Armistead, D. (2009, July 21). Examining 'United breaks guitars' – lessons learned the hard way. Retrieved from http://socialwebstrategies.com/2009/07/21/examining-united-breaks-guitars-lessons-learned-the-hard-way/

leader in branded journalism. Coca-Cola wanted to better tell its own story. As a result, it launched a new company website rebranded as "Coca-Cola Journey" with the tagline "Refreshing the world, one story at a time." It was an out-of-the box approach to online communication. Contributors were trained and oriented as publishers instead of Web masters. The purpose of the new site and content is not to directly drive sales, but to drive social media interaction and develop long-term brand relationships that would eventually drive sales offline. Some of the stories you could experience on the Coca-Cola Journey include: Willie Mays Says "Hey": Baseball Legend Brings His Story to Coca-Cola; 10 Reasons Why the 2014 FIFA World Cup Was Truly the #WorldsCup; and Tackling Youth Unemployment: What the World Can Learn from Germany's Apprenticeship Program. Almost every article is embedded with a unique social media plugin.

The Coca-Cola Company's Head of Digital Communications Ashley Brown says, "I'm on a mission. What I want to do is kill the press release." And if you can build a newsroom and staff it with trained writers, what's to stop you? The new site looks more like a newsmagazine chock-full of proprietary content than a corporate landing page. Coca-Cola seems to once again be forging new ground with its push into content marketing.

The practice of creating and sharing valuable free content to draw and convert prospects into customers and loyal fans is growing. Content marketing or communications marketing is perfect for social media because it's fresh and so easy to share. But it's not unique to social media. Content marketing is used for live events, case studies and branded content tools. These things probably deliver more value, brand awareness, backlinks and discussion than simple social media sharing.

Supplementing traditional media

In 2009, two Domino's pizza employees were fired after one filmed the other preparing sandwiches for delivery while putting cheese up his nose and nasal mucus on the sandwiches as well as violating other health code standards. The employee doing the filming was kind enough to narrate the video. Although both employees ended up with felony charges for delivering prohibited foods, the damage to Domino's had already been done once the video went viral on YouTube and the story was picked up by the national mainstream media. The incident had such broad exposure that five of the 12 top Google search results for Domino's brought up nose-picking.

In response, Tim McIntyre, vice president of communication for Domino's, did a series of TV interviews explaining that the company would hold the franchise owner accountable for hiring poor employees, one of which also turned out to be a registered sex offender. The company then shifted its focus to regaining customer trust and rebuilding its brand. This required a mix of social and traditional media to broadly communicate what the company was doing. Domino's announced that it had changed its recipe, offered money-back guarantees and set up a site for customers to share photos of their food. The company tracked public opinion and customer sentiment in real time via social media listening. This allowed it to make adjustments and fine-tune different aspects of the campaign. Sales at U.S. locations increased 14 percent in the quarter after the campaign launched, and the company's share price the following year was up an amazing 75 percent.

Social media tools

Social media listening

One of the advantages of social media is the opportunity to receive immediate feedback. This allows organizations to monitor what is being said about them. Dell computers, for example, receives more than 25,000 mentions per day. The company uses various listening tools and filters to separate what they deem as important messages from background noise. Dell has been pretty successful at finding the messages that actually matter. These are messages from influential Twitter users with thousands of followers, stories posted on top tech blogs and forums, and urgent customer requests.

Similarly, Southwest Airlines is a very active brand on social media. The low-cost airline is becoming a leader in customer service and social media interaction. It scored No. 1 in customer service in the 2013 Airline Quality Ratings and has nearly 1.7 million Twitter followers. When winter storms in early 2014 caused hundreds of cancellations in the Midwest and Northeast, the company's online reservation system and phone lines were jammed. And it received 12,000 tweets over a six-day period — twice as many as normal. *USA Today* highlighted the plight of one of Southwest's travelers. Ryan, a 32-year-old consultant and frequent flier was stranded like thousands of others because of the weather. He tried unsuccessfully to make a reservation online and then phoned the reservation center, only to get a busy signal. So, he tweeted, "Why is your reservation number busy? Had a flight canceled today and can't seem to get through to reschedule. Ridic." Southwest's social media team responded within two minutes.

Social media listening can quickly tell you when you have a problem or weakness in your system. It can also point out opportunities that may have previously gone unnoticed.

Social media ROI

Return on investment is the gain from an investment minus the cost of the investment. Many people think social media is free media. Nothing could be further from the truth. Managing and succeeding in social media takes time, people and technology — all of which are limited resources with associated costs. It takes time to listen. It takes people to generate the massive amounts of necessary content. And it takes technology to analyze the results and adjust your strategy. We're going to focus briefly on the need to measure results to determine if your organization is getting a solid return on its social media investment.

One of the first things we need to clearly understand is what is meant by the term **Web analytics**. According to the Web Analytics Association, "Web analytics is the measurement, collection, analysis and reporting of Internet data for the purpose of understanding and optimizing Web usage." Some other terms you may encoun-

WEB ANALYTICS
The measurement, collection, analysis and reporting of Internet data for the purpose of understanding and optimizing Web usage.

KPI (KEY PERFORMANCE INDICATOR)
An important measure tied to a campaign or social media objective and used to evaluate its success.

CTR (CLICK-THROUGH RATE)
A way of measuring the success of an online advertising or communications campaign by the number of users that click on a specific link.

ter are **KPI** and **CTR**. KPI stands for key performance indicator. Examples include click-through rates, brand awareness and engagement. CTR stands for click-through rate or how often someone clicked on your ad or content to learn more or make a purchase.

The rise of social media has caused some to question the validity of CTR as a measure. Opponents of CTR, including social networking giants like Facebook, argue that you can see an ad, not click on it and still be influenced by it. You wouldn't click on a billboard, after all, and it may still influence your behavior.

What we are seeing is the rise of better measurement tools that don't just track clicks and likes, but rather look at real measures of engagement in the form of discussion, shares across multiple platforms/channels and actions taken as a result of shares.

Olivier Blanchard, principal at BrandBuilder Marketing and author of "Social Media ROI", recommends the following practices:

- Maintain a list of everything you can measure.
- Maintain a list of everything you must measure.
- Stay current on the best measurement tools.
- Ensure the neutrality of the employee(s) tasked with measuring your social media program.
- Tie everything you measure to business objectives.
- Test, measure, learn, adapt, repeat.

As you consider different measures to evaluate your social media success, make sure you tie your measures to the objectives you've already established. You will need a number of different measures to determine engagement, which is categorized by several different behaviors. According to Drew Meyers, president of ad agency Gyro's San Francisco office, the typical online marketing campaign these days usually has about five KPIs. However, it's not unusual for there to be more. "There's a tendency toward a profusion of KPIs," he says. This leads to "an increase in noise versus an increase in intelligent analysis."

Measuring the impact of your social media efforts requires upfront planning. You will need several tools to accurately determine engagement and how far users' actions take them. Engagement isn't worth much if it doesn't lead your key publics to action that accomplishes your objectives and goal.

Summary

Social media has become a critical component of effective communications campaigns. It is powerful because of its immediacy as well as its ability to engage with customers and stakeholders, engender loyalty and develop trust.

One of the biggest trends in social media is the move to mobile devices. This holds true for the consumption of news and branded content as well. Public relations and marketing practitioners should consider planning content first for mobile usage and second for laptop and computer usage.

There are six factors you should study when choosing which social media channels to use for message delivery: users, usage, engagement, compatibility, SEO and potential. Make sure you understand each of these elements. It's also important for social content to be fresh, concise, visually interesting and highly shareable.

In addition, don't miss out on the opportunity to learn what your customers are thinking and doing through social media listening. This is one of the underused and undervalued social media tools.

Finally, you will need several KPIs to determine the success of your social media tools. Make sure you tie KPIs to your objectives and that your measurement of ROI includes all costs including time, people and technology.

Exercises

1. Do some social media listening of your own. Pick a social media channel and industry (e.g., automobiles) and see if you can find out what people are talking about by "listening."

2. Look up an NGO and see what social media tools it is currently employing. Use the six factors outlined in the text to evaluate whether you think it has the right mix of channels.

3. Take a look at a new social media platform with which you are not familiar. Become a user. Then determine four or five different KPIs you could use to measure engagement on that platform.

References and additional readings

Ballve, M. (2014, July 7). The Snapchat report: Audience numbers, demographics, and brands' early marketing efforts. Retrieved from: http://www.businessinsider.com/a-primer-on-snapchat-and-its-demographics-2014-6

Blanchard, O. (2014, March 4). Social media ROI: Managing and measuring social media efforts in your organization. Que Publishing: London.

Cameron, D. (2013, September 23). I've just chaired a meeting of COBRA-tragically the latest reports are that 6 British nationals have been killed in the Kenya terror attacks. [Tweet]. Retrieved from https://twitter.com/David_Cameron/status/382211485264785408

Clifford, S. (2009, April 15). Video prank at Domino's taints brand. Retrieved from http://www.nytimes.com/2009/04/16/business/media/16dominos .html?_r=2&ref=business&

Duggan, M. (2013, December 30). Social media update 2013. Retrieved from http://www.pewinternet.org/2013/12/30/social-media-update-2013/

Flandez, R. (2009, April 20). Domino's response offers lessons in crisis management. Retrieved from http://blogs.wsj.com/independentstreet/2009/04/20/dominos-response-offers-lessons-in-crisis-management/

Gilbertson, D. (2014, January 8). Airline passengers increasingly vent on social media sites about travel woes. [*The Arizona Republic* article]. Retrieved from http://www.usatoday.com/story/travel/flights/2014/01/08/frustrated-fliers-turn-to-twitter/4368629/

Holcomb, J., Gottfried, J., & Mitchell, A. (2013, November 14). News use across social media platforms. Retrieved from http://www.journalism.org/2013/11/14/news-use-across-social-media-platforms

Holmes, R. (2014, March 4). 4 Ways to actually use big data. Retrieved from http://www.inc.com/ryan-holmes/4-ways-to-use-big-data.html

Honigman, B. (2104). 8 Ways social media affects your SEO. [Blog post]. Retrieved from http://blog.sumall.com/journal/8-ways-social-media-affects-seo.html

Oremus, W. (2014, February 4). The half-decent Oreo tweet that dazzled a nation. Retrieved from http://www.slate.com/blogs/future_tense/2013/02/04/oreo_super_bowl_blackout_tweet_dazzles_twitter_reveals_low_bar_for_brands.html

Sisson, N. (2014, February 12). Which social media sites should you be on, and why? Retrieved from http://www.socialmediatoday.com/content/which-social-media-sites-should-you-be-and-why

Scott, R. (2014, March 6) Case studies showing how early adopters benefit from new social media platforms. Retrieved from http://www.smartinsights.com/social-media-marketing/social-media-governance/case-studies-early-adopter-social-media-platforms

Truong, A. (2014, February 13). This report shows why brands should embrace Instagram (if they haven't already). Retrieved from http://www.fastcompany.com/3026419/fast-feed/this-report-shows-why-brands-should-embrace-instagram-if-the-havent-already

Wasserman, T. (2013, May 11). KPI: What is a key performance indicator? Retrieved from: http://mashable.com/2013/05/11/kpi-definition/

Wigmore, I. (2014, July). Part of the personal computing glossary: Social media. Retrieved from http://whatis.techtarget.com/definition/social-media

Yeung, K. (2013, May 5). LinkedIn is 10 years old today: Here's the story of how it changed the way we work. Retrieved from http://thenextweb.com/insider/2013/05/05/linkedin-10-years-social-network/

CHAPTER 10

CALENDARING AND BUDGETING

"Do not squander time, for that is the stuff that life is made of."

—Benjamin Franklin

AMERICAN INVENTOR, JOURNALIST AND STATESMAN

LEARNING IMPERATIVES

- To learn a format for calendars and budgets that supports strategic planning.

- To understand the importance of calendaring interactivity among tactics.

- To learn the value of creativity in the calendaring and budgeting processes.

I n all relationships, timing is everything. Whether responding to a crisis or pursuing an opportunity, timing plays a crucial role in the strategic planning process.

The next step in the Strategic Planning Matrix — calendaring activities and budgeting for their cost — requires very specific detail. With so much information available in the communications and business literature about calendaring and budgeting, only a few important points need to be emphasized here.

Primarily, it is important to remember that a calendar and a budget are not just strategic planning tools. As we see in the next chapter, they are also important tools to manage the implementation of a plan. They must be considered carefully so that timing and cost are addressed within the overall framework of the organization's goals as well as the plan's objectives. They require meticulous attention to detail. If timing is off, your plan may fail. If you have not budgeted precisely, you will have cost overruns that may have long-term consequences.

Electronic tools for calendaring and budgeting abound. One of the best for a calendar is a Gantt chart (see Figure 10.1) that allows you to view the schedule for each public by day, week or month. Budgeting programs should perform calculations automatically to ensure accuracy. If you use an Excel spreadsheet, make sure you check your formulas.

As shown in the teaching case in this chapter, both the calendar and budget should detail tactics by public and strategy so your client or executive can quickly determine what tactics will target a specific public and how much each will cost. It also makes you much more aware of the cost of information and persuasion efforts among each of your key publics, and you are conversant in the interactive scheduling of the campaign by public. It provides an easy "line-item veto" when your client or executive wants to eliminate a public or strategy for any reason. It is a simple matter to delete that section of your plan and subtract the cost from the total.

STRATEGIC PLANNING MATRIX

ACTION PLANNING

6. CALENDAR AND BUDGET

Calendar   Calendars show when each tactic begins and ends and the relationship of tactics to each other in a time continuum. Calendars are organized by public and strategy to show the work required. A Gantt chart is recommended.

Budget   Budgets are also organized by public and strategy. The budget projects the cost of each tactic. It also indicates where costs will be offset by donations or sponsorships. Subtotals are provided for each strategy and public.

Calendaring

Never forget that a calendar is strategic. When you calendar a plan, you are not just picking dates; you are finding the premier moment for an event to be held, social media to spread the word virally or an ad campaign to launch. Timing is critical to success. A few important guidelines can help make sure your calendaring is effective.

Interactivity is key. The timing of tactics should be such that you magnify, reinforce and build on other tactics within publics and across publics. Schedule the grade school poster contest to conclude in time to use the winning posters in your efforts to solicit sponsorships from local businesses. Time your viral communication to peak when publics are getting messages in more formal channels.

Check for conflicts seasonally and within communities. It is difficult to compete with traditional events and efforts. The annual Oktoberfest is probably not the time to schedule the launch of the hospital's new alcoholic rehab wing.

Build on tradition and other regularly scheduled events. While you need to avoid conflicting events, building upon related traditions can leverage awareness and motivation. The beginning of a new school year might be a great time

Figure 10.1
What is a Gantt chart?

A Gantt chart is a horizontal chart (usually a bar chart) developed as a production control tool in 1917 by Henry L. Gantt, an American engineer and social scientist. Frequently used in project management, a Gantt chart provides a graphical illustration of a schedule that helps to plan, coordinate and track specific tasks in a project. Gantt charts may be simple versions created on graph paper or more complex automated versions created using project management applications such as Microsoft Project or Excel. Dozens of other software packages are also available to help build effective Gantt charts.

Simple Gantt Chart

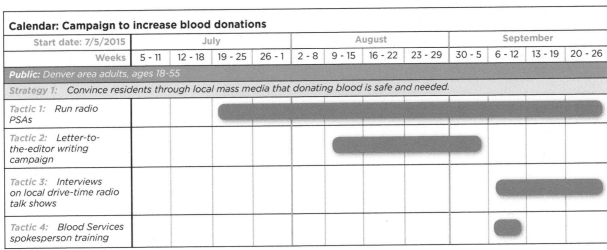

Calendar: Campaign to increase blood donations												
Start date: 7/5/2015	July				August				September			
Weeks	5 - 11	12 - 18	19 - 25	26 - 1	2 - 8	9 - 15	16 - 22	23 - 29	30 - 5	6 - 12	13 - 19	20 - 26
Public: Denver area adults, ages 18-55												
Strategy 1: Convince residents through local mass media that donating blood is safe and needed.												
Tactic 1: Run radio PSAs												
Tactic 2: Letter-to-the-editor writing campaign												
Tactic 3: Interviews on local drive-time radio talk shows												
Tactic 4: Blood Services spokesperson training												

A recipe for Cool Whip's success

MINI CASE

HUNTER PR

BACKSTORY

Despite the fact that this case is more than 15 years old, it remains a great example of how to leverage strategic calendaring.

In early 1995, Kraft Foods approached Hunter PR with the question of how to dramatically increase sales of its whipped-topping product, Cool Whip, during the coming summer. With stiff competition in the dessert toppings market from name brands such as Reddi-wip, as well as store brands like Kroger and Western Family, Kraft needed to come up with a campaign that would brand it as the nondairy whipped topping of choice among consumers.

The Hunter team brainstormed what to do and came up with an idea to capitalize on an undercelebrated American holiday: Flag Day, June 14th. Between 1995 and 1997, Hunter built three different "America's Grandest Flag Cakes" at key patriotic locations: the Washington Monument (1995), Independence Hall (1996) and the Statue of Liberty (1997). In each location, ginormous United States flag cakes were assembled — catching not only the attention of local residents, but national media outlets looking for interesting stories and visuals.

KEY FACTS

- The Flag Day events required numerous permissions and the coordination of hundreds of volunteers.
- Weighing more than 20,000 pounds, the flag cakes measured approximately 60 feet by 90 feet — roughly the size of one and a half tennis courts.
- Helicopters were hired to keep birds from spoiling the cakes.
- Slices of the cake were soon distributed to the crowd, and the remaining cake was donated to local food banks.

How would you use a national holiday to increase product usage?

AP Photo/HO/Larry Lettera

Hunter's Liberty Island flag cake weighed 21,140 pounds and covered 5,500 square feet.

HUNTER'S STRATEGY

In order to reduce costs in producing the cakes, Hunter gained sponsorship from Sara Lee, who provided the pound cakes, and Comstock, who contributed the pie filling. These brand names, along with Cool Whip, were listed as the primary ingredients in flag cake recipes highlighted by the media. Hunter was able to tie Cool Whip to a relatively unknown holiday in mid-June just in time to promote a fun, patriotic recipe for Independence Day, summer barbecues and family reunions.

Understanding that local and national media held the key to reaching Kraft's customers, Hunter initiated an aggressive campaign to contact as many news outlets as possible. The PR firm then beamed B-roll via satellite to 700 affiliates nationwide. Hunter also arranged product placements on the TODAY show, featuring flag cake recipes that customers could make at home. Hunter even arranged for patriotic signing groups, local and national officials, Scout troops, descendants of the signers of the Declaration of Independence and Daughters of the American Revolution to participate in the events.

RESULTS

- Without any paid advertising, Hunter's PR stunt successfully motivated consumers to make their own flag cakes using Cool Whip. In 1995, an additional 8,000 cases of the topping were sold during the week of the event.
- Nearly 100 newspapers across the United States ran articles including the Los Angeles Times and Philadelphia Daily News.
- Coverage of "America's Grandest Flag Cake" increased each year, reaching a crescendo in 1997 with more than 82 million media impressions.

WORKS CITED

Hunter PR (2009). Celebrating Flag Day in a grand way — Cool Whip style. Case study provided by Hunter PR.

---

to launch an effort to change a habit or routine. Perhaps when the kids go off to school is the best time for the local library to start a women's readers' circle.

Always provide enough lead time for production and other arrangements. Plan for collateral material to be complete far in advance of the time it is needed. Make all reservations and invitations to key participants well in advance of the event. Doing so will leave time to reprint or rebook, if needed. Major conferences reserve venues years in advance. Most campaigns cannot be pulled off overnight.

Plan backward from the implementation date. If the launch is in July, when should the media pieces be prepared and placed to support the launch? Is the media element a promotion or a followup? When should collateral material be completed to be available at the launch? When should invitations be printed and mailed to ensure people have time to schedule it and RSVP?

An implementation calendar is obviously much more detailed than a calendar for a proposed plan. While the latter simply schedules the date each tactic will be used, the former requires scheduling of all efforts leading up to the date of implementation.

Calendar

The calendar below maps out an American Dental Association (ADA) campaign to decrease the incidence of tooth decay among elementary school children by motivating them to practice good dental hygiene. The communication confirmation table for this example is in Chapter 11.

		Month:	September
		Week:	1 2 3 4
Key public: Students			
Strategy: Motivate brushing/flossing through classroom activities			
Tactics:	Bulletin board		
	Chart to mark daily brushing		
	Disposables for those who didn't brush/floss		
	Interactive tablet app with activities for kids		
	Mr. Tooth screensaver		
	Mr. Tooth erasers		
Strategy: Motivate through class lesson on dental hygiene			
Tactics:	Video on how to brush/floss		
	Art activity/Mr. Tooth	X	
	Visit from dentist		
	Learning activity on dental hygiene		
Key public: Parents			
Strategy: Promote through PTA			
Tactics:	Email on negative effects on learning		X
	PTA Facebook social plug-ins		
	Brochure at parent/teacher conferences		
	Classroom displays at parent/teacher conferences		
	Mailer on cumulative costs of dental work		X
Strategy: Remind through take-home collateral			
Tactics:	Brush/floss kit sent home		
	Flyer sent home		
	"I'm a good brusher" stickers		
	Invitation to classroom dentist visit		
Key public: Teachers			
Strategy: Motivate by providing classroom resources			
Tactics:	Lesson plans on website	X———	
	Dentist available to visit class		
	Bulletin board material	X———	
	Mr. Tooth models	X———	
	Learning activity ideas	X———	
	Classroom brushing chart	X———	
	YouTube videos	X———	
Strategy: Motivate through ADA appeal			
Tactics:	Dimensional mailer requesting cooperation	X	
	Magnet with website for campaign resources/FAQs	X	
	Online survey to measure participation	X	
	Follow-up email		
	Resource website	X———	

October	November	December	January	February	March	April	May	June
1 2 3 4	1 2 3 4	1 2 3 4	1 2 3 4	1 2 3 4	1 2 3 4	1 2 3 4	1 2 3 4	1 2 3 4

Budgeting

The budget should also be considered strategically. The issue should not only be total cost but also who will pay and how. Highly creative plans find solutions to budgetary limitations, many of which result in greater creativity and persuasive power. Recruiting volunteers to do work that would have been a budgetary item results not only in lower cost but also in greater support and advocacy from opinion leaders in a community. Building **partnerships** between organizations — whether business-to-business or corporate-to-nonprofit — often strengthens the credibility of the appeal. Combining with other actors in a cooperative cost-sharing effort provides a unity of action that is more persuasive and far-reaching than acting unilaterally.

Even requesting small contributions from target publics (e.g., $2 admission to an event with the proceeds donated to a relevant local charity) can be effective. Making something free doesn't always make it appealing. In fact, many people consider that something free may not be worth their time. Among certain publics, you are more likely to get attention and participation if there is some monetary investment — even if only small.

Your budget should have eight columns. This format is easy to set up in a spreadsheet. The first column identifies the public and strategy. The second column identifies the tactics that fall under each strategy. The third column provides a little detail about each tactic (e.g., 40-page, full-color brochure; two-minute YouTube video; custom-designed iPhone cases). The fourth column gives the quantity needed. The fifth column provides the cost per unit. The sixth column is the total projected cost for that budget item. The seventh column identifies the sponsored credit (i.e., how much of the given tactic will be donated). The eighth column provides the actual projected cost of each tactic (i.e., number of units times per item cost, minus sponsored credit equals actual cost). Each column is important. They show the scope and cost of each tactic as well as external support in terms of offsetting discounts and sponsorships. It is crucial for clients or supervisors to know how much your creativity and partnerships have saved.

This format breaks the cost of your campaign down by public, strategy and tactic. You can quickly see where your resources have been allocated. It is critical to know what it will cost to reach a particular public or to see quickly that one strategy is going to cost more than the rest of the campaign. Good budgeting makes it relatively easy to do a mental cost-benefit analysis to determine if each expenditure is worth the gain. The strategic planning process is dynamic. Proper budgeting will help you identify potential areas of concern. It should also help you to identify areas where greater creativity might be needed to do things differently and for a lower cost. Executives expect this kind of analysis.

Nevertheless, don't automatically reject a public because of cost. Be creative in finding ways to do what you have planned more frugally, like using volunteers or collaborating with other organizations to share costs. Also, don't forget to seek out sponsorships. Strategic partnerships and sponsorships can foster win-win relationships and in many ways buy you influence you couldn't afford and/or acquire on your own.

PARTNERSHIP
A mutually beneficial short- or long-term cooperative relationship to reach common goals.

TIPS FROM THE PROS

Spending your money strategically

Judith T. Phair, APR, Fellow PRSA, president of PhairAdvantage Communications, former vice president of communications for the Graduate Management Admission Council and former PRSA president, tips you off on budgeting so your first-rate public relations programs don't end up as exercises in "what might have been."

Effective budgeting is one of the most strategic things you can do to advance your department and organization — and your career. To be valued as a trusted adviser and counselor, a public relations professional needs to know the business side of the client or organization. Carefully building, justifying, maintaining and monitoring a budget is a critical part of strategic planning. A well-constructed budget provides a built-in method for setting expectations and evaluating results. Here are some things to keep in mind when crafting a financial scenario that will truly show return on investment and set the stage for gaining funding for future projects.

Know the organization's business plan. Understand the relationship of your work to key elements of the business. What are the top priorities, including financial priorities?

Budget strategically. Think about why dollars will be spent, as well as how. Justify each expenditure with measurable results.

Budget realistically. Match the budget to expectations. If the organization doesn't have the resources to meet its expectations, show what would be required as well as what can be done within existing boundaries. Offer alternative scenarios, along with a strategic analysis of what the return on investment would be with greater expenditures.

Consider both direct and indirect costs. Staff labor is not "free," nor is the use of equipment, office space and the like.

Measure the return on investment. Remember, also, that the return does not need to be monetary to provide real value. If you invest in a program to create the climate for an effective fundraising campaign or to boost public support for (or against) legislation, that ultimately contributes to the organization's bottom line.

Budget

The school district and ADA are collaborating together to improve adolescent dental hygiene. This budget does not include the ADA's portion of the campaign; it is for the school district's costs only. The district has 10 elementary schools, a total of 200 teachers and 3,500 children. The communication confirmation table for this example is in Chapter 11.

Key public: Students	
Strategy: Motivate brushing/flossing through classroom activities	
Tactics:	Bulletin board
	Chart to mark daily brushing
	Disposables for those who didn't brush/floss
	Interactive tablet app with activities for kids
	Mr. Tooth screensaver
	Mr. Tooth erasers
Strategy: Motivate through class lesson on dental hygiene	
Tactics:	Video on how to brush/floss
	Art activity/Mr. Tooth
	Visit from dentist
	Learning activity on dental hygiene
Key public: Parents	
Strategy: Promote through PTA	
Tactics:	Email on negative effects on learning
	PTA Facebook social plug-ins
	Brochure at parent/teacher conferences
	Classroom displays at parent/teacher conferences
	Mailer on cumulative costs of dental work
Strategy: Remind through take-home collateral	
Tactics:	Brush/floss kit sent home
	Flyer sent home
	"I'm a good brusher" stickers
	Invitation to classroom dentist visit
Key public: Teachers	
Strategy: Motivate by providing classroom resources	
Tactics:	Lesson plans on website
	Dentist available to visit class
	Bulletin board material
	Mr. Tooth models
	Learning activity ideas
	Classroom brushing chart
	YouTube videos
Strategy: Motivate through ADA appeal	
Tactics:	Dimensional mailer requesting cooperation
	Magnet with website for campaign resources/FAQs
	Online survey to measure participation
	Follow-up email
	Resource website

Detail	Quantity	Per Item Cost	Total Projected	Sponsored Credit	Actual Projected
Download from ADA website		$0.00	$0	$0	$0
Download from ADA website		$0.00	$0	$0	$0
Local dentists provide	10,500	$0.25	$2,625	$2,625	$0
Download from ADA website		$0.00	$0	$0	$0
Download from ADA website		$0.00	$0	$0	$0
20 percent discount from national supplier	31,500	$0.10	$3,150	$630	$2,520
Strategy subtotal			*$5,775*	*$3,255*	*$2,520*
Download from ADA YouTube channel		$0.00	$0	$0	$0
Download from ADA website		$0.00	$0	$0	$0
Local dentist volunteers		$0.00	$0	$0	$0
Download from ADA website		$0.00	$0	$0	$0
Strategy subtotal			*$0*	*$0*	*$0*
Public subtotal			**$5,775**	**$3,255**	**$2,520**
Download from ADA website/PTA email		$0.00	$0	$0	$0
Embedded from website/blog		$0.00	$0	$0	$0
Provided by ADA	4,500	$0.00	$0	$0	$0
Download from ADA website, district prints	200	$2.75	$550	$0	$550
Design, printing and mailing	7,000	$0.76	$5,320	$0	$5,320
Strategy subtotal			*$5,870*	*$0*	*$5,870*
Local dentists subsidize 50 percent	7,000	$1.50	$10,500	$5,250	$5,250
ADA provides flyer, district pays for mail	31,500	$0.26	$8,190	$0	$8,190
Provided by ADA. Sent home monthly, 9 months	31,500	$0.00	$0	$0	$0
Email	3,500	$0.00	$0	$0	$0
Strategy subtotal			*$18,690*	*$5,250*	*$13,440*
Public subtotal			**$24,560**	**$5,250**	**$19,310**
Download from ADA website		$0.00	$0	$0	$0
Local dentists		$0.00	$0	$0	$0
Download from ADA website		$0.00	$0	$0	$0
Download from ADA website		$0.00	$0	$0	$0
Download from ADA website		$0.00	$0	$0	$0
Download from ADA website		$0.00	$0	$0	$0
Download from ADA YouTube channel		$0.00	$0	$0	$0
Strategy subtotal			*$0*	*$0*	*$0*
ADA designs, district prints and mails	200	$0.50	$100	$0	$100
ADA provides	200	$0.00	$0	$0	$0
Sent by ADA		$0.00	$0	$0	$0
PTA send out email	200	$0.00	$0	$0	$0
Maintained by ADA		$0.00	$0	$0	$0
Strategy subtotal			*$100*	*$0*	*$100*
Public subtotal			**$100**	**$0**	**$100**
Campaign total			**$30,435**	**$8,505**	**$21,930**

Summary

Strategic planning does not end at tactics. Your approach to calendaring and budgeting must also be strategic. Tactics should be timed to gain maximum benefit from other tactics in the plan and from external events and annual community calendars. Strategic budgeting allows you to creatively manage cost while leveraging other relationships. The calendar and budget should be just as much a part of your strategic and creative planning as are the other elements of the plan.

Exercises

1. Examine a local annual event, and identify what publics are being targeted. Put together a Gantt chart for preparations and tactics. What are all the elements of the event, including partnerships, media and collateral materials?

2. Look online and make some phone calls to estimate the cost of the tactics identified for the above event. Categorize the budgetary items by public to determine a cost per public. Identify where the organizers might have negotiated discounts or contributions and where partnerships have mitigated the cost.

References and additional readings

Gantt.com. (2012, June 20). What is a Gantt chart? Retrieved from www.Gantt.com

CHAPTER 11

IMPLEMENTATION AND COMMUNICATIONS MANAGEMENT

"There is a logic of language and a logic of mathematics. The former is supple and lifelike, it follows our experience."

—Thomas Merton
AMERICAN MONK, WRITER AND POET

LEARNING IMPERATIVES

- To learn how to synthesize a plan into a confirmation table to check your plan's logic.

- To learn how to use a calendar and communication confirmation table to manage the production and implementation of tactics.

- To understand the importance of measurement and flexibility in the process of implementation.

COMMUNICATION CONFIRMATION TABLE

A visual tool used to validate the logic of a communications plan.

Two of the most valuable tools for managing the implementation of a plan are the strategically planned calendar and the **communication confirmation table**. The calendar keeps all strategies and tactics for all publics coordinated and on schedule. The communication confirmation table helps you check to make sure you are accomplishing what your analysis and plan say you needed to accomplish with each public in order to reach the goal. Nevertheless, remember this is a planning matrix; you should complete every step of the planning — through evaluation criteria and tools — before you begin to implement the plan. Once you have done that, use the calendar and the communication confirmation table as your management maps.

TIPS FROM THE PROS

How to manage integrated campaigns

Andy Hopson is executive director of the University of Florida's Strategic Communication Agency housed within the School of Journalism and Communications. He was previously president of Publicis Dialog, a "holistic" agency he helped launch in the U.S. Andy tips you off on how to integrate public relations, advertising, digital, social and marketing services into successful campaigns.

Now, more than ever, consumers are barraged with marketing messages, not only from traditional and digital media channels but also from user-generated content and social media. We don't differentiate where we get information. We take it in holistically to form opinions and brand preferences as well as to make decisions. Successful public relations practitioners understand that holistic, integrated marketing strategies are critical to successful brand management.

Integrated marketing communications is all about building brands through consistent messaging across all communication channels and touching consumers wherever they are in ways most meaningful to them individually. Successful campaigns cohesively communicate consistent messages at every point of contact with consumers, whether through a 30-second television spot, news article, event, YouTube video or social media post.

Advertising allows control of the message. Public relations enables brand storytelling. Targeted content marketing informs, and social media engages. Campaigns that successfully integrate multiple disciplines surround consumers in a way that generates a distinct understanding of the brand essence.

The following are components of successful integrated campaigns:

Holistic training. Communicators from all disciplines must be trained to think broadly. They must possess an open mind to recognize the role each discipline can play in an integrated campaign.

Holistic planning. Successful integrated marketing communications campaigns start with planning, extend to the creative process and continue through execution. Advertising, marketing, public relations, content and social marketing must have equal status as each play a role in creating equity and brand preference among consumers.

Multidisciplinary creative development. A really big idea is one that can be effectively applied across many marketing disciplines and extended to all channels of communication. Ideas must be drawn from a broader range of perspectives — not devised by one discipline and later adapted to others.

Whole-picture measurement. An integrated campaign can be more readily held accountable for business performance. Holistic strategists must measure the effectiveness of each channel of communications so they can modulate the marketing mix for optimal return on investment.

Managing by calendar

To manage a project well, you must be able to visualize the outcome in your head. You must be able to see how an effort comes together to communicate messages to an individual public and across all your publics. The Gantt chart format recommended for the calendar helps you identify tasks and preparation by public throughout the entire timeframe of the project or campaign. You can manage (or delegate management) by public if needed.

The same format allows you to identify a selected timeframe — for example, the first week of June — and consider every tactic being implemented among all publics within that timeframe. It provides a holistic view of every tactic integrating across all publics; it displays the whole picture of the campaign among all publics for that timeframe. As a management tool, it helps you keep all the balls in the air because you visualize the entirety of events, but it still allows you to narrow your focus to one public as needed.

MINI CASE

QANTAS

How did the world's safest airline fare in a crisis?

BACKSTORY

On Nov. 4, 2010, just four minutes after takeoff from Singapore's Changi Airport, passengers on board Qantas' flight 32 to Sydney heard two loud bangs. They watched helplessly as flames and debris shot from one of the plane's four engines, damaging the wing and fuselage. Rumors that the plane had crashed began to spread across social media as residents of Batam — a small island south of Singapore — uploaded images to Flickr and Twitter of mangled Qantas airplane parts that had fallen from the sky.

The Airbus A380, the world's largest passenger aircraft, was forced to make an emergency landing back in Singapore an hour and 40 minutes after the incident. With its reputation for safety on the line, Qantas needed to respond quickly, and effectively implement crisis communications plans.

KEY FACTS

- Beginning service in September 2008, Qantas became one of the first companies to fly the giant Airbus A380, which carries up to 525 passengers.
- All 459 passengers and crew onboard QF32 disembarked unharmed following the engine explosion.
- It took Qantas just 30 minutes to release its first statement after becoming aware of the incident.
- At the time of the explosion, Qantas had six A380s in its fleet.
- Qantas resumed A380 services on Nov. 27, more than three weeks after the troubled flight.

Barcroft Media/Getty Images

Local police check debris from Qantas A380 in Batam, Indonesia.

How would you respond in such a crisis?

QANTAS' STRATEGY

Following QF32's safe landing, the airline immediately released a written statement confirming that an engine had failed and denied tweets that the plane had crashed. By the end of the day, Qantas had released additional information about the explosion. Knowing the safety of its six super jumbos would be called into question, CEO Alan Joyce also hosted a media conference where he announced the temporary grounding of all Qantas A380s.

Operationally, Qantas began substituting several of its Boeing 747 fleet to carry passengers previously booked on A380 flights. The airline also leased a Boeing 777 from British Airways.

Although operationally Qantas was quick in responding to the challenges that came with flight 32, its social media responses were slow and weak. In the 24 hours following the incident, the airline failed to provide sufficient information on its Facebook page, writing only one post, which included a dead link. Qantas also ignored its Twitter followers completely and failed to upload much to its YouTube channel.

RESULTS

- The A380 incident was deemed Australia's biggest PR disaster of 2010.
- The International Air Transportation Association created new universal guidelines for the use of social media in the event of a crisis.
- Although Qantas' communications efforts via traditional media were prompt and transparent, it grossly underestimated the importance of leveraging social media in a crisis. As Qantas reacted slowly to videos, pictures and stories posted online, it allowed "citizen journalists" to not only break the story, but to determine its impact and duration. Joyce admitted, "We were ready for traditional media … but we'd missed this whole social media end of communication."

WORKS CITED

ABC News (Australia). (2010, November 4). Joyce discusses A380 engine failure [Video file]. Retrieved from https://www.youtube.com/watch?v=rtdiOx0Q4CU

Anonymous. (2010, November 4). Qantas grounds all A380s after engine failure. *The Guardian.* Retrieved from http://www.theguardian.com/world/2010/nov/04/qantas-plane-emergency-landing-singapore

Anonymous. (2010, November 20). Airbus A380: Facts and figures. *The Telegraph.* Retrieved from http://www.telegraph.co.uk/finance/newsbysector/industry/engineering/8147589/Airbus-A380-facts-and-figures.html

Bailey, J. (2013, April). Crisis communications in the age of social media: How the aviation industry woke up to the power of citizen journalists. International Public Relations Association. Retrieved from http://www.ipra.org/itl/04/2013/crisis-communications-in-the-age-of-social-media-how-the-aviation-industry-woke-up-to-the-power-of-citizen-journalists

Business Insider Australia. (2013, June 30). Frightening photos from the report on the Qantas A380 incident show exactly what happened. *Business Insider.* Retrieved from http://www.businessinsider.com/frightening-photos-from-the-report-on-the-qantas-a380-incident-show-exactly-what-happened-2013-7#!I8W4P

Govindasamy, S. (2010, November 23). Qantas to resume limited A380 services. *Flightglobal.* Retrieved from http://www.flightglobal.com/news/articles/qantas-to-resume-limited-a380-services-350061/

La, J. (2008, April 20). The Airbus A380's suite ride. *Los Angeles Times.* Retrieved from http://www.latimes.com/travel/la-tr-airbus20apr20-story.html

McCusker, G. (2012, January 9). Australia's 2011 PR disasters awards announced. *PR Disasters.* Retrieved from http://prdisasters.com/?p=944

Smith, M. (2010, November 8). Qantas finds A380 engine issues, keeps fleet grounded. *Reuters.* Retrieved from http://uk.mobile.reuters.com/article/topNews/idUKTRE6A62P320101108?i=3

Managing by communication confirmation table

The steps in the planning section of the Strategic Communications Planning Matrix have required an analytical approach to answer these four questions:

- What needs to be accomplished?
- Who needs to be reached and motivated?
- What messages need to be sent to get our publics to act?
- How can we most effectively send those messages?

The planning is analytical and is completed one public at a time using your research and knowledge about a particular public to formulate and deliver messages to that public. Because planning is naturally linear, it is helpful — particularly to students learning the strategic process — to create an abbreviated and more visual tool to validate the viability of your plan. This process helps to ensure the plan follows logically from the analysis of publics. That is the purpose of the communication confirmation table. It presents the logic across a single line of vision to confirm that planning decisions employ good reasoning. By abbreviating your analysis in key words across the matrix categories, the communication confirmation table presents your logic as the answers to the four questions above.

The communication confirmation table identifies each key public and shows you which objectives each public will help you fulfill. It then summarizes the self-interests of a public and shows in the next column how those self-interests are incorporated into the message appeal. It identifies the opinion leaders — or influentials — of the public that should be used to reach them. It then uses key words to highlight the strategies and supporting tactics necessary to achieve the objective. Viewing this

STRATEGIC PLANNING MATRIX

COMMUNICATION

7. COMMUNICATION CONFIRMATION

The confirmation table checks the logic of your analysis in formulating a persuasive plan. The action plan is reduced to a format that shows the alignment of strategies and tactics with key publics and opinion leaders; messages with self-interests; and all of these components with the objectives. The completed table becomes a tool to manage implementation of the campaign.

Key Public	Objectives	Self-interests	Primary Messages	Opinion Leaders	Strategies	Tactics

shorthand version of your plan helps you confirm that sound logic and analysis have been applied to your strategic plan. It also demonstrates how well the plan flows and ensures that all elements of the matrix action planning process are aligned.

It is not unusual for the confirmation table to reveal discrepancies in logic that were not apparent while the plan was being written. Have you selected midday television talk shows to reach high school students? Did you plan to run PSAs during drive time to reach housewives? Have you designed a message about money-saving features to target a public that is less concerned about money and more concerned about safety? Are you using video news releases to send a complicated message

better conveyed in magazine feature stories or blogs? Are you trying to reach teens on Facebook when you might better reach them through Instagram, Snapchat or Vine? Check your logic, and then go back and make any appropriate changes to your plan before you begin executing it. As intimated in the quotation at the beginning of the chapter, language is fluid and logical — especially words defining a strategic plan which effectively builds on itself.

Ongoing monitoring and feedback

These two management tools — the Gantt chart calendar and the communication confirmation table — are the maps you use to manage your efforts. The calendar tells you what is coming up to help you be prepared and on top of your campaign. The confirmation table is a continual reminder — not just of the tactics you need to implement but also of the messages you are trying to convey to secure action from your publics.

These tools add the flexibility that is often missing from the planning process. When you plan the evaluation (the final step in the Strategic Communications Planning Matrix), you will plan for measurement throughout the implementation phase. These measurements provide checkpoints for your progress toward reaching the objectives and goal. But what if your measurements reveal that you are not on track? Because you have strategically planned a calendar and thoughtfully prepared the communication confirmation table, you have the flexibility to go back to those two documents to rework and refine your plan to get back on track.

The necessary alteration may be as simple as adding or changing a single tactic or as grand as revamping an entire public. The confirmation table also provides the flexibility to quickly add or delete a public. You don't have to rewrite the whole plan. You have a summary of your plan by public, most particularly of the logic of the plan based on your analysis. Use it to determine what you need to change to reach your objectives on time and within budget.

Communication confirmation table

This communication confirmation table maps out the entire campaign to decrease the incidence of tooth decay among elementary school children by motivating them to practice good dental hygiene.

Key public	Objectives	Self-interests	Primary messages
Students	Increase brushing	Pleasing parents/ teachers	Mom says brush and floss every day
	Increase flossing	Peer acceptance	Your friends like you better when your teeth are clean
	Reduce decay		
		Avoiding discomfort	Clean teeth won't get cavities that hurt
Parents	Increase brushing	Children's health	Brushing/flossing prevents kids' cavities
	Increase flossing	Saving money	Preventing cavities saves money
	Increase annual exams		Annual exams help stop decay before it gets expensive
	Reduce decay		
		Children's school performance	Kids with healthy teeth do better in school
Teachers	Increase brushing	Healthy children	Kids with healthy teeth learn better and behave better
		Children's school performance	
	Increase flossing		
	Increase annual exams	Reducing behavioral problems	Kids with decayed teeth are suffering
	Decrease decay		

Opinion leaders	Strategies	Tactics
Parents Teachers Peers	Motivate brushing/flossing through classroom activities	Bulletin board Chart to mark daily brushing Disposables for those who didn't brush/floss Interactive tablet app with activities for kids Mr. Tooth screensaver Mr. Tooth erasers
	Motivate through class lesson on dental hygiene	Video on how to brush/floss Art activity/Mr. Tooth Visit from dentist Learning activity on dental hygiene
Dentists Teachers Other parents	Promote through PTA	Email on negative effects on learning PTA Facebook social plug-ins Brochure at parent/teacher conferences Classroom displays at parent/teacher conferences Mailer on cumulative costs of dental work
	Remind through take-home collateral	Brush/floss sent home Flyer sent home Sticker on kids "I'm a good brusher" Invitation to classroom dentist visit
Administrators Dentists Children	Motivate by providing classroom resources	Lesson plans on website Dentist available to visit class Bulletin board material Mr. Tooth models Learning activity ideas Classroom brushing chart Youtube videos
	Motivate through ADA appeal	Mailer requesting cooperation Magnet with website for campaign resources/FAQs Online survey to measure participation Follow-up email Resource website

Summary

The communication confirmation table is a planning tool that becomes a management tool once you have begun the actual implementation of your communications plan. As a planning tool, it confirms the logic of your plan for each public according to the analysis completed in your research. As a management tool, it provides the flexibility to change your plan quickly and effectively to make progress toward your objectives. The strategically planned calendar becomes the other key management tool in the implementation process. Use it to manage your efforts for each public as well as to manage the whole campaign from a macro perspective. In the implementation process, these two management tools provide the capability for measurement and feedback to adjust the plan and keep it on track.

Exercises

1. Use one of the partial plans or analyses completed in the exercises from prior chapters and create a communication confirmation table that will help you evaluate the logic of the plan.

2. Select a public that was not used in the above table and add them to it as a viable part of the plan.

CHAPTER 12

COMMUNICATIONS MEASUREMENT AND EVALUATION

"In reality, the lines are now so blurred between social and traditional media that we really have to change the entire [measurement] conversation."

—K.D. Paine

PUBLIC RELATIONS MEASUREMENT GURU AND CEO OF PAINE PUBLISHING, LLC

LEARNING IMPERATIVES

- To understand the importance of evaluation in demonstrating results.

- To understand how to plan evaluation based on what you are trying to accomplish.

- To understand how to determine evaluation criteria and the appropriate measurement tools.

A little over a decade ago, surveys among public relations professionals found that they generally "lacked confidence to promote evaluation methods to employers and clients" (Watson, 2001). Lack of knowledge and understanding of evaluation models and techniques seemed to be the primary reason practitioners did not propose or conduct evaluation.

What a phenomenal difference a decade makes! Finally, measurement has become the watch word and "results, results, results" the mantra of executives.

Instead of viewing an organization's communication as a kind of mystical intangible — intangible methods, intangible effects and intangible results — we now measure everything in our effort to build strong relationships with key publics and contribute to our organization's success. This crucial step has finally made us strategic.

We must be focused on what we are trying to accomplish, who we need to reach to do that, what messages will motivate them and how best to send those messages so they pay attention and act. Executives demand hard data measuring our results in each one of those key elements to success. They use data to evaluate success and to drive decision-making.

Organizations — commercial, governmental and nonprofit — are managed to produce results and to accomplish their missions. Each function of the organization must be able to demonstrate its contribution to the accomplishment of its mission. The ability to prove results is critical not only for the organization but also for the employees doing the work. There is little reward to working daily in efforts that you cannot be sure are making a contribution.

Evaluation models

The literature of communication contains several models of evaluation. They basically all evaluate success along three standards. The first is success that justifies the budget expenditure. The second is effectiveness of the program itself. The third is whether objectives were met. While these standards are all worthwhile gauges of success, put yourself in the CEO's place. What is he/she looking for? In a word, results.

Results may mean meeting the objectives, they may mean success that justifies the budget expenditure or they may mean effectively carrying out a program. But

STRATEGIC PLANNING MATRIX

EVALUATION

8. EVALUATION CRITERIA AND TOOLS	Evaluation criteria are the desired results established by the objectives.
	Evaluation tools are the methodologies you use to gather the data. These tools must be included in the calendar and budget.

Is it time for a breakup?

BACKSTORY

T-Mobile — the fourth largest wireless network company in America — has suffered in recent years from stagnant customer growth and diminishing market share as customers moved to market leaders: Verizon, AT&T and Sprint. In an attempt to regain market share and revitalize its brand, T-Mobile has unveiled a program to transform ordinary cell phone contracts: the "un-carrier revolution." The program invited customers to "break up" with their current carrier, post their breakups to social media sites and start a relationship with T-Mobile.

KEY FACTS

- T-Mobile — which announced the un-carrier revolution March 26, 2013 — was the first in the industry to do away with annual contracts.
- While struggling somewhat in the U.S. with only 49.1 million subscribers, T-Mobile is one of the strongest international network companies.
- Total net customer additions for T-Mobile in 2012 reached only 203,000, compared with AT&T's 3.7 million.
- Market share in 2012 dropped from 12.7 percent to 11.6 percent, despite a massive increase in ad spending.

How would you respond?

T-MOBILE'S STRATEGY

In March 2013, T-Mobile announced phase one of its four-phase strategy: a service plan which no longer required an annual contract. In June 2013, phase two allowed customers to upgrade their handset twice a year rather than every two years. Phase three, released in October, provided unlimited data and texting worldwide at no extra cost, and phase four, released in January 2014, introduced the "break-up letter" concept and offered to pay early termination fees of customers who switched to T-Mobile.

T-Mobile kept the buzz of the un-carrier revolution alive and gained greater exposure through its use of social media. CEO John Legere refuted claims and threats of competitors on Twitter while advocating the T-Mobile brand, retweeted comments that indicated brand loyalty and personally responded to customer complaints. An app was created on

David Becker/Getty Images News/Getty Images

T-Mobile CEO, John Legere, speaks at the 2013 International Consumer Electronics Show in Las Vegas.

T-Mobile's Facebook page, which helped customers write and share their break-up letters on social media. A Facebook quiz — which portrayed T-Mobile as the rebel of the wireless network industry — also offered prizes.

RESULTS

- The success of the un-carrier program transformed T-Mobile from being the slowest growing carrier in the U.S. to the fastest in nine months. The company added a record-breaking 2.4 million new customers in the first quarter of 2014 — more than 11 times the amount it added in all of 2012.
- Share value increased 7.3 percent the morning the quarterly report was announced. Revenue rose 47 percent to $6.88 billion, compared with $4.68 billion in the same quarter of the previous year.
- T-Mobile's BrandIndex score measuring value perception matched that of the market leader Verizon's. YouGov's survey showed that customers were most likely to choose T-Mobile if they were to switch carriers in the next six months. To date, more than 80,000 people have shared their break-up letters through social media.

WORKS CITED:

Bunton, C. (2014, January 16). 80,000 "break-up" letters later, T-Mobile widens ETF payment program to include U.S. Cellular and others. *TmoNews*. Retrieved from http://www.tmonews.com/2014/01/80000-break-up-letters-later-t-mobile-widens-etf-payment-program-to-include-u-s-cellular-and-others/

Cheng, R. (2014, May 1). T-Mobile swings to loss on cost of exploding customer growth. *CNET*. Retrieved from http://www.cnet.com/news/t-mobile-swings-to-loss-on-cost-of-exploding-customer-growth/

Lopes, M. (2014, May 1). T-Mobile's discounted plans boost subscriber adds. *Reuters*. Retrieved from http://www.reuters.com/article/2014/05/01/us-tmobile-results-idUSBREA400812014O501

Marek, S. (2013, July 9). T-Mobile's increased ad spend in 2012 didn't result in market share gains. *FierceWireless*. Retrieved from http://www.fiercewireless.com/story/t-mobiles-increased-ad-spend-2012-didnt-result-market-share-gains/2013-07-09

Marzilli, T. (2014, March 4). T-Mobile's value strategy pays dividends. *YouGov BrandIndex*. Retrieved from http://www.brandindex.com/article/t-mobiles-value-strategy-pays-dividends

McDuling, J. (2014, April 4). Here's more evidence that T-Mobile's crazy strategy might just be working. *Quartz*. Retrieved from http://qz.com/195641/heres-more-evidence-that-t-mobiles-crazy-strategy-might-just-be-working/

T-Mobile. (2014, May 1). T-Mobile US reports first quarter 2014 results and best ever quarterly performance in branded postpaid net customer additions. [Press Release]. Retrieved from http://investor.t-mobile.com/Cache/1001186494.PDFY=&O=PDF&D=&fid=1001186494&T=&iid=4091145

T-Mobile US, Inc. Annual Report (2013). Retrieved from http://www.google.com/url?sa=t&rct=j&q=&esrc=s&source=web&cd=2&sqi=2&ved=0CDcQFjAB&url=http%3A%2F%2Fphx.corporate-ir.net%2FExternal.File%3Fitem%3DUGFyZW50SUQ9NTA2MDIyfENoaWxkSUQ9NTQ3NjI4fFR5cGU9MQ%3D%3D%26t%3D1&ei=NNxrU5mPHojwoATuvlDQDw&usg=AFQjCNF76YJu8hT_X9IVQwU04NRdlKptOQ&sig2=H0pOY1NHD8heP-DRUUhiow&bvm=bv.66330100,d.cGU

what we should focus on as our organization's marketing, public relations and advertising communication specialists is setting objectives that are measured in terms of results. We also need to justify budget expenditures in terms of results and determine program effectiveness in terms of results.

Evaluation of program effectiveness simply measures whether our tactics succeeded in delivering the right motivational messages to the right publics and caused them to act. Action should bring the results needed to meet the objectives. Were attitudes, opinions and behaviors changed? Did those changes produce the desired outcome and satisfy the goal within the allocated budget? Evaluation that does not measure end results simply cannot stand the test of today's organizational managers. And communication professionals who cannot demonstrate that their efforts produce the desired outcomes within acceptable expenditures are themselves expendable.

Pamela Vaughan, HubSpot's lead blog strategist, identifies the top five social media ROI metrics. In examining those metrics, we see validated Katie Paine's statement at the beginning of this chapter. Measuring ROI of social media differs little from measuring ROI of traditional media. The tools may be different, but the criteria or metrics are essentially the same. According to Vaughan, we should:

> *First measure reach* — How far your message spreads.
> *Second measure traffic* — Does your reach generate traffic to websites or other places, virtual or physical, where you market your product or idea?
> *Third measure conversion of traffic to leads* — How much traffic is converted to interest or leads?
> *Fourth measure conversion of leads to customers* — How many of the leads are becoming customers or supporters?
> *Fifth compare conversion rates of different tactics* — Which tactics had the highest conversion rate of traffic to leads and leads to customers?

Essentially, Vaughan is suggesting we measure whether the tactics we are using are getting the right messages to the key publics and motivating them to act so we achieve results. Regardless of the channels we use — traditional media, social media or any other channels and tactics — we must measure the effectiveness of our communication. Any other criteria or metric is meaningless.

Evaluation is actually relatively easy if it is planned from the beginning of a campaign using the Strategic Planning Matrix. Good evaluation owes a lot to good objectives. If the objectives are written as outcomes to be accomplished in order to reach the goal, then the evaluation will be results-oriented. Two steps must be considered in evaluating any plan. First, by what criteria should we judge success (or what are the metrics)? Second, what are the best tools to measure those criteria?

Evaluation criteria

It is particularly important in this era of "big data" to set clear objectives that then become the metrics or **evaluation criteria** by which we measure success or results. According to Ash Ashutosh, CEO of Actifio, a provider of data management software,

Evaluation criteria and tools

A regional banking institution's research shows that while the public perceives it is financially strong, well-managed and safe, brand loyalty even in the financial industry is dependent upon perceptions of the quality of customer service and the involvement of the organization in its local communities. The bank implemented a campaign highlighting community relations efforts and improved customer service. It had four objectives, each of which becomes a criterion to measure success.

Objective one: Improve the bank's overall customer service ratings from 4.8 on a seven-point scale to 5.8 within six months (21 percent increase).

> *Criteria:* Customer service ratings are 5.8 or higher on June 1, 2015 (six months after campaign begins).

> *Tool:* We'll plan to use the bank's automated email survey system to measure customer satisfaction ratings two weeks before and two weeks after June 1, 2015, and take the aggregate score. As an additional step, we will monitor monthly customer satisfaction scores to gauge our progress during the campaign.

Objective two: Improve the public perception of the bank as customer-service oriented from 40 percent using that descriptor to 60 percent using that descriptor within one year (50 percent increase).

> *Criteria:* Sixty percent of customers will feel the bank is customer-service oriented on Jan. 1, 2016 (one year after the campaign begins).

> *Tool:* Replicate the values perception survey upon which the campaign was built in June 2015 to measure progress toward the objective and the first week of January 2016 to determine if the objective was met.

Objective three: Raise awareness of the bank's local contributions to the community to 60 percent within six months.

> *Criteria:* Sixty percent of customers will know about at least one of the bank's contributions to the community on June 1, 2015.

> *Tool:* Add an unaided recall question to the values perception survey upon which the campaign was built. Determine progress toward the objective with the interim survey in June 2015 and a final survey the first week of January 2016.

Objective four: To maintain a 94 percent customer retention rate during 2015 and a 95 percent retention rate for the four years after that (through 2019).

Criteria: The bank loses less than 6 percent of its current customers in 2015 and less than 5 percent of its customer base each year from 2016 to 2019.

Tool: Use the bank's customer records to determine what percent of current customers remain each year. The number of customers on the first day of January each year will serve as the benchmark.

"Organizations must find smarter data management approaches that enable them to effectively corral and optimize their data." One of the best ways to do this is to clearly define success in terms of specific, measurable objectives so it becomes clear what data is relevant.

Criteria are automatically determined when objectives are set. Objectives are designed to provide direction to planning and to identify the results that define success. Clients and managers will judge success by the criteria (objectives) you have set. In this step of your plan, restate your objectives in terms of success, and designate an appropriate method for measuring each one, including a date. For example, if one of your objectives is to increase name recognition of your client from 30 to 80 percent, the metric for success would be written, "Achieve 80 percent name recognition of the client's name among key publics by June 30, 2015."

The successful achievement of all campaign objectives should result in the accomplishment of the goal, which may or may not be directly measurable. If you have followed the planning matrix, accomplishing the overall goal will signify to management that you have achieved success in all three standards identified above. You can justify the expenditure because you reached your goal within proposed budget. You demonstrate effectiveness because your strategies and tactics combined to accomplish the goal. And, you met the campaign objectives, which resulted in the accomplishment of the goal.

Make sure to establish meaningful measures of success. Message exposure doesn't mean message receipt. Always keep in mind that behavior is the ultimate measure.

In addition to evaluating campaign results, you should look at the effectiveness of different parts of your plan, including how well strategies and tactics performed. You should also evaluate your own performance: your professionalism, creativity and ability to direct or implement a communication effort. You can add evaluation factors that specifically address your success and effectiveness in community relations, media relations or some other skill area. While media placement is not a measure of whether a public received and acted upon a message, it is still a factor to be evaluated within the context of effective strategies and tactics. Only through honest self-evaluation will you improve your skills. What did you do well? What could you have done better? Where do you need more training or experience? These are primarily internal measures and do not usually become part of the formal campaign put together using the Strategic Planning Matrix. But they are, nonetheless, important.

Converting your objectives to evaluation criteria is your primary evaluation of results. Additional criteria that address your team's specific capability and expertise are highly useful secondary criteria to measure your effectiveness and improve your performance.

Evaluation tools

EVALUATION TOOLS

Methods used to gather data needed to assess whether evaluation criteria were met.

Each objective must be converted to an evaluation criterion or metric, and each criterion must be measurable by an **evaluation tool**. Measurement tools are essentially research tools. They are the same kinds of methodologies used in research, but they focus on outcomes. They include surveys, sales measures, vote counts, dollars raised or saved, legislative bills passed or failed and hundreds of other concrete outcomes. The rules of research apply in evaluation. Sound methodology will not only give you credibility but also reliable and valid data on which to base future efforts.

Typically, evaluation measurements require a benchmark measurement before the program begins, during the program or both. Without adequate planning for the evaluation process, the benchmarks are often not taken before the campaign starts, resulting in no data for comparison. Unless you know where you started, you cannot determine how far you've come.

Although measurement tools are essentially the same as research methods, many research organizations have specialized in evaluative methods. It would be wise to access the websites and newsletters on evaluation and measurement produced by specialty firms like Paine Publishing or Cision. While evaluation tools for some objectives may be obvious, others may require complicated formulas that would, for example, combine measures of sales, media placements and social media referrals in some kind of sliding scale that measures the effect of communications, marketing and customer engagement on product sales.

Clearly articulated evaluation tools must include the source of information and how it will be obtained. Include all necessary tasks when describing the evaluation tool for each criterion. If you are measuring the criteria mentioned above, your evaluation tool would read something like this: "Conduct a random, statistically viable, telephone survey of the key public population June 28 to 30, 2015, to determine what percent recognize the client's name." This data could then be compared to the survey conducted at the beginning of the campaign Jan. 1 to 3, 2015, which indicated 30 percent name recognition for the client.

Adding evaluation tools to calendars and budgets

The evaluation process necessitates reviewing your calendar and budget to ensure that all evaluation tools are scheduled and costs estimated. You can designate a separate section of the calendar and budget to specifically address the planned evaluation. A wiser choice might be to include evaluation as part of the planned strategies and tactics for each public. Only with this kind of planning can you ensure

Measuring social media

Katie Delahaye Paine, CEO of Paine Publishing, LLC, an online publisher of magazines and e-books about PR and social media measurement, tips you off on rethinking your approach to measurement.

There are key stakeholders, and then there's everyone else. In that key stakeholder group are probably a number of influential journalists who publish their stories in a blog, on Facebook or via a link on Twitter. And there are customers and employees who increasingly get information about buying decisions from social media. Innumerable others have influence to one degree or another. Measuring social media, therefore, requires a variety of tools including employee surveys, customer surveys, content analysis and Web analytics. Regardless of what you are measuring, you can set up a perfect measurement system by following these steps:

Use industry standards. Dozens of corporations — like GM, GE, Southwest Airlines, McDonald's and Procter & Gamble — as well as leading industry associations have published standards for social media. Read them. Use them. It will save you a ton of arguments. http://painepublishing.com/wp-content/uploads/2013/10/Complete-standards-document.pdf

Establish SMART objectives: specific, measurable, achievable, relevant and time-bound. Start with clear goals and objectives and an understanding of how your program contributes to their accomplishment. No longer does generating awareness in likes or links cut it.

Identify influentials. According to established Social Media Measurement Standards, influentials have reach, frequency and relevance. In other words, they have an audience and produce good content frequently enough to have some impact. Identify these people.

Establish benchmarks. When someone asks, "How did my campaign do?" Your question should be, "Compared to what?" Without realistic and relevant benchmarks against which to measure success, all metrics are meaningless.

Get consensus on the metrics. Make sure your boss, your boss's boss and everyone else that will see your metrics has a common understanding of what "success" looks like. Social media success is often ill-defined and poorly understood. Gather everyone together and agree on the desired results.

Determine from where the data will come. Some 500 or more tools today purport to "measure" social media. Until you know what you're measuring, you can't even begin to know what tools you need. If the goal is awareness, you need a survey instrument. If it's return on investment, you need both budget and sales numbers. If it's engagement, agree on what "engagement" looks like.

Analyze and report insights. Data without insights is only trivia. Dig into your data to figure out what it means and what it tells you about improving your program. Measurement can continuously improve your efforts — but only if you really learn from the data. Examine trends over time. Do complaints go up or down? Do relationships get better or worse? If someone consistently writes about you, what do they say? Do not report results in pie charts. They do not show progress or trends. Tell a story with data, and figure out how best to illustrate it.

Repeat regularly.

that appropriate benchmark research is done in the beginning and throughout the campaign to compare with evaluation research. It also enables you to incorporate appropriate evaluation in the detailed planning for tactics. For example, if you need to measure the number of attendees at events, or traffic to a blog, you will build into the tactic a method for tracking those numbers. Trying to guesstimate such figures later only causes your evaluation to be inadequate and your claim to success suspect. Finally, including the evaluation tools in the calendar and budget for each public ensures that funding is available for this critical function.

Summary

Communication and marketing professionals cannot expect to be taken seriously unless they positively demonstrate the results of their efforts. Measuring the effectiveness of communication efforts can be a straightforward process if you use the Strategic Communications Planning Matrix. The matrix focuses your efforts to set objectives that are the outcomes which will combine to reach the overall goal. Evaluation of the objectives should be as strategic a function as any part of the process. Objectives become the evaluation criteria or metrics and must meet the highest standards of evaluation measurement. Effective planning will also include determining how to measure the effectiveness of specific strategies and tactics as well as your own performance.

Tools for measuring success are basically the same as the methodologies used in research. Nevertheless, many professional research firms now specialize in evaluative research and can design specific tools for your needs. Make sure to include the evaluation tools needed in the calendar and budget for each public so this critical process is not overlooked.

Exercises

1. Ask a local nonprofit to share with you its objectives from a strategic plan, and check to see if evaluation measurement is included in the plan. Ask about the process for evaluating success, and assess what tools will be necessary to determine if the overall goal was truly achieved.

2. Examine several of the research methodologies identified in Chapter 3 and determine how each could be converted to an evaluation tool.

3. Do a Web search for research companies and find those that advertise evaluation measurement. Try to find specific descriptions of the kinds of tools they use. Also search for communications research and/or evaluation newsletters that are available on the Web.

References and additional readings

Ashutosh, A. (2012). Best practices for managing big data. [Guest post]. Retrieved from www .forbes.com

Kaushik, A. (2014). Occam's razor. [Web analytics blog]. Retrieved from http://www.kaushik .net/avinash

Paine, K. D. (2014). The Measurement Advisor. Retrieved from http://painepublishing.com/ measurementadvisor/

The Measurement Standard (2014). *The Newsletter of Public Relations and Social Media Measurement from Salience Insight*. Retrieved from http://kdpaine.blogs.com/themeasurement-standard/

Vaughan, P. (2011). Top 5 metrics for auditing your social media marketing ROI. Retrieved from blog.hubspot.com

Watson, T. (2001). Integrating planning and evaluation: Evaluating the public relations practice and public relations programs. In R. L. Heath (ed.), *Handbook of public relations* (pp. 259-268). Thousand Oaks, CA: Sage Publications, Inc.

CHAPTER 13

RESPONDING TO RFPs

"So the writer who breeds more words than he needs, is making a chore for the reader who reads."

—Dr. Seuss
(THEODOR SEUSS GEISEL)
AMERICAN WRITER AND CARTOONIST

LEARNING IMPERATIVES

- To be able to develop effective client pitches.

- To understand how to use the Strategic Communications Planning Matrix in crafting a persuasive pitch.

- To learn to prioritize the material essential to winning business.

Recently, one of the authors of this book accompanied the CEO of a mid-sized finance company on visits to three different public relations agencies. Each of the agencies was pitching the company to win its business. The finance company already had a strong reputation in its home state but wanted to update its logo, brand identity and messaging in preparation for expansion to neighboring states. The CEO listened attentively to the various proposals and at the conclusion of each was handed a pitch book summarizing what each of the agencies proposed to do for the finance company.

The first pitch book was a stack of about 30 pages stapled in the corner that focused on how connected the company was to reporters in the company's home state. The second pitch book was about 70 pages and spiral bound with nearly 20 pages of secondary research charts and tables. The third pitch book was short — only about a dozen smartly designed pages.

The CEO said, after leaving the second presentation, "Do they think I'm going to read all this? I don't have that kind of time." But after the third presentation, she leafed through and analyzed each of the pages in the professionally designed, short pitch book. She said, "I like that firm. I think we might go with them." It took one more follow-up meeting and they were hired.

Sometimes winning business is as much about what you leave out as it is about what you put in a proposal. Learning to prioritize information and appeal to the self-interest of an individual or organization will often mean the difference between winning and losing business. Using the Strategic Planning Matrix to help you analyze what clients want and what they need can reduce your anxiety and keep you focused on your potential client's self-interests.

RFPs

A request for proposal or RFP is a solicitation made by a company or organization for services to be performed by a supplier. Suppliers in communication are usually agencies, consultants or freelancers offering specific services. Most RFPs go through a bidding process where potential suppliers can bid against other suppliers to win the business. But communications services such as strategic planning, message design and the development of creative tactics are not commodities that are easy to compare and value. That's why it's critical to develop proposals that clearly sell your experience and capacity to provide the best service available.

The RFP process

RFPs are often managed by a third-party procurement system such as Bidsync. This is particularly the case with government agencies at the local, state and federal level. Governments are hypersensitive to issues of fairness and nearly always use a third party, or an independent contracting office within government, to solicit and process bids to avoid accusations of favoritism. Government agencies also follow a strict set of protocols to ensure fair treatment in selecting and awarding work once proposals are received. Many use a weighted point system — assigning each section of the RFP response a different number of points based on its importance and value to the organization. Proposals from suppliers such as public relations agencies are evaluated and awarded a percentage of points possible in each category. The firm with the highest total points wins the contract.

Those competing for business are usually given two to four weeks after the RFP is distributed to submit their proposals. The first step, however, is to indicate that you or your agency is interested in competing for the contract. Once you've indicated a desire to submit a proposal, you are permitted to ask questions to help clarify the request. This is an opportunity to make a great impression before you even begin your proposal by asking smart, relevant questions (see Figure 13.1). The converse is also true. If you ask an unintelligent question, it will show that you either haven't read the RFP very carefully or that you don't understand the request. But be careful that the

Figure 13.1
Potential questions to ask RFP issuers

Responding to an RFP is a time-consuming process. Before you invest that time, make sure that you have a good chance of winning by discovering if it is an open competition, what the client is really looking for and what it will take to make you and your firm stand out.

1. **Why are you conducting this RFP?**
   There are many reasons to conduct RFPs. Knowing the client's motivation helps determine what's needed and how serious they are about awarding the business. If they can't answer this to your satisfaction, you may not want to participate.

2. **What criteria are important to you in selecting a firm? How would you rank the criteria?**
   This will help you craft a focused response, honing in on the issues that are most important to them.

3. **Do you have a timeline for making the decision?**
   If they don't have a timeline, they may not be particularly serious, and you may want to reconsider your participation.

4. **Are there any special circumstances of which we should be aware?**
   Forewarned is forearmed.

5. **What role will pricing play in the decision?**
   Not all RFPs are about cost reduction, and even those that are may define cost reduction in different ways. Knowing the answers to these questions will help you determine the pricing structure that will appeal most to the client. Many an RFP response has included an alternate fee proposal that the client was uninterested in.

6. **Are there additional documents we should review or people we should speak with before responding?**
   The more information you can gather, the better you can address their concerns.

7. **Who is responsible for managing the RFP process? Who else will be involved in making the decision?**
   You need to know who your audience is to craft the most appropriate response. If the chief marketing officer is managing the process, there's a lot of information in that fact.

8. **How many other firms are competing? Which other firms are competing?**
   In order to differentiate yourself from your competition, you need to know who that competition is. Some people won't answer these questions, but it never hurts to ask.

Source: Adapted from Are RFPs worth responding to? *by C. Dixon*

questions you ask don't reveal things about you as a competitor or don't result in the client disclosing more than you want them to. Answers to all questions are distributed to all those competing for the business as addendums to the original RFP. This process ensures that everyone trying to win the business is operating with the same information and receiving it at the same time. But if you ask the wrong questions, it may result in loss of your competitive advantage when the client discloses information to all competitors that previously only you knew.

Parts of an RFP response

Although the specific requirements for marketing and communications RFPs vary widely, the most common categories of information required are: executive summary, team bios, detailed response, case studies, portfolio of work and budget.

Executive summary. This is typically the first thing a client will read in your proposal. Make sure it is well-written, engaging and concise. We recommend no more than a page including graphics. Use short sentences and bullet points. Don't worry if it feels a little choppy. You won't have room for a lot of transitions. A good executive summary has four basic characteristics:

- **It immediately engages the attention of the reader.** Either by an incisive restatement of the problem or challenge, a vision of what could be created or some other attention-getting device, the executive summary must grab the reader and entice him/her to read on.
- **It provides a broad solution to the problem.** Your summary should demonstrate how you plan to integrate different elements of a campaign together into a creative solution. Provide just enough detail to keep the reader engaged but not so much that he/she will get bogged down.
- **It contains visual words and phrases.** Use smart language that will enable the executive to actually visualize the plan — including the creative work — that will secure the attention of key publics.
- **It provides concise rationale for acceptance of the solution.** Appeal to logic and reason as well as emotion in presenting your case. Include a few key facts to demonstrate your understanding of the issue at hand.

About the agency/team bios. Keep these brief. You only need a couple of short paragraphs to describe the agency. With the team bios, include those who will actually be working on the account. This is a very important part of your RFP response. Managers and directors want to know who they will be interfacing with and what experience they're actually buying. Don't simply put the top management and senior people in the organization; this could be seen as a bait-and-switch when a junior team is assigned to the project.

Detailed response. This is typically where you show your plan. Use the Strategic Planning Matrix to help you think through and summarize the situation as well as to clearly identify goals. Some RFPs may ask you to include specific measures (objectives), but most won't ask for that level of detail. It is important, however, to identify the key publics you think need to be reached, some of the important messages that need to be sent, how you will approach your publics and through which channels you plan to deliver your messages. This part of the plan must be founded on research, and it must address the client's perceived need and his/her research-based actual need. You will also want to include a sampling of tactics that could be employed to demonstrate your strategic thinking and creativity. In some instances, where you have sizeable accounts at stake, you'll want to invest enough time and research to flesh out the core opportunity/problem and identify a big idea to carry your campaign.

Case studies. Most of those putting work out for bid will want to see a proven track record. Government entities, in particular, usually ask for three case studies. Carefully select projects where you or your agency demonstrated solid measurable results. Try to find cases where you successfully met challenges similar to those outlined in the solicitation. Look for instances where you not only changed perceptions but also motivated publics to change their behaviors. Keep these case studies simple and short, but be sure to include relevant photos, charts and graphs to visually show your successes.

Portfolio of work. RFPs will usually recommend including other examples of your work beyond the requested case studies. Use this section to highlight your unique experience and expertise. Do not include too many additional samples. A few key selections will suffice in showing the scope and quality of work you're capable of producing. Tailor your portfolio material to the self-interests of the requesting organization. Offer to provide additional examples upon request rather than cluttering your RFP response with voluminous and unrelated portfolio pieces.

Budget. This may be the trickiest section to compile. Sometimes you'll be given a budget of say $150,000 and asked to show what you can do for that amount. More often than not, you'll be asked to propose a budget for the project. This is nearly impossible if you don't know what the organization putting out the RFP has in mind or is able to commit. Whenever possible, try to get a ballpark figure or benchmark from which to start. You could put together a new product launch for $25,000 or $250,000, depending on how much coverage, social media exposure and buzz the company wants. There is always, at some level, a point of diminishing returns and you don't want to go too far beyond that. The other tricky part of budgeting is whether to propose a retainer, project fee or billable hours. Check the RFP for guidance on this. You will want your proposed budget to be competitive because this is one of the sections given the most weight in selecting a winning bid.

Finally, we strongly recommend that you include a brief explanation of your plan to evaluate your success. Include the evaluation criteria and tool as outlined in the matrix. If you don't feel like it fits in the budget section, you can insert the evaluation at the end of your detailed response. We like it next to the budget because it shows what the client is paying for.

Deciding when to respond to an RFP

When should you take the time to respond to an RFP? Assembling a proposal may take only a few hours, or it may take as many as 50 to 100 hours. You can't and won't want

TIPS FROM THE PROS

A strategic response to RFPs

Chris Thomas, owner of Intrepid, a hybrid communications agency founded in 1995, tips you off on how to successfully win clients by balancing strategy with big ideas in your response to RFPs.

Requests for proposals, or RFPs, typically require and reward a tactical approach to communications. The issuing organization or department is seeking concrete direction and ideas in order to justify the investment with upper management, boards or superiors. Additionally, many government entities are required to follow a specific format in developing an RFP, which stifles the strategic process.

The very nature of most RFPs does not, at face value, allow for the strategic process to be effectively implemented. The notion is that big ideas win RFPs but are often of little consequence to the bottom line — while the development and execution of solid strategies influences perceptions, changes behaviors and achieves objectives.

The challenge for strategic communicators is how to navigate the RFP process to allow for strategy while providing sufficient ideas and direction. The following are three tips for agencies and consultants when responding to an RFP.

1. Do your homework and learn as much as possible about the prospective client/project — including asking for clarification to understand its goal and objectives. This will often help to differentiate you from the competition.
2. Work to educate the client about the strategic process and how it is the most effective vehicle for meeting the goal and objectives. Communicate your strategic approach and experience as well as how you would tailor the process to the client's needs.
3. Work to develop appropriate concepts, including a "big idea," that align with the client's goal and objectives. Provide a caveat when introducing concepts that explains that the research outcome and resulting strategies will dictate tactics; however, the concepts and ideas presented are examples of some initial thinking.

to respond to all requests. But here's a story that might make you think twice about not responding.

Some time ago, the city of Austin, Texas, issued an RFP for a website overhaul. It went to about 100 companies nationwide, including about 50 in the state of Texas. Because it went to so many companies, everyone kind of laughed it off thinking it would be too much of a crapshoot. In the end, only three companies bid on the project. Their bids ranged from $600,000 to $1.2 million. Of those three companies, only one of them conformed to the requirements set forth in the RFP. That company won the project for $1.1 million. Sometimes you win just by showing up. Other times you can spend countless hours responding to RFPs that you have little chance of winning.

Begin with some math

Deciding when to respond to an RFP should begin with some simple math. Is the number of bids times the average cost of bidding greater or less than the average profit times the number of wins?

The formula for successful bidding is:

$$bids \times ave.\ cost\ of\ bidding < profit \times wins$$

The key questions are:

- What is the cost of bidding?
- What is your probability of winning?
- How profitable will the project be if you win?

Small projects with slim margins decrease the time you should spend pursuing the opportunity. On the flip side, big projects with long-term agreements are worth spending more time and energy to go after. And a weak or half-baked proposal will almost always be time wasted. Most agencies allocate a portion of their budget to new business development, which includes responding to RFPs. The real decisions are how to choose which projects to bid on and how much effort to invest. To stay competitive, every agency and consultant needs to continually add new clients.

Evaluate your position

One recent study showed that you are not likely to win a bid if you don't have previous involvement with a prospective client. Only 10 to 15 percent of companies without prior experience won contracts.

Nonetheless, you should consider responding if you:

- Have a positive relationship with the customer issuing the RFP.
- Understand the customer's needs and preferences.
- Have experience doing what the customer needs done.
- Understand the customer's procurement, evaluation and selection methods.
- Are able to engage with the customer to discuss the request and clarify needs.
- Have detailed knowledge of the competitive environment.
- Believe there is potential for additional work beyond the scope of the RFP.

Improving your win rate

The difficulty with RFPs is they are all over the board. They come in more varieties than breakfast cereal. However, one of the keys to all successful RFP responses

is brevity. No proposal ever needs to be more than 10 pages. Do your research. Evaluate results. Make it visual.

Do your research

Sarah Maronn, media and public relations professional with Red Jeweled Media, says, "You wouldn't want to get into a long-term relationship without having dated the person first, right? The same goes for a long-term working relationship." You must invest in order to get to know an individual or organization first. Maronn shares some ways to do this as you prepare for an RFP response:

1. Look at every page of their website.
2. Search for news or blogs and forum comments mentioning the company, both positive and negative.
3. Check out their social media pages: Are they on Facebook, Twitter, Pinterest, LinkedIn? Who is following them and how many?
4. What are the company's core values, interests and community engagements, and who is their ideal customer or client?
5. Talk to them . . . which leads to my next tip: "I just called to say, 'I love you.'"

She concedes that maybe you don't need to say, "I love you," or sing for that matter, but you do need to show the company that you like them, and you do need to really find out if you do.

Carefully evaluate

There are really only two ways to improve your RFP win rate. Number one: Respond to fewer, more qualified, RFPs. Number two: Improve the quality of your responses. Keep your efforts focused by spending more time on the RFPs with high potential. Most organizations could toss out up to one-third of the RFPs they responded to last year because they already knew they wouldn't win. Some experts suggest coming up with a scoring system to evaluate the potential merits of an RFP. One example is found in Figure 13.2. Another suggestion is to track your success rate with each organization, since historical performance is the best predictor of future success. Stop responding to companies that don't select you. Institute a three- or four-strike rule. If you don't win business after four attempts, you are probably not a good fit. Once you win a contract, the count is reset to zero strikes.

Another recommendation is to define what constitutes a win up front. Some RFPs are cancelled and contracts never awarded. Other RFPs are put on hold. John Care, managing director of Mastering Technical Sales, says, "Use a simple rule: Win rate = number of RFPs awarded divided by number of RFP responses. No special cases, exceptions or asterisks." He then suggests publishing a league table showing wins, losses, responses, costs and revenue from each RFP. The benefit, he says, comes from publicizing what is working and what is not.

Figure 13.2
RFP score card

Client and project name:		SCORE:	51.0
Opportunity information			
Is the company a previous/current client?	y	Score +15	15
If yes, do we have a successful track record with the client?	y	Score +/−5	5
If no, has a relationship been established with the client before this RFP?	y	Score +10	10
Will the project be profitable for our agency?	y	Score +15	5
Is there potential for follow-up work with the issuing firm?	y	Score +/−10	8
Are response timelines understood and achievable?	y	Score +/−10	−5
Have we successfully implemented similar projects for other clients?	y	Score +/−10	7
Will the project give us a good case study or enhance our reputation?	y	Score +/−10	6
Competition			
Company 1	n	Score −5	0
Company 2	n	Score −5	0
Company 3	n	Score −5	0
Company 4	n	Score −5	0
Total:			51

Make it visual

Realtors understand the power of curb appeal in moving a house. Communications professionals should also understand the importance of visual appeal in selling their ideas. Most people are visual learners. People absorb about 75 percent of what they learn visually. The rest comes from what they hear, smell, touch and taste. We want to keep potential clients looking longer. Ironically, a shorter proposal (10 pages maximum) will enable them to absorb more than a 100-page document.

Making a presentation visually appealing requires professional design. Develop a sexy template, and customize the content within the template for each proposal. Use a grid to ensure your design has clean lines and good alignment. Establish a hierarchy within the document that clearly leads the reader through in the sequence you desire. Use photos and imagery to convey emotion. This can also be done with the effective use of charts and graphs to communicate data. Carefully select your fonts and typography to assist with the hierarchy and tone. And establish a color palette that you will use throughout the template. These are the basic elements of good design that will assist you in creating a sweet template for winning presentations. You can then populate the template with your persuasively written response to the RFP. Anyone that submits a text-based proposal is just shooting themselves in the foot. Don't do it.

Remember the example at the beginning of the chapter. The concise pitch book essentially won the work. Clients will choose based on the pitch book and presentation (if you are allowed to make one). If those don't impress, they won't look any further.

Summary

Responding to RFPs is an essential part of winning business for many companies. Knowing when to respond and how to respond strategically will make the difference between being successful in acquiring new clients or wasting valuable time and resources responding to countless requests. Be selective in which RFPs you choose to respond to. Prior experience with a potential client is almost essential to winning a bid. A clear understanding of a potential client's needs and expectations will also aid you in determining whether it is worth your time to respond.

When you choose to respond, keep your pitch short — no more than 10 pages. You also need to tailor your response to the specific needs and self-interests of the client. Prioritize information, and make sure it is presented in a graphically compelling fashion.

Exercises

1. Use the Internet to find a typical RFP response. Analyze the information provided and highlight what you'd keep if you were reducing it to a 10-page pitch.

2. Next, select three elements that you've highlighted, and determine how you could present the information graphically.

3. Pull a dozen communications RFPs together, and select a local firm that you'd like to work for. Now, assuming you work for the firm, determine which RFPs you'd respond to and explain why.

References and additional readings

Care, J. (2013, March).Winning the RFP game: How to increase your win rate and decrease your costs. Retrieved from http://www.masteringtechnicalsales.com/files/Winning_The_RFP_Game.pdf

French, G. (2014). RFPs — Love 'em or leave 'em? GFA Sales Improvement. Retrieved from http://www.sellingcoach.co.uk/gfa_newsletter-RFP_love_em_or_leave_em.htm

Maronn, S. (2013, April 16). How to win a public relations agency RFP. [Web blog post]. Retrieved from http://www.redjeweledmedia.com/blog/bid/177170/How-to-Win-a-Public-Relations-Agency-RFP

Dickson, C. (2013). Are RFPs worth responding to? Retrieved from http://www.captureplanning.com/articles/are-rfps-worth-responding-to.cfm

Kutcher, D. (2014, June 2). Requests for proposals (RFPs) - and why your business should pay attention to them. Retrieved from https://www.youtube.com/watch?v=J68RHdUW3I4

Holtz, S. (2008, March 26). How to respond to RFP with all the information you need. Retrieved from http://practice.findlaw.com/law-marketing/how-to-respond-to-rfp-with-all-the-information-you-need.html

CHAPTER 14

PRESENTATIONS

"The ability to present is probably the number one skill lacking today. If you can't present well, you're not going to move up in the company."

—Cindy Peterson

FOUNDER OF PRESENTATIONS FOR RESULTS, A COACHING AND CONSULTING FIRM

LEARNING IMPERATIVES

- To understand how to create and give a presentation that achieves positive results.

- To understand that a presentation does more than sell an idea—it convinces the client of your ability to implement that idea.

Nearly all of today's practitioners would admit to losing a client to someone else, not with a better idea or plan, but simply with a better presentation. Most decisions, whether to fund an in-house corporate campaign or to outsource work, are based more on a presentation than on substance. In fact, more often than firms would care to admit, agencies are selected based on their presentation and then asked to implement not their own proposal, but someone else's idea. This reality has led to firms actually copyrighting their proposals to prevent ideas from being taken without compensation. The problem is, you can't copyright ideas—only the tangible or recorded expression of them. So shady business people simply find another way to "express" your idea.

Why would an executive like someone's idea but not choose him/her to implement it? The simple answer: presentation. You cannot view a presentation as simply giving the substance of your idea or proposal. A presentation is a visual and personal demonstration of your capability, personality, capacity and creativity. It must inspire confidence and create chemistry between you and a potential client or executive.

Following a strategic planning approach

The reality of today's business environment is that few executives have the time or patience to read lengthy reports or proposals. Hopefully someone on the project team will read the entire proposal or communications plan, but that cannot be guaranteed. The only two probable points of exposure to your plans, campaigns or ideas are the executive summary (addressed in the previous chapter) and the client presentation. If these two things are engaging and to the point, an executive might take the time to look deeper into your plan. If not, you will lose his/her attention and support.

© Pressmaster/Shutterstock.com

The key to the success of a presentation is the strategic planning approach. Your goal is to grab their attention and convince them to not just adopt your proposal, but to have you implement it. With that goal in mind and specific objectives to support that, analyze the public(s) to be addressed, your relationship with them and their motivating self-interests. Then design your presentation to deliver those messages and lead your audience—perhaps only one key decision-maker—to the conclusions you want them to reach. Remember you aren't just selling your idea; you are selling your creativity and ability to implement that idea better than anyone else. You must appeal directly to the

Overcoming presentation anxiety

Lenny Laskowski, president of LJL Seminars, international professional speaker and author of the best-selling book, "10 Days to More Confident Public Speaking," tips you off on how to keep those nerves in check.

TIPS FROM
THE PROS

The majority of speaking anxiety comes from nervousness. I employ a variety of physical and mental techniques to calm nerves.

PHYSICAL TECHNIQUES:

Take a brisk walk before you speak. Physical activity will loosen up your entire body and get your blood circulating. If you are speaking in a large hotel, as I often do, take a walk around the hotel and burn off some nervous energy. Just don't get lost, and keep an eye on the time.

Loosen up your arms and hands. While sitting in your seat before you speak, dangle your arms at your sides—letting blood flow to the tips of your fingers. When blood flow is directed away from your skin, fingers and toes, you often feel a tingling sensation, and your skin may begin to look pale and feel cold. Dangling your arms and hands reestablishes blood flow; you will start to feel better and more relaxed. Also while sitting, turn your wrists and shake your fingers to force the blood to flow to your hands and fingers.

Don't sit with your legs crossed. Stand up well in advance of being introduced and walk around so the blood flows in your legs. This will also prevent leg cramping when you first stand.

Scrunch your toes. But be careful not to scrunch so tightly that you get a cramp.

Loosen up your facial muscles. Wiggle your jaw back and forth gently. Yawn (politely, of course).

Use deep-breathing exercises.

MENTAL TECHNIQUES:

Prepare and rehearse. This is the single-most important thing you can do.

Visualize success. Think "success" using visualization techniques. Visualize the audience applauding you when you are done.

Be natural but enthusiastic.

Be personal. Be conversational, and include some personal stories during your speech.

Focus on your message, not on your nervousness.

decision-maker's self-interests, creating a personal connection or chemistry and inspiring confidence in you. Weaving in the influence of opinion leaders may also be useful.

Respecting your audience

Knowing that your audience has little time, you must get to the key points and solutions quickly in order to capture and retain interest. You must show the logic and the creativity that make the proposal workable. Give just enough detail to sell the plan but not so much as to lose the interest of the target audience. A few details, carefully inserted, will help add credibility. Always include the cost in terms of time and resources (money). Remember that an executive decision-maker typically has only three questions that matter:

1. Is this the best solution or plan (i.e., is there really a need, and will it work)?
2. How much will it cost?
3. Is this the right team to accomplish it?

To convince an executive to spend time and money on your plan, you must address the core of the challenge or opportunity and the macro-level logic, creativity and appropriateness of the solution proposed. Your big idea may be in the form of branding, identification with a key societal issue, a change in the logo or slogan, a new focus on community relations or a number of other overarching ideas. Just remember that executives usually have a broad, holistic view of problems, opportunities and programs. Their vision encompasses the whole organization, not just your part of it. They want to see the grand solution and creative integration of that solution across organizational functions and publics. They also want to know if it is the most cost-effective approach to the situation and why they should support the plan. Remember, in order for them to internalize your plan, you must first capture their attention and make them want to work with you.

Presenting your plan

A presentation of your solution or plan is a multisensory version of an executive summary. A presentation is not a speech. You can't just stand up and talk. By its nature, a presentation is visual. The visual elements can add emotion and help create impressions of capacity, dependability and competence. They must be very carefully considered and developed to support your approach, not detract from it.

No matter how much time you have to make your presentation, you must capture the attention of your audience in the first few seconds. Establish the need and the broad solution immediately. Then sketch in the details as time and interest permit. Make sure to show creative work—slogans, logos, visual tactics—to engage and excite the target audience, but don't continue describing details after interest in them wanes. Get back quickly to the rationale for selecting this plan and the cost of doing so. Also address the cost of not embracing your solution. Then end on a positive note and with the only wise course of action: hiring you.

Figure 14.1
Sample organization of a business presentation

1. Capture attention.

2. Introduce yourself and review the agenda.

3. Review the opportunities and problems, demonstrating understanding of the potential client's position through research.

4. Present your unique approach for solving the problem.

5. State the objectives and publics/messages necessary to accomplish them.

6. Show some of the creative work. Planning typically has no visual appeal and must be accompanied by creative work to sell your solution.

7. Overview the budget using simple graphics.

8. Provide the rationale for implementing the plan, as well as the inherent difficulties and the cost of not accepting your proposal.

9. Summarize the campaign and ask for the contract or business.

Here are some general principles for presentation success:

- *Immediately engage attention and hold it.* If attention wanes, do something to engage the audience.
- *Keep the end result in mind at all times.* The goal is to gain approval and selection of your plan and your team by the decision-makers. Everything you do and say in the presentation must be focused on that goal.
- *Establish a relationship.* Try to bond with the key decision-maker whether he/she is a client or an executive in your organization. Inspire confidence. Demonstrate capability and creativity. Create chemistry. If they don't like you personally, they won't choose to work with you. Create an excitement for the collaboration.
- *Keep it short, concise and to the point.* Long presentations will lose the audience. Set a time limit for each discussion point in the presentation and stick to it. Keep the presentation moving and the ideas flowing. If you sense your audience is losing interest, shift your style to liven up the presentation, or better yet, move on.
- *Use logical and customized organization.* Use a research-based, analytical approach to problem-solving that the client will understand. Focus on opportunities and solutions. Customize the presentation to meet the self-interests and needs of the target audience. A sample format for a business presentation is found in Figure 14.1, but remember to tailor the format

to your specific audience. Use examples relevant to the target audience's experience. And keep it visual and memorable.

- *Be prepared.* Organize well. Use appealing visual aids. Rehearse thoroughly. An audience can always tell when someone is unprepared. Further, your ability to improvise when unexpected problems arise (such as your software not being compatible with the provided technical equipment) is directly related to how well prepared you are. Don't expect to be able to ad-lib in an emergency if you haven't thoroughly prepared and practiced.

Using technology

In today's high-tech environment, expectations for professionalism are high. Presentation software abounds. You should know the different programs, along with their features and capabilities, and not be tied to any one program. Use the program that best meets the needs of the presentation. While Prezi is impressive in its movement and progression features, it doesn't show information in charts and graphs as clearly as is necessary in some presentations. PowerPoint is still a better choice if you have a lot of data in graphs. Using animation of some kind is almost an imperative in any presentation. Animation software like GoAnimate or Sliderocket is continually being created and improved. Become proficient with many programs. Remember that you will be selected based on the quality and impressiveness of the presentation. You can't just have good ideas; you have to be able to present those ideas in a creative, innovative way.

Remember also that high-tech presentations have their pitfalls. Computer-designed and driven presentations are absolutely requisite, but when the technology fails, for whatever reason, the failure reflects on the presenter. While a great presentation can demonstrate the creativity, capability and innovativeness of a team, a poor presentation can ruin any chance of success.

Technical difficulties are unacceptable. If you are using technology of any kind in a presentation, make sure you know the equipment or computer programs, how to operate them and how to quickly troubleshoot problems. Make sure every link and program is compatible. Make sure the presentation area has sufficient power outlets and is wired to support the technology. Arrive early to set up and test the technology. Always carry a selection of connectors and spare cords, bulbs and other small replacement parts. Nonetheless, be well prepared enough to give your presentation without the visuals if necessary.

Recognize also that technology has a tendency to reduce and sometimes eliminate the personal connection between the presenter and the client or executive. The presenter must be conscious of the relationship and work to maintain the personal connection. When possible, use a remote or have someone advance your slides. Most remotes, like those made by Logitech, have a small USB stick transmitter that plugs easily into a MAC or PC. Using a remote will allow you to move freely about the room, cutting the invisible tether that keeps so many people tied to a podium or laptop. By moving around, using hand gestures and pointing out significant information or visuals on the screen, you can help your audience engage not only with the presentation but also with you.

The presentation is an opportunity to interact with the client or executive and begin to build trust. Technology should support but never drive a presentation. Presentations should always be driven by purpose and content. In today's business climate, a good presentation is your key to opening the door. A bad presentation means your ideas may never see the light of day, or you may sit by and watch as some other team executes them.

Summary

Presentations are the most significant channels used to communicate almost every public relations or marketing plan. No matter how revealing the research, no matter how creative and ingenious the strategic plan, no change will occur unless you effectively communicate the plan or solution to the decision-makers. You must also demonstrate the criticality of their expending resources on this plan or solution and convince them that you are the person or team to pull it off. As with all communication, your target audience must first be persuaded to pay attention to the message and then be persuaded to act on the content. Persuading decision-makers to use your solutions requires the same two-step process. You must gain their attention and then their approval.

In our fast-paced world, presentations are the key to getting decision-makers to pay attention to and more deeply examine a proposal. They should be approached with the same care and analysis used in your planning and response to an RFP.

Exercises

1. Select any of the plans you have prepared for the exercises in other chapters of this book and create a short presentation that would engage a decision-maker and cause him/her to listen to your ideas. Follow the steps in Figure 14.1, and make sure you have an attention-getting tactic at the beginning of the presentation.

2. Visit other classes within which presentations are being given. Do your own analysis of their effectiveness. What techniques worked well, and why? What did not work, and what would you have done differently?

3. Create a chart that analyzes the features, benefits and negative aspects of a variety of presentation software programs. Analyze what they do well and where they fall short, and describe the kind of plan they are most appropriate to present.

References and additional readings

Boylan, B. (2001). *What's your point?: The 3-step method for making effective presentations.* Avon, MA: Adams Media Corporation.

Daum, K. (2013). 5 tips for giving *really* amazing presentations. Retrieved from www.inc.com/kevin-daum/5-tips-for-giving-really-amazing-presentations.html

Leech, T. (2004). *How to prepare, stage, and deliver winning presentations.* New York: AMACOM.

VideoMaker Tips. (2013). The 6 best business presentation software alternatives to PowerPoint. Retrieved from www.goanimate.com/videomakertips

Young Entrepreneur Council. (2013). 13 tips for giving a killer presentation. [Blog article.] Retrieved from www.huffingtonpost.com

CHAPTER 15

ETHICS AND PROFESSIONALISM

"A little integrity is better than any career."

—Ralph Waldo Emerson
AMERICAN POET

LEARNING IMPERATIVES

- To understand that your career success depends upon the quality of your ethical and professional behavior.

- To understand the values and ethical standards upon which to base decisions and behavior.

- To be cognizant of professional codes of ethics and resolve to abide by them.

- To understand the characteristics of professionalism and begin to develop behaviors consistent with those characteristics.

- To appreciate the contributions of diverse individuals and adopt an attitude of acceptance.

ETHICS
Personal and professional value systems and standards that underlie decisions and behavior.

As you begin to read this chapter, many of you are thinking, "Really? Do I need to read more bunk about **ethics**?"

But before you answer, ask yourself:

- Do I care that my behavior could cost thousands of people — myself included — to lose hundreds of millions of dollars saved for retirement?
- Do I care that my actions not only caused me but also many others to lose their jobs because my company went out of business?
- Do I care that nobody will hire me because of my poor reputation?
- Do I care that I might lose everything and end up in prison?

These are only a few of the documented consequences suffered many times over in the last few years by real business and communications professionals — people just like you — who didn't give much thought to ethics. You may think that you would **never** do anything that drastically unethical or unprofessional. They didn't think so, either. Their road to professional and personal disaster began with a tiny step — a small, seemingly insignificant breach of ethics or **professionalism**.

PROFESSIONALISM
Characteristics and behavior befitting a professional.

It is unfortunate that even with increased emphasis on and discussion regarding professional ethics in the last couple of decades, we seem to have had a greater number of high profile incidents rather than fewer. Studies show a continual decline in ethical behavior. Cases in point are the incidents of public relations professionals compensating media professionals (including bloggers) to endorse products or ideas without full disclosure. What these incidents indicate is that some communications professionals still do not understand the disastrous consequences for our profession of corrupting the societal channels of communication. And now mistrust of media, to which the previously mentioned behavior contributes, has sunk lower still. If the major channels for information dissemination in our society are not trusted, how can we possibly expect our messages will be trusted?

Advocacy is a critical function in a free market economy and a free society. Without advocacy, people are unaware of the full range of choices available to them from consumer products to political opinions. Because some organizations have abused the public trust by using manipulative communication and marketing practices and sometimes even deceit, communicators today are often labeled "flacks" or "spin doctors," implying the less than trustworthy practices of advocating questionable causes and twisting the truth. Because of past abuses perpetrated by a few, almost all organizations, corporations and institutions continue to face an uphill battle to gain the trust of their publics.

In his book, "The Cheating Culture: Why More Americans Are Doing Wrong to Get Ahead," David Callahan presents dozens of examples of people who attained great professional success only to take devastating falls because their success came at the expense of their integrity. He demonstrates how our business culture, and even American culture, condones cheating — a little fudging on your tax return, failure to return the excess change you get at the grocery store or lying on a resume. He argues that our culture is breeding dishonesty and ethical breaches as necessary and acceptable in order to achieve success. That is until the perpetrators crash and burn. Callahan asserts:

> Human beings are not simply creatures of their economic and legal environment. We don't decide whether to cut corners based only on a rational calculus about potential gains and losses. We filter these decisions through our value

systems. And while more of us will do wrong in a system where cheating is normalized or necessary for survival or hugely profitable, some of us will insist on acting with integrity even if doing so runs counter to our [short-term] self-interest (p. 105).

Ethics

The ethics and behavior of organizations and individuals have come to the forefront in terms of the expectations of an organization's stakeholders. According to Wilcox, Cameron and Reber:

> Ethics refers to the value system by which a person determines what is right or wrong, fair or unfair, just or unjust. It is expressed through moral behavior in specific situations. An individual's conduct is measured not only against his or her own conscience but also against some norm of acceptability that has been societally, professionally, or organizationally determined.

As the statement implies, ethical decisions are made at a number of different levels. At the highest level, every society has an implied ethical standard. American culture has some basic societal values — like honesty, integrity, fairness and equity — that are still considered universal, values we should not lightly abandon. Nevertheless, societal standards of ethics often deteriorate to become the equivalent of legal standards.

With trust at a premium now in our society, the second level of ethical standard-setting is in organizations that have formulated their own **ethical codes** based on core corporate or organizational values. The goal is to guide employees to comply in programs, procedures and practices. To be credible, the values and codes must permeate the organization's communication practices.

At the third level, communications and marketing professionals may choose to subscribe to professional codes of behavior like those provided by the American Marketing Association, the American Advertising Federation, the Public Relations Society of America or other similar professional organizations (see Appendix C: Professional Codes of Ethics.) Finally, underlying each of these ethical levels are personal standards of behavior based on individual value systems.

ETHICAL CODES
Written and formalized standards of behavior used as guidelines for decision-making.

Organizational ethics

Today's issue for organizations is "transparency." Transparency requires organizations to openly align their behavior and their communication with a set of core values that are societally accepted and important to their key publics. According to Stoker and Rawlins (2004):

> By revealing the organization's motives, the [organization] becomes accountable to the public. Transparency then becomes self-regulating, encouraging organizations to choose only practices they could publicly justify. By being transparent, the organization puts its credibility on the line by aligning its communication with its ethics.

Gertz (1998) goes a step further by providing two moral rules that must be inviolate. The first is "do not disable." To disable is to diminish a person's ability to choose or act voluntarily. People have a right to the information they need to make reasoned, rational decisions for their own lives. The second rule is "do not deprive of freedom." This rule requires organizations to disclose any information on practices that may affect stakeholders. Gertz includes in this rule any action that would limit someone's ability to act freely, depriving him/her of control over personal actions.

Gertz applies some additional moral rules to transparency: Don't deceive, don't cheat, keep promises, obey laws and do your duty. Stoker and Rawlins (2004) comment that, "These rules directly apply to the communication process. It would be hard to imagine transparency without abiding by these rules. But these are the [minimum] expectations for [communications professionals]."

While ethical communication with our publics is of primary importance, customer service has become the face of most organizations. And it seems to be the area most difficult to manage. Outsourcing customer service, even offshoring it to other nations, has become the punchline of jokes about high-tech and credit-card customer service. In many industries, customer service lines are typically staffed by hourly employees, some making not much more than minimum wage. The result is a low level of competence and high turnover as employees seek for better jobs with better pay and advancement potential. But what could be more important in establishing trust than quality customer service? The example set by Nordstrom is widely known. Stories abound of the upscale retail clothing giant allowing customers to return virtually any item — even items obviously not purchased in their stores! On industry trust scales, Nordstrom always ranks at the top.

Yet most industries have been slow to learn. They say they understand the importance of customer service, but haven't been able to resolve issues with the age-old system of entry-level, minimum-wage employees. They add layers of supervision and management, building their customer service around a hierarchical reporting structure rather than focusing on building a trust-based relationship with crucial publics. A case in point is media giant Comcast. Their customer service difficulties have become legend with the YouTube video of a serviceman napping on a customer's couch while on hold with the Comcast service line. In a more recent case, a Comcast customer called to get an improper $35 charge reversed. Five phone calls and nine different customer service representatives later, the customer was being billed for hundreds of dollars more, and the charge was still not reversed. Finally, after threats to publicize the company's incompetence, the corporate public relations department intervened to resolve the issue.

Customers armed with social and new media tools can wield a lot of power. The "United breaks guitars" case discussed in Chapter 9 is a prime example. The airline's customer service failure cost the company millions of dollars.

Comcast is a fast growing company, and it is difficult to manage customer service for tens of millions of customers. But it is crucial that this frontline communication function is structured and managed effectively. A company may allocate huge budgets for public relations to build trust with its key publics, but all that will be for naught if trust is not maintained at other touch points. Quality, respectful customer service is one of the foundations of trust required in today's marketplace.

Codes of ethics and professional standards

Because our effectiveness as professionals is directly dependent upon whether we are trusted, professional ethical standards are critical to the strength of our profession. (See examples in Appendix C.) But professional ethical codes are not without problems. By their nature, such codes tend to establish the basest acceptable behavior, bordering on legality rather than morality. Over time, such standards tend to reduce the overall level of ethical practice to that minimally acceptable expectation. To quote James E. Faust in an address given to law students in 2003:

> There is a great risk of justifying what we do individually and professionally on the basis of what is "legal" rather than what is "right. ..." The philosophy that what is "legal" is also "right" will rob us of what is highest and best in our nature. What conduct is actually "legal" is, in many instances, way below the standards of a civilized society. ... If [we] accept what is legal as [our] standard of personal or professional conduct, [we] will rob [ourselves] of that which is truly noble in [our] personal dignity and worth.

Further, it is usually quite difficult for a professional organization to enforce a code of ethics. Much has been written about ethical codes and their problems. Nevertheless, professionally it is deemed important for organizations to establish ethical codes for their members. Such codes are seen as crucial for maintaining professional status, respect and legitimacy. They are also guidelines to entry-level professionals seeking to establish their own ethical standards based on a personal value system. Most professional codes of ethics incorporate stated values that include truth, honesty, fairness, good taste and decency. Basing behavior on these values will always provide a solid foundation of personal ethics for any communications professional.

Personal ethics and decision-making

Our personal ethics are based on our system of values and beliefs. According to Davis Young, you cannot be forced to lose your values; they are only lost if you choose to relinquish them. As was discussed in the chapter on persuasion, values and beliefs are the building blocks for attitudes that direct behavior. Although a very personal determination, our values and ethics are heavily influenced by our culture and background. In American culture, truth, freedom, independence, equity and personal rights are highly valued and contribute to the formulation of most of our value systems and resultant ethical standards. But another important influence on our value systems is our personal and societal definition of success.

In the late 1980s, Amitai Etzioni, having just completed a book on ethics, prepared to teach the subject to students at Harvard Business School. After a semester of effort, he lamented that he had been unable to convince classes full of MBA candidates that "... there is more to life than money, power, fame and self-interest." Etzioni's experience is disconcerting but not surprising. The situation is no better to-day. Our society has put such an emphasis on money, power and fame as measures of success that these factors have become the decision-making criteria for genera-tions of professionals. Yet those same professionals, at the ends of their careers (and usually in commencement speeches to graduating college students), regret not hav-ing spent enough time with family or serving the community. Our analysis of key publics' self-interests should lead us to the conclusion that money, power and fame are usually secondary motivators when placed next to important life issues.

Perhaps our personal definitions of success and the pressure to reach the per-ceived societal definition of success have caused us to neglect those things in life that really matter. Those definitions necessarily affect our ethical standards and decisions. It would, therefore, seem important to take another look at our measure of personal success, and reestablish basic values to shape moral and ethical behavior. Ralph Waldo Emerson's definition of success (Figure 15.1) may be a viable starting point.

Consistent with contemporary measures of success, most decisions to behave unethically seem to be based primarily on financial considerations and secondarily on power considerations. Most professionals find the temptation to behave unethi-cally becomes overwhelming only when money is the decision factor. The more there is to gain or lose financially, the greater the temptation to behave contrary to what the individual and organization know to be ethical. When your ability to sup-port and feed your family and keep a roof over head is threatened, you become more open to an unethical alternative. And increasingly, the more chance there is to gain significant amounts, the more likely some people are to throw ethics and profes-sionalism to the wind — and personal integrity with it.

According to Stephen Carter, a Yale University law professor, acting with integ-rity is comprised of three steps: discerning what is right and what is wrong, acting on the basis of that assessment and openly expressing that your actions are based on your own personal understanding of what is right and wrong.

Now is the time, as you prepare to launch your career, to make the commit-ment to act with integrity in everything you do. Just like you believe none of the disasters at the beginning of this chapter will ever plague your career, so did each of the many people who ended up in prison or in the unemployment line. Choose

⬡ Figure 15.1 _____
An enduring definition of success

"To laugh often and love much; to win the respect of intelligent persons and the affection of children; to earn the approbation of honest citizens and to endure the betrayal of false friends; to appreciate beauty; to find the best in others; to give of one's self; to leave the world a bit better, whether by a healthy child, a garden patch, or a redeemed social condition; to have played and laughed with enthusiasm and sung with exultation; to know that even one life has breathed easier because you have lived, this is to have succeeded."

—Ralph Waldo Emerson, 1803–1882

now to act with integrity. Thomas Friedman, author of "The World is Flat," says that globalization and technology have made us **hyperconnected**. People can easily find out where you live, how old you are, how much your house is worth, what you watched, what you bought and on and on. In other words, you can't hide from the decisions you make.

Choose now to understand the ethical standards of public relations and marketing and to follow them assiduously. Choose now to maintain a professional reputation that causes people to want to be associated with you, to want to work with you and to feel confident about hiring you.

Once you have compromised, you can expect the demand for compromise to continue. Even changing jobs doesn't necessarily free you.

Whatever reputation you establish will follow you to at least some degree for the rest of your professional life. In the communications profession where personal credibility and trustworthiness is an imperative, reputation can mean the difference between success and failure. All professional codes and standards aside, ethics come down to our personal decisions of appropriate behavior. The six simple rules in Figure 15.2 may help you to protect yourself against situations which will compromise your ethics and your professionalism.

HYPERCONNECTED

When people are connected to organizations and society through multiple means such as email, phone, social media and instant messaging.

Characteristics of professionalism

Professional reputation is one of the few enduring possessions. Businesses may come and go. Circumstances may, at times, cause difficulties in your career. Your professional success is dependent upon your building a good reputation; it is a critical element of professionalism.

Obviously, ethical behavior is one of the most important attributes of a solid professional. But it is not the only attribute. In fact, lists of characteristics and attributes necessary for professional survival abound. Four key categories of attributes deserve attention.

Personal and professional development

A professional should never stop learning. Take advantage of formal and informal means of education, and follow these tips to help you build a sound reputation and a successful career:

- Strengthen your skills and keep up with changes and innovations, particularly in the areas of technology and social media.
- Read profusely both in and out of the field. One of the reasons behind the broad liberal arts curriculum in communication programs is the need for communicators and business professionals to be familiar with other areas of knowledge. The skills needed to communicate come from the communication curriculum. Background in what you will be communicating comes from other fields of study.
- Obtain membership in at least one professional association, and actively pursue the educational opportunities offered therein.

Figure 15.2
Wilson's six rules for ethical decision-making

1. **Make your ethical decisions now.** Examine your value system, and define your personal and professional ethics now, before you are in a situation where you are pressured to succumb. Examine current case studies of ethical dilemmas and make decisions about what your own conduct will be. It is much easier to stick to ethical decisions you have already made based on personal and professional values than it is to make those decisions in the face of pressure and financial need.

2. **Develop empathy.** Treat others as you would expect to be treated. Don't judge others too harshly, and lend a helping hand. You may be fortunate not to have faced their dilemmas, but it may only be a matter of time. A little empathy and compassion go a long way and increase the chance of receiving compassion and assistance when you need it.

3. **Take the time to think things through.** Don't be railroaded or rushed into making decisions. When you are pressured to make a quick decision about something and you feel uncertain or confused, take your time. Chances are that if you feel rushed when making an ethical decision, you are being railroaded into doing something unethical and unwise, something you would not do if you had more time to think it through.

4. **Call a "spade" a "spade."** Lying, cheating and stealing by any other names are still lying, cheating and stealing. In today's complex business environment, we have an incredible ability to sanitize issues and rationalize behavior by using less poignant terms like "white lies" or "half-truths" or "omission" or "creative storytelling." But deception of any kind is lying; winning by anything but honest and ethical means is cheating; and appropriating anything that does not rightfully belong to you or your employer is stealing. Applying the terms that most people agree are prohibited by both personal and professional standards will help you make ethical decisions in complex or confusing situations.

5. **Recognize that every action and decision has an ethical component.** Ethical dilemmas seldom emerge suddenly. They are the culmination of several seemingly innocuous decisions and actions leading to the point of ethical crisis. Every decision you make has an ethical component even if it is not immediately obvious. Make sure to review the ethical ramifications of actions and decisions along the way. Project where a given decision will lead. Doing so will help you avoid many ethical crises that might otherwise "sneak up" on you.

6. **Establish a freedom fund.** Start today to save some money from each paycheck you receive. Establish a separate savings account and habitually contribute to your freedom fund. Much unethical behavior is a result of feeling you simply cannot afford to behave otherwise. You have financial obligations in life, and losing your job may mean you will lose your car or your home or that you won't be able to feed your family. If you are asked to do something that violates your personal or a professional code of ethics, you should first try to reason or negotiate not to do it. If you are unable to convince your employer, a freedom fund allows you to quit a job rather than compromise standards and jeopardize your professional reputation. Initially, plan to accumulate the equivalent of three to six months net salary in your freedom fund. As you are promoted to higher professional levels, raise the balance to a year or more of net income. A freedom fund is designed to pay the bills until you find another job. The greater your professional stature, the longer you should expect to look before finding an acceptable position. Plan accordingly, and never withdraw money from your freedom fund for anything else. If you do, it won't be there when you need it. In today's environment, it is almost certain that you will need to rely on your freedom fund to preserve your ethical standards.

- Read the news, blogs and professional journals. Read the important new books that everyone is reading. Read national and international publications that broaden your knowledge of current events and world information. You will be interacting with people in personal, professional and social situations. It is imperative that you be able to converse about current events, new discoveries, important studies and research, politics, sports, entertainment and other topics. Thoroughly knowing your profession will not only impress the decision-makers you work with but also help you keep your job.

- Learn from your colleagues and fellow professionals. Be actively involved in professional organizations that provide networking opportunities. Be willing to serve in those organizations and diligently do good work. Call professionals you meet to gain information and advice, and be available to mentor. Send them appropriate notes of congratulations, thanks and encouragement. Send out lots of Christmas cards. Keep your network vital and alive by developing relationships that demonstrate your care and respect for others.

- Finally, don't be afraid to ask questions. Have confidence in yourself, your knowledge and your ability, but remain humble and teachable. Overconfidence often masks incompetence. Don't be afraid to admit you have more to learn.

Work habits and job performance

Know your own strengths and weaknesses, and own up to your mistakes. Otherwise, you'll never overcome your challenges. Prioritize tasks, allocate time and work within constraints. Don't be concerned with the number of hours worked, but with the results and successes. Be goal-oriented, not just task-oriented. Pay attention to details, and always deliver work on time. Work hard and be absolutely dependable.

If you want to be promoted, do your job well and then help do the job of the person you would like to replace. Help that person whenever possible. When people are promoted, they often have a hand in selecting a replacement. Make yourself the obvious choice.

Personal conduct

Always act in a professional manner, and dress professionally. Always be on time. Be aware of what goes on around you. Observe procedures and power structures (formal and informal) and work within them. Always be ethical, and never allow yourself to be persuaded to compromise your personal standards. The respect of others is directly proportional to your respect for yourself and your respect for them. Work toward a balance in your life. Don't live to work or you'll be too stressed to maintain other vital relationships in life. If all you have in life is your job, you might be good at what you do, but you'll be very dull. Cultivate other interests and relationships. Be a generous contributor and serve in your community.

TIPS FROM THE PROS

How to preserve your reputation

Anthony D'Angelo, APR, Fellow PRSA, is senior manager of communications for ITT Corporation and chair of the Public Relations Society of America's College of Fellows. His opinion pieces on the value of public relations to organizational leadership have been published in Businessweek and the Financial Times. He tips you off on how to safeguard your reputation.

Trust is the *sine qua non* — absolute necessity — of the public relations profession, and reputation its stock in trade. Ethics and professionalism, therefore, are not optional. Without those attributes reflected in consistent behavior, a public relations professional will certainly fail. Here are the implications if you're pursuing a public relations career:

Trust and credibility are hard won and easily lost. No organization can exist without trust from the publics, internal and external, on which its survival depends. Trust and credibility are earned, daily, by people and organizations whose words and actions are in harmony. The video matches the audio, the product matches the claim, the delivery matches the promise, every time. In an increasingly cynical and disillusioned world, organizations that operate according to an ethical code and strive to live according to stated values have the best shot at succeeding. It's hard to do, and every person and organization makes mistakes. Still, public relations and message strategies not grounded in ethical behavior will undoubtedly implode. Without trust, they're just noise. Audiences are too sophisticated and perceptive to be duped.

It's not enough to have good intentions. The marketplace does not reward those who merely intend to behave ethically. Ethical action is expected and required. PR professionals must, therefore, know what they stand for personally, as well as on behalf of the organizations they represent. They must also always behave that way — even in environments that have different rules than they are used to, such as in crisis situations or in foreign countries. Fortunately, you don't have to make up your own professional code; you can study the PRSA Code of Ethics and similar industry guideposts to learn the foundational principles of our profession. They will help you navigate very complex, contentious issues that you will inevitably encounter in your career.

Professionalism is an extension or expression of an ethical foundation. Indeed, treating others with civility, courtesy and respect is not "nice to do," it is professionally imperative. Recognize that you teach people how to treat you through your behavior, as do organizations. If you supply courtesy and respect in your public relationships, you will find it returned.

The same holds true for inconsiderate behavior, rudeness and animosity. Furthermore, there is a direct relationship, too often overlooked, between courtesy and credibility. The high road to a satisfying career is demanding, but the people you meet there are inspiring and helpful.

Warren Buffet was wrong, at least when he said, "It takes 20 years to build a reputation and five minutes to ruin it." Thanks to social media, it takes less than five minutes. Stay vigilant.

Human relations

Courtesy is fast becoming a lost art in our culture. A few years ago, Ann Landers provided a concise perspective of **professional courtesy** in one of her columns:

> When you get right down to it, good manners are nothing more than being thoughtful and considerate of others. They are the principal lubricant of the human machinery we use when we interact with others.

Be personable and likeable. Learn to work well with people, treating them as equals. Work with and respect administrative assistants and other staffers. They can help you succeed or cause you to fail. Develop relationships that win loyalty and dedication. Know people's names (and the proper spelling) and use them. Be a mentor to newcomers.

Keep a sense-of-humor and of perspective. Don't hold grudges, and stay out of office politics for at least the first year in any company. It will take that long to figure out the informal power and communications structure. Never allow yourself to believe the job couldn't be done without you. Remember that cooperative effort is the key to success. Always be grateful and show that gratitude openly and often. Give others credit freely for their contributions.

PROFESSIONAL COURTESY
Exhibiting good manners by being thoughtful and considerate of others.

Embracing diversity

In today's world, both ethics and professionalism demand that we embrace **diversity**. Because issues of diversity in our society have come to the fore as trendy and politically correct, detractors may scorn their importance. More damaging though are those who have taken up the cause because it is trendy, rather than because it is morally right and a critically important part of the essence of our humanity.

Often, we wrongly equate diversity with equal employment opportunity and hiring quotas, failing to recognize that diversity celebrates the differences in all people, uniting them for better solutions and a brighter future. Harnessing diversity in our organizations and communities means creating an environment in which all individuals, regardless of difference, can work toward reaching their personal

DIVERSITY
Appreciating differences in culture, gender, race, background and experience.

potential while serving the common good. Diversity does not focus just on race or gender. It addresses the contributions all individuals have to make because of their differences, not in spite of them. The following quote is often attributed to Nelson Mandela, but it was actually written by The New York Times bestselling author, Marianne Williamson. She wrote in her book "A Return to Love:"

> Our deepest fear is not that we are inadequate. Our deepest fear is that we are powerful beyond measure. It is our light, not our darkness, that most frightens us. We ask ourselves, who am I to be brilliant, gorgeous, talented and fabulous? Actually, who are you not to be? You are a child of God. Your playing small doesn't serve the world. There's nothing enlightened about shrinking so that other people won't feel insecure around you. We were born to make manifest the glory of God that is within us. It's not just in some of us; it's in everyone. And as we let our own light shine, we unconsciously give other people permission to do the same. As we are liberated from our own fear, our presence automatically liberates others.

Diversity demands we examine privilege in our lives and accept the responsibility that comes with that privilege. It requires that we set aside "tolerance" in preference of acceptance. It requires that we not identify one right way, one mainstream to which all others must conform, but that we recognize myriad viable paths to a solution. It means we must set aside ethnocentrism and learn to appreciate the variety of our world and its inhabitants.

In the workplace, issues of diversity become even more critical. In today's environment, employers seek not only trained and skilled individuals; they are looking for versatility, flexibility and skill in operating in diverse environments. They require not only job skills, but skills in communication and human relations. Preparing for the workforce, especially as a communicator, means preparing for work in diverse environments with individuals who are different in many ways, among them culture, race, gender, religion, sexual orientation, physical ability, age, national origin and socioeconomic status. The following are some guidelines to developing characteristics to embrace diversity:

> ***Understand yourself and your history.*** The first step to embracing diversity is to understand yourself and the part played in your life by culture. Culture largely determines behavior. When we accept something as correct, right or proper, we have usually made a cultural judgment. Understand also the privileges and opportunities you have been afforded that have contributed to the person you are now. Recognize that with those privileges come responsibilities, and own up to those responsibilities. Also identify situations in which you were disadvantaged and how they have contributed to who you are. Rather than feeling self pity, use those circumstances to develop empathy for others. We have all experienced both privilege and disadvantage to some degree. Reaching out to join cooperatively in the elimination of disadvantages of any kind is a positive way to deal with our own disadvantages.
>
> ***Shed the guilt, and stop the blame.*** One of the biggest barriers to embracing diversity is guilt. Guilt is manifested in defensive postures. "It's not my

fault," is heard all too often when we deal with issues of diversity. Learn to recognize a statement of fact without feeling blamed. It is a fact that certain groups in our society have been disadvantaged in ways that have been difficult to overcome. Supporting their efforts is not an admission of guilt. It is an attempt to prevent further pain and suffering by helping overcome disadvantages, regardless of their cause. On the other hand, do not become engaged in blaming behaviors. It does no good to blame people and drive them into a defensive posture. Blame and guilt are divisive, not unifying or productive.

Minimize ethnocentrism. Although ethnocentrism is typically manifested between national cultures, it is present within nations as well. Ethnocentrism, or identifying our own particular culture and circumstance as the ideal to which all others should strive, is like wearing blinders. Different doesn't mean wrong or less effective. It just means different. Just as there is not only one right answer in creatively solving problems, there is not just one "right" culture. Appreciate your own culture but recognize it is not better — just different — than other cultures.

Avoid stereotypes. Stereotyping is sometimes a useful tool in understanding publics, but when we talk about diversity it is almost always harmful. Don't assume stereotypical characteristics about people with whom you have not worked or become acquainted. Also avoid the tendency to classify people as valuable members of a team just because of their membership in a particular group that may be a target public. Their value as a skilled communicator transcends the traits that classify them. All trained communicators should be able to marshal the resources and research to target any public.

Appreciate different ways of doing things. Learn not only that there is more than one right answer or way to accomplish something but also that different ways of doing something may have advantages not evident at first glance. Appreciate that using different approaches may enhance the creativity of the whole team. And, recognize that sometimes a different approach has a contribution to make that standard methods could not. Western medicine is a typical example of ethnocentrism and stereotyping that has hindered the widespread use of less traumatic treatments that work. Eastern-trained healers who work with the nervous system, the body's electrical impulses and pressure points have been successful time and time again at curing ailments Western medicine pronounced incurable.

Recognize professionalism and ability. Stereotypes often prevent us from recognizing the skills and competence of individuals. Professional communications and marketing skills are not genetic. If we begin to look at colleagues as fellow professionals instead of classifying them by their differences, we will find we have more in common than we thought.

Learn to develop relationships with individuals. Begin to see people as individuals: living, breathing and pursuing a quality-of-life similar to that which you pursue. Friendships be-

gin when people take the time to get to know one another as human beings. Ask questions if you are uncertain how to behave. Whereas "Blacks" used to be appropriate terminology, many now refer to themselves as African-Americans. Many Native Americans prefer to be addressed by tribal affiliation. Hispanics include Puerto Ricans, Cubans, Mexicans and Mexican-Americans, to name only a few. Ask people how they define themselves, and then show respect for the individual by adopting that definition in your interactions with them. It is the same personal respect you would wish to be accorded.

In the marketing, communications and advertising professions, more often than not, we work in teams. Seldom is a solution developed or implemented by one person in isolation from others. Learning to harness diversity means learning to let differences work for you, allowing diversity to enhance solutions and performance. In today's world, those who excel professionally will be those who have learned to appreciate and embrace diversity.

Summary

It is only logical to conclude our examination of strategic communications planning with a discussion of professionalism and ethical practice. Without these elements, no communications effort will succeed over the long term. Successful communication is based on trust, and trust is built by exhibiting professional and ethical behavior. Ethics are based on individual and group value systems (ethical codes) governing acceptable behavior. Value systems must place a premium not only on ethical behavior but also on diversity. True professionals exhibit a sincere commitment to an environment in which all may reach their potential while contributing to the overall goals.

Exercises

1. Do some thinking about your own personal value system and how it will drive your ethical choices in the professional world. Develop your own definition of success, and identify the ethical standards it implies.

2. Look up the codes of ethics in Appendix C and decide which one best exemplifies your approach to the profession.

3. Open a savings account designated as your freedom fund.

4. Initiate a serious discussion with one or two friends about diversity. Explore your similarities and your differences. Speak honestly about how you have been advantaged as well as disadvantaged.

References and additional readings

Callahan, D. (2004). *The cheating culture: Why more Americans are doing wrong to get ahead.* Orlando, FL: Harcourt, Inc.

Carter, S. L. (1997). *Integrity.* New York: HarperPerennial.

Etzioni, A. (1989). Money, power and fame. *Newsweek,* 18 September, 10.

Faust, J. E. (2003, February 28). Be healers. [Address given to the J. Reuben Clark Law School at Brigham Young University]. Provo, UT.

Friedman, T. L. (2007). *The world is flat (3.0).* New York: Farrar, Straus and Giroux

Gertz. B. (1998). *Morality: Its nature and justification.* New York: Oxford.

Howard, C., & Mathews, W. (1994). *On deadline: Managing media relations* (2nd ed.). Prospect Heights, IL.: Waveland Press.

Stoker, K., & Rawlins, B. (2004, March 10-14). Light and air hurt no one: The moral and practical imperative for transparency. [Paper presented at the International Public Relations Research Conference]. Miami, FL.

Tannen, D. (1994). Gender games. *People.* 10 October, 71-74.

Wilcox, D. L., Cameron, G. T., & Reber, B. H. (2014). *Public relations: Strategies and tactics* (11th ed.). Upper Saddle River, NJ; Pearson Education.

Young, D. (1987, November 8-11). Confronting the ethical issues that confront you. [Address given at the 40th Annual PRSA National Conference]. Los Angeles.

APPENDIX A
TIPS FROM THE PROS

APPENDIX B
STRATEGY BRIEFS

Strategy brief — backgrounder/brief history

Key public (brief profile including motivating self-interests):

Secondary publics (if any):

Action desired from public(s):

Focus on an event, organization or issue:

Proposed title:

Primary messages (two-five short statements, similar to sound bites)

Secondary messages (bulleted supporting data, facts, examples, stories, testimonials, etc.)

   1. Primary:

      Secondary: ·
            ·
            ·

   2. Primary:

      Secondary: ·
            ·
            ·

   3. Primary:

      Secondary: ·
            ·
            ·

Opinion leaders and how they will be used (testimonials, quotes, etc.):

Photos/charts/graphics (if any):

Where and when distributed:

Additional uses after distribution:

Timeline/deadline:

Strategy brief — billboard/poster

Key public (brief profile including motivating self-interests):

Secondary publics (if any):

Action desired from public(s):

Slogan, if any (should tie to overall big idea):

Primary message (usually one short primary message, similar to a sound bite)

Secondary messages (bulleted supporting data, facts, examples, stories, testimonials, etc.)

    1.   Primary:

        Secondary: ·
             ·
             ·

Opinion leaders and how they will be used (testimonials, quotes, etc.):

Color palette:

Art:

Size(s) of billboard/poster:

Location(s) of billboard/poster:

Print quantity and offset printing spot colors (if applicable):

Method and timing of distribution:

Additional uses after distribution:

Timeline/deadline:

Tip: Use this strategy brief to create a wireframe before designing your billboard/poster.

Strategy brief — blog post

Key public (brief profile including motivating self-interests):

Secondary publics (if any):

Action desired from public(s):

Overriding message (should tie to overall big idea and appeal to self-interest):

Proposed headline:

Proposed lead:

News hook:

Embedded links to internal and external sites:

SEO terms (10-20 key words or phrases) and tags:

Primary messages (two-five short statements, similar to sound bites)

Secondary messages (bulleted supporting data, facts, examples, stories, testimonials, etc.)

1. Primary:
    Secondary: ·
               ·
               ·

2. Primary:
    Secondary: ·
               ·
               ·

3. Primary:
    Secondary: ·
               ·
               ·

Opinion leaders and how they will be used (testimonials, quotes, etc.):

Photos/charts/graphics (if any):

Distribution contact (blog, blogger's name, email and phone):

Distribution once published:

Additional uses after publication:

Timeline/deadline:

Tip: If you are managing a blog, you should do a strategy brief for every blog post, and you must also create and maintain an editorial calendar.

Strategy brief — brochure

Key public (brief profile including motivating self-interests):

Secondary publics (if any):

Action desired from public(s):

Overriding message (should tie to overall big idea and appeal to self-interest):

Primary messages (two-five short statements, similar to sound bites)

Secondary messages (bulleted supporting data, facts, examples, stories, testimonials, etc.)

1. Primary:
    Secondary: •
    •
    •

2. Primary:
    Secondary: •
    •
    •

3. Primary:
    Secondary: •
    •
    •

Opinion leaders and how they will be used (testimonials, quotes, etc.):

Color palette:

Cover title and cover copy:

Cover photos/graphics (if any):

Internal photos/graphics:

Brochure size, paper (weight, finish):

Print quantity and offset printing spot colors (if applicable):

Where and when distributed:

Additional uses after distribution:

Timeline/deadline:

Strategy brief — direct mail piece

Key public (brief profile including motivating self-interests):

Secondary publics (if any):

Action desired from public(s):

Overriding message (should tie to overall big idea and appeal to self-interest):

Tone:

Proposed p.s.:

Primary messages (two-five short statements, similar to sound bites)

Secondary messages (bulleted supporting data, facts, examples, stories, testimonials, etc.)

1. Primary:
   Secondary: •
   •
   •

2. Primary:
   Secondary: •
   •
   •

3. Primary:
   Secondary: •
   •
   •

Opinion leaders and how they will be used (testimonials, quotes, etc.):

Color palette:

Cover title and cover copy:

Cover photos/graphics (if any):

Internal photos/graphics:

Print quantity and offset printing spot colors (if applicable):

Mailer size and paper (weight, finish, etc.):

Postage:

Source of mailing list:

Where and when distributed:

Additional uses after distribution:

Timeline/deadline:

Strategy brief — email news pitch

Publication:

Reporter/editor being pitched:

Email contact:

Related stories published by reporter:

Reporter beat/assignments:

Story being pitched:

Proposed email subject line:

News angle and primary message (including appeal to reporter's self-interest):

Secondary messages that support the news angle and primary message (bulleted supporting data, facts, examples, stories, testimonials, etc.):

-
-
-
-

Photos /charts/graphics:

Timing of pitch:

Planned follow-up with media:

Timeline/deadline:

Tip: Reporters typically will not open attachments.

Strategy brief — fact sheet

Key public (brief profile including motivating self-interests):

Secondary publics (if any):

Action desired from public(s):

Overriding message (should tie to overall big idea and appeal to self-interest):

SEO terms (10-20 key words or phrases):

Primary messages (two-five short statements, similar to sound bites)

Secondary messages (bulleted supporting data, facts, examples, stories, testimonials, etc.)

1. Primary:
   Secondary: •
   - •
   - •

2. Primary:
   Secondary: •
   - •
   - •

3. Primary:
   Secondary: •
   - •
   - •

Opinion leaders and how they will be used (testimonials, quotes, etc.):

Color palette:

Graphics/charts (if any):

Finished size:

Where and when distributed:

Additional uses after distribution:

Timeline/deadline:

Strategy brief — feature story

Key public (brief profile including motivating self-interests):

Secondary publics (if any):

Action desired from public(s):

Overriding message (should tie to overall big idea and appeal to self-interest):

Tone:

Proposed headline:

Proposed lead:

News hook:

SEO terms (10-20 key words or phrases):

Primary messages (two-five short statements, similar to sound bites)
Secondary messages (bulleted supporting data, facts, examples, stories, testimonials, etc.)

1. Primary:
    Secondary: •
               •
               •

2. Primary:
    Secondary: •
               •
               •

3. Primary:
    Secondary: •
               •
               •

Opinion leaders and how they will be used (testimonials, quotes, etc.):

Photos/graphics/art:

Distribution contact (publication, editor's name, email and phone):

Distribution once published:

Additional uses after publication:

Timeline/deadline:

Strategy brief — infographic

Key public (brief profile including motivating self-interests):

Secondary publics (if any):

Action desired from public(s):

Overriding message (should tie to overall big idea and appeal to self-interest):

Primary messages (In an infographic, these are categories of information used as subheads — usually two-six categories.)

Secondary messages (In an infographic, these are the hard data or facts that fit under each primary category. Use vector elements such as avatars, ideograms, ribbons and speech bubbles to convey information quickly.)

1.   Primary Message Category:
     Secondary Messages: •
                         •
                         •

2.   Primary Message Category:
     Secondary Messages: •
                         •
                         •

3.   Primary Message Category:
     Secondary Messages: •
                         •
                         •

Graphs and charts to be used (for comparison use column and bar charts; for transition use line or area charts; for composition use pie or waterfall charts):

Other images or icons to be used (photos, avatars, ideograms, illustrations, ribbons, speech bubbles and word clouds):

Color palette:

Fonts:

Where posted/distributed:

Additional uses after distribution:

Timeline/deadline:

Strategy brief — letter to the editor

Key public (brief profile including motivating self-interests):

Secondary publics (if any):

Action desired from public(s):

News reference (previous story and publishing date):

Primary messages (two-five short statements, similar to sound bites)

Secondary messages (bulleted supporting data, facts, examples, stories, testimonials, etc.)

   1.   Primary:
       Secondary: •
             •
             •

   2.   Primary:
       Secondary: •
             •
             •

   3.   Primary:
       Secondary: •
             •
             •

Opinion leaders and how they will be used (testimonials, quotes, etc.):

Length (newspaper's suggested word count):

Distribution contact (publication, editor's name, email and phone):

Distribution once published:

Additional uses after publication:

Timeline/deadline:

Note: Use a typical letter format complete with your signature, title, city, state and contact information.

Strategy brief — media advisory

Key public (brief profile including motivating self-interests):

Secondary publics (if any):

Action desired from public(s):

Overriding primary message (should tie to overall big idea and appeal to self-interest):

Media contact and email address:

Proposed email subject line:

Proposed headline:

Key information (use these categories as subheads in your advisory):

Who:

What:

Where:

When:

Why:

How:

Opinion leaders and how they will be used (testimonials, quotes, etc.):

Photos/charts/graphics:

Where and when distributed:

Planned follow-up with media:

Timeline/deadline:

Strategy brief — media kit/online newsroom

Key public (brief profile including motivating self-interests):

Secondary publics (if any):

Action desired from public(s):

Opinion leaders and how they will be used (testimonials, quotes, etc.):

Special event or reason to distribute kit:

Proposed content (fact sheet, executive bios, infographics, videos, backgrounders, photos, etc.) and how it appeals to the key public's self-interests. Each communications piece should have its own strategy brief.

a.

b.

c.

d.

e.

Proposed packaging (location on Web, folder, box, envelope, etc.):

Color palette:

Packaging graphics (logo, photo, etc.):

Method and timing of distribution (digital, sent with story, handed out at event, etc.):

Print quantity (if applicable):

Specific media to receive kit:

Proposed follow-up with media (if any):

Timeline/deadline:

Tip: Today's media environment requires most organizations to maintain at least a basic online newsroom presence.

Strategy brief — news release

Key public (brief profile including motivating self-interests):

Secondary publics (if any):

Action desired from public(s):

Proposed headline:

Proposed lead:

News hook:

SEO terms (10-20 key words or phrases):

Primary messages (two-five short statements, similar to sound bites)

Secondary messages (bulleted supporting data, facts, examples, stories, testimonials, etc.)

1. Primary:
    Secondary: •
    •
    •

2. Primary:
    Secondary: •
    •
    •

3. Primary:
    Secondary: •
    •
    •

Opinion leaders and how they will be used (testimonials, quotes, etc.):

Photos/charts/graphics (if any):

Where and when distributed:

Additional uses after publication:

Timeline/deadline:

Tip: Use the strategy brief for an email news pitch to send your news release to targeted reporters, bloggers, etc.

Strategy brief — newsletter

Key public (brief profile including motivating self-interests):

Secondary publics (if any):

Action desired from public(s):

Overriding message (should appeal to self-interest):

Overall tone:

Masthead text and graphics:

Lead story:

Lead story graphics:

Regular features or sections — special columns, reports and letters — and how they appeal to the key public's self-interests. Each feature and story should have its own strategy brief.

    a.

    b.

    c.

    d.

Other stories or articles (each should have its own strategy brief):

Color palette:

Photos/graphics:

Opinion leaders and how they will be used (testimonials, quotes, etc.):

Finished size, number of pages and paper (weight, finish, etc.):

Print quantity and offset printing spot colors (if applicable):

Where and when distributed:

Additional uses after distribution:

Timeline/deadline:

Editorial calendar:

Strategy brief — op-ed piece

Key public (brief profile including motivating self-interests):

Secondary publics (if any):

Action desired from public(s):

Overriding message (should appeal to self-interest):

Tone:

Proposed headline:

Proposed lead:

Primary messages (two-five short statements, similar to sound bites)

Secondary messages (bulleted supporting data, facts, examples, stories, testimonials, etc.)

1. Primary:
   Secondary: •
   •
   •

2. Primary:
   Secondary: •
   •
   •

3. Primary:
   Secondary: •
   •
   •

Opinion leaders and how they will be used (testimonials, quotes, etc.):

Distribution contact (publication, editor's name, email and phone):

Distribution once published:

Additional uses after publication:

Timeline/deadline:

Strategy brief — print ad

Key public (brief profile including motivating self-interests):

Secondary publics (if any):

Action desired from public(s):

Overriding message (should tie to overall big idea and appeal to self-interest):

Tone:

Slogan or tagline (if any):

Primary messages (two-five short statements, similar to sound bites)

Secondary messages (bulleted supporting data, facts, examples, stories, testimonials, etc.)

1. Primary:
   Secondary: ·
   - ·
   - ·

2. Primary:
   Secondary: ·
   - ·
   - ·

3. Primary:
   Secondary: ·
   - ·
   - ·

Opinion leaders and how they will be used (testimonials, quotes, etc.):

Color palette:

Photos/graphics:

Target publication(s):

Ad size, format and resolution:

Ad placement (publications):

Additional uses after publication:

Timeline/deadline:

Strategy brief — radio ad or PSA

Key public (brief profile including motivating self-interests):

Secondary publics (if any):

Action desired from public(s):

Overriding message (should tie to overall big idea and appeal to self-interest):

Tone:

Format (jingle, single voice, dialogue, etc.):

Length (10 seconds, 15 seconds, 30 seconds, 60 seconds, etc.):

Slogan or tagline (if any):

Primary messages (two-five short statements, similar to sound bites)

Secondary messages (bulleted supporting data, facts, examples, stories, testimonials, etc.)

1. Primary:
    Secondary: •
               •
               •

2. Primary:
    Secondary: •
               •
               •

3. Primary:
    Secondary: •
               •
               •

Opinion leaders and how they will be used (testimonials, quotes, etc.):

Title:

Proposed voice actors:

Sound effects:

Music:

Permissions:

Production quantity:

Where and when distributed:

Additional uses after airing:

Timeline/deadline:

Strategy brief — social media posts (Facebook, Instagram, Google +, Twitter)

Key public (brief profile including motivating self-interests):

Secondary publics (if any):

Action desired from public(s):

Overriding message for series of posts (should tie to the overall big idea and appeal to self-interest):

Photo or graphics (if applicable):

Hashtags and/or text links (if applicable):

SEO terms (10-20 key words or phrases):

First five posts (include primary/secondary message elements; may not include all elements below):

1. Message:
   Art:
   Links:
   Hashtags:

2. Message:
   Art:
   Links:
   Hashtags:

3. Message:
   Art:
   Links:
   Hashtags:

4. Message:
   Art:
   Links:
   Hashtags:

5. Message:
   Art:
   Links:
   Hashtags:

Analytics to monitor posts:

Editorial calendar:

Strategy brief — special event

Key public (brief profile including motivating self-interests):

Secondary publics (if any):

Action desired from public(s):

Tentative event date/deadline:

Event location:

Event theme (should tie to overall big idea):

Slogan or tagline (if any):

Primary messages (two-five short statements, similar to sound bites)

Secondary messages (bulleted supporting data, facts, examples, stories, testimonials, etc.)

1. Primary:
    Secondary: ·
    ·
    ·

2. Primary:
    Secondary: ·
    ·
    ·

3. Primary:
    Secondary: ·
    ·
    ·

Opinion leaders and how they will be used (testimonials, quotes, etc.):

Desired atmosphere/tone:

Key visual elements:

Interactive activities (if any):

Collateral pieces (print, multimedia, Web, etc.). Each will need individual strategy briefs:

Takeaways (gifts, mementos, swag, etc.):

Special guests:

Targeted media to invite:

Planned promotion:

Tip: Always use a detailed checklist and calendar when planning and executing a special event.

Strategy brief — speech

Key public (brief profile including motivating self-interests):

Secondary publics (if any):

Action desired from public(s):

Speaker:

Venue:

Length:

Audience (the key public may be broader than the physical audience of the speech):

Overriding message (should tie to overall big idea and appeal to self-interest):

Proposed title:

Opening attention-getting device (humor, story, statistics, etc.):

Primary messages (two-six main ideas or points in the speech)

Secondary messages (bulleted supporting data, facts, examples, stories, testimonials, etc.)

1. Primary:
   Secondary: ·
   - ·
   - ·

2. Primary:
   Secondary: ·
   - ·
   - ·

3. Primary:
   Secondary: ·
   - ·
   - ·

Opinion leaders and how they will be used (testimonials, quotes, etc.):

Visuals and/or video to be used, if any:

Conclusion:

Speech publication or distribution:

Additional uses after delivery:

Timeline/deadline:

Strategy brief — video

Key public (brief profile including motivating self-interests):

Secondary publics (if any):

Action desired from public(s):

Overriding message (should tie to overall big idea and appeal to self-interest):

Tone:

Format (jingle, voice-over, situation, etc.):

Length (30 seconds, 60 seconds, up to three minutes maximum):

Slogan or tagline (if any):

Primary messages (two-five short statements, similar to sound bites)

Secondary messages (bulleted supporting data, facts, examples, stories, testimonials, etc.)

1. Primary:
   Secondary: •
   •
   •

2. Primary:
   Secondary: •
   •
   •

3. Primary:
   Secondary: •
   •
   •

Opinion leaders and how they will be used (testimonials, quotes, etc.):

Title:

Proposed actors:

Location(s):

Props/equipment needed:

Photos/graphics:

B-roll:

Sound effects:

Music:

Permissions:

Where and when distributed:

SEO description for posting:

Additional uses after posting:

Timeline/deadline:

Tip: Always create a storyboard and shot list before you begin shooting video.

Strategy brief — video news release (VNR)

Key public (brief profile including motivating self-interests):

Secondary publics (if any):

Action desired from public(s):

Proposed headline:

Proposed lead:

News hook:

Primary messages (two-five short statements, similar to sound bites)

Secondary messages (bulleted supporting data, facts, examples, stories, testimonials, etc.)

1. Primary:
    Secondary: •
               •
               •

2. Primary:
    Secondary: •
               •
               •

3. Primary:
    Secondary: •
               •
               •

Opinion leaders and how they will be used (testimonials, quotes, etc.):

Desired length (30 seconds, 60 seconds, 90 seconds, etc.):

Proposed spokespersons:

Visuals:

Filming location(s):

Equipment needed:

B-roll:

Sound effects:

Music:

Permissions:

Where and when distributed:

SEO description for posting:

Additional uses after airing:

Timeline/deadline:

Tip: Always create a storyboard and shot list before you begin shooting video.

Strategy brief — website

Key publics (brief profiles including motivating self-interests of each key public):

Secondary publics (if any):

Action desired from publics:

Overriding message and tone (should tie to overall big idea and appeal to self-interest):

URL:

SEO terms (10-20 key words or phrases):

Opinion leaders and how they will be used (testimonials, quotes, etc.):

Primary messages for the home page (two-five short statements, similar to sound bites):

1. Primary message:

2. Primary message:

3. Primary message:

Primary navigation categories and subcategories (indicate how they appeal to the key publics' self-interests):

A.
1.
2.
3.

B.
1.
2.
3.

C.
1.
2.
3.

D.
1.
2.
3.

Visual design elements (logos, pictures and illustrations):

Color palette:

Fonts:

Interactive Elements:

Promotion to drive traffic to URL:

Social media links:

Timeline/deadline:

APPENDIX C
PROFESSIONAL CODES OF ETHICS

Principles and practices of advertising ethics

Created by the Institute for Advertising Ethics, administered by the American Advertising Federation (AAF).

Adopted by the Advisory Council of the Institute for Advertising Ethics, April 14, 2011.

Principle 1

Advertising, public relations, marketing communications, news and editorial all share a common objective of truth and high ethical standards in serving the public.

Principle 2

Advertising, public relations, and all marketing communications professionals have an obligation to exercise the highest personal ethics in the creation and dissemination of commercial information to consumers.

Principle 3

Advertisers should clearly distinguish advertising, public relations and corporate communications from news and editorial content and entertainment, both online and offline.

Principle 4

Advertisers should clearly disclose all material conditions, such as payment or receipt of a free product, affecting endorsements in social and traditional channels, as well as the identity of endorsers, all in the interest of full disclosure and transparency.

Principle 5

Advertisers should treat consumers fairly based on the nature of the audience to whom the ads are directed and the nature of the product or service advertised.

Principle 6

Advertisers should never compromise consumers' personal privacy in marketing communications, and their choices as to whether to participate in providing their information should be transparent and easily made.

Principle 7

Advertisers should follow federal, state and local advertising laws and cooperate with industry self-regulatory programs for the resolution of advertising practices.

Principle 8

Advertisers and their agencies, and online and offline media, should discuss privately potential ethical concerns, and members of the team creating ads should be given permission to express internally their ethical concerns.

Code of ethics — Association of Institutional Research

Adopted by the AIR membership on December 18, 1992, and updated most recently on May 2, 2013.

Preamble

The Code of Ethics and Professional Practice (Code) of the Association for Institutional Research (AIR) was developed to provide members of the association with some broad ethical statements with which to guide their professional lives and to identify relevant considerations when ethical uncertainties arise. It also provides a means for individuals new to the profession to learn about the ethical principles and standards that should guide the work of institutional researchers.

Although the association also serves those institutions that employ our members, our primary service to those institutions is achieved through our individual members. Hence this Code is directed to individuals and not institutions although basic tenets contained within the Code are also applicable to our colleges and universities and should be compatible with institutional codes and values.

The persons who practice institutional research (IR) are a diverse group from many different academic backgrounds and from many different professional experiences. Add to this diversity among IR practitioners the tremendous variation in the practice of IR as defined at individual colleges and universities, and IR professionals would seem to have little common ground. It is precisely for these reasons that this Code of Ethics and Professional Practice is important.

Many of the professions from which IR practitioners come have their own standards or codes for acceptable and even expected performance. This Code adds to those existing documents in recognition of the special and different demands inherent in the practice of institutional research. In many institutions the institutional researcher is viewed as the "guardian of truth" or the "conscience" of the institution. This is an extra burden for institutional researchers, and this Code provides some guidance to practitioners who bear that burden. Along with the other professional standards, this Code defines a normative expectation for institutional researchers in their work. At the same time, the Code provides the foundation for institutional research as a profession.

Although it provides standards, the Code does not provide a set of rules. Reasonable differences of opinion can and do exist with respect to interpretation, and specific application must take into account the context of a given behavior. Adoption of a code of ethics cannot guarantee ethical behavior or resolution of all disputes. Rather, it sets forth standards to which professionals aspire and against which their actions can be judged (both by themselves and others.) Ethical behavior should result from a personal commitment to engage in ethical practice and an attempt to act always in a manner that assures integrity. All members of AIR should pledge to maintain their own competence by continually evaluating their research for scientific accuracy, by conducting themselves in accord with the ethical standards expressed in this Code, and by remembering that their ultimate goal is to contribute positively to the field of postsecondary education.

Finally, this Code is a living document that must change and be shaped as the practice of institutional research continues to evolve and develop.

Section I — competence

a. **Claims of competence.** The institutional researcher shall not, in job application, resume, or the ordinary conduct of affairs, claim or imply a degree of competency he/she does not possess.

b. **Acceptance of assignments.** The institutional researcher shall not accept assignments requiring competencies he/she does not have and for which he/she cannot effectively rely upon the assistance of colleagues, unless the supervisor has been adequately apprised or unless he/she would acquire the necessary competence prior to doing the research. The institutional researcher should use methodologies or techniques that are new to him/her only after appropriate study, training, consultation and supervision from people who are competent in those methodologies or techniques.

c. **Training of subordinates.** The institutional researcher shall provide subordinates with opportunities for professional growth and development.

d. **Professional continuing education.** The institutional researcher has the responsibility to develop his/her own professional skills, knowledge and performance and to keep abreast of changes in the field.

Section II — practice

a. **Objectivity.**

  i. Unbiased attitude. The institutional researcher shall approach all assignments with acknowledgement of personal biases and make all attempts to minimize the effect of such biases in the conduct of the work.

  ii. Conflicts of interest. The institutional researcher should disclose situations in which financial or other personal considerations may compromise, or have the appearance of compromising, decisions or the performance of services. Disclosure and proper management of such situations assures that unavoidable conflicts do not interfere with the integrity of performance of duties.

b. **Use of accepted technical standards.** The institutional researcher shall conduct all tasks in accordance with accepted technical standards.

c. **Initial discussions.** Before an assignment is begun, the institutional researcher shall clarify with the sponsor and/or major users the purposes, expectations, strategies and limitations of the research.

  i Special care shall be taken to recommend research techniques and designs that are appropriate to the purposes of the project.

  ii. Special care shall be taken to advise the sponsor and/or major users, both at the design phase and, should the occasion arise, at any time during the execution of the project, if there is reason to believe that the strategy under consideration is likely to fail or to yield substantially unreliable results.

d. **Identification of responsibility.** The institutional researcher shall accept responsibility for the competent execution of all assignments which he/she or a subordinate undertakes, and shall display individual and/or office authorship, as appropriate, on all such reports.

e. **Quality of secondary data.** The institutional researcher shall exercise reasonable care to ensure the accuracy of data gathered by other individuals, groups, offices or agencies on which he/she relies, and shall document the sources and quality of such data.

f. **Reports.** The institutional researcher shall ensure that all reports of projects are complete; are clearly written in language understandable to decision-makers; fully distinguish among assumptions, speculations, findings and judgments; employ appropriate statistics and graphics; adequately describe the limitations of the project, of the analytical method and of the findings; and follow scholarly norms in the attribution of ideas, methods and expression and in the sources of data.

g. **Documentation.** The institutional researcher shall document the sources of information and the process of analysis in each task in sufficient detail to enable a technically qualified colleague to understand what was done and to verify that the work meets all appropriate standards and expectations.

Section III — confidentiality

a. **Atmosphere of confidentiality.** The institutional researcher shall establish clear guidelines about confidentiality issues within the institutional research office.

b. **Storage and security.** The institutional researcher shall organize, store, maintain, analyze, transfer and/or dispose of data under his/her control in such a manner as to reasonably prevent loss, unauthorized access or divulgence of confidential information.

c. **Release of confidential information.** The institutional researcher shall permit no release of information about individual persons that has been guaranteed as confidential, to any person inside or outside the institution except in those circumstances in which not to do so would result in clear danger to the subject of the confidential material or to others; or unless directed by competent authority in conformity with a decree of a court of law.

d. **Special standards for data collection.**

   i. Balancing privacy risks against benefits. The institutional researcher shall, at the design stage of any project, thoroughly explore the degree of invasion of privacy and the risks of breach of confidentiality that are involved in the project, weigh them against potential benefits, and make therefrom a recommendation as to whether the project should be executed, and under what conditions.

   ii Developing specific guidelines. Where appropriate, the institutional researcher shall adopt a written description of any specific steps beyond the regular guidelines within the institutional research office that are necessary during a specific assignment to ensure the protection of aspects of privacy and confidentiality that may be at specific risk.

   iii. Disclosure of rights. The institutional researcher shall ensure that all subjects are informed of their right of refusal and of the degree of confidentiality with which the material that they provide will be handled, including where appropriate, the implications of any freedom of information statute. Any limits to confidentiality should be made clear.

   iv. Appraisal of implications. The institutional researcher shall apprise institutional authorities of the implications and potentially binding obligations of any promise to respondents regarding confidentiality and shall obtain consent from such authorities where necessary.

Section IV — relationships to the community

a. **Equal treatment.** The institutional researcher shall promote equal access and opportunity regarding employment, services and other activities of his/her office, without regard to race, creed, gender, national origin, disability or other accidental quality; and in analysis, demeanor and expression shall be alert to the sensitivities of groups and individuals.

b. **Development of local codes of ethics.** The institutional researcher should develop and promulgate a code of ethics specific to the mission and tasks of the institutional research office and should strive to cooperate with fellow practitioners in the institution in developing an institution-wide code of ethics governing activities in common. The institutional researcher should take reasonable steps to ensure that his/her employers are aware of ethical obligations as set forth in the AIR Code of Ethics and Professional Practice and of the implications of those obligations for work practice.

c. **Custody and archiving.** The institutional researcher shall apply all reasonable means to prevent irrevocable loss of data and documentation during its immediately useful life, and, being aware of the role of data as institutional historic resource, shall act as an advocate for its documentation and systematic permanent archiving.

d. **Assessment of institutional research.** The institutional researcher shall develop and implement regular assessment tools for the evaluation of institutional research services.

e. **Institutional confidentiality.** The institutional researcher shall maintain in strict confidence and security all information in his/her possession about the institution or any of its constituent parts, which by institutional policy is considered to be confidential, and shall pursue from Section III of this Code all processes for that purpose as are appropriate.

f. **Integrity of reports.** The institutional researcher shall make efforts to anticipate and prevent misunderstandings and misuse of reports within the institution by careful presentation and documentation in original reports, and by diligent follow-up contact with institutional users of those reports. If an institutional research report has been altered, intentionally or inadvertently, to the degree that its meaning has been substantially distorted, the institutional researcher shall make reasonable attempts to correct such distortions and/or to insist that institutional research authorship be removed from the product.

g. **External reporting.** The institutional researcher has an obligation to the broader community to submit and/or disseminate accurate information and engage in responsible reporting when requested by legitimate authority, including federal, state, and other governmental agencies and accrediting bodies. With respect to private inquiries, such as those from guidebook editors, journalists or individuals, the institutional researcher, should he/she respond, is bound by the same standards of accuracy, confidentiality and professionally responsible interpretation.

Professionally responsible interpretation includes consideration of how the requesting individuals or organizations will employ the information. A sound understanding of how information will be used is fundamental to decisions regarding what type of information and supporting materials is appropriate and whether to participate with the request, if such reporting is not mandatory.

Section V — relationships to the craft

a. **Research responsibilities.**

    i. The institutional researcher shall seek opportunities to contribute to and participate in research on issues directly related to the craft and in other professional activities, and shall encourage and support other colleagues in such endeavors.

    ii. The institutional researcher should take responsibility and credit, including authorship credit, only for work actually performed and to which he/she has contributed. The institutional researcher should honestly acknowledge the work of and the contributions made by others.

b. **Integrity of the profession.** The institutional researcher should work toward the maintenance and promotion of high standards of practice.

    i. The institutional researcher should uphold and advance the values, ethics, knowledge and mission of the profession. He/she should protect, enhance, and improve the integrity of the profession through appropriate study and research, active discussion and responsible criticism of the profession.

    ii. The institutional researcher should contribute to the knowledge base and share with colleagues knowledge related to practice, research, and ethics. He/she should seek to contribute to the profession's literature and to share knowledge at professional meetings and conferences.

c. **False accusations.** The institutional researcher shall take care not to falsely demean the reputation or unjustly or unfairly criticize the work of other institutional researchers.

d. **Incompetence of colleagues.** The institutional researcher who has direct knowledge of a colleague's incompetence should consult with that colleague when feasible and assist the colleague in taking remedial action. If efforts to change a colleague's incompetent behavior or practice are unsuccessful, the institutional researcher has an ethical and professional obligation to use the institutional or agency guidelines for reporting such conduct.

e. **Unethical conduct of colleagues.**

    i. The institutional researcher shall take appropriate measures to discourage, prevent, identify and correct unethical conduct of colleagues when their behavior is unwittingly or deliberately in violation of this code or of good general practice in institutional research.

    ii. The institutional researcher who believes that a colleague has acted unethically should seek resolution by discussing the concerns with the colleague when feasible and when such a discussion is likely to be productive.

    iii. If efforts to change a colleague's unethical behavior or practice are unsuccessful, the institutional researcher has an ethical and professional obligation to use the institutional or agency guidelines for reporting such conduct.

Code of ethics — American Marketing Association

Adopted by members of the American Marketing Association (AMA) in 2008.

Ethical norms and values for marketers

Preamble

The AMA commits itself to promoting the highest standard of professional ethical norms and values for its members (practitioners, academics and students). Norms are established standards of conduct that are expected and maintained by society and/or professional organizations. Values represent the collective conception of what communities find desirable, important and morally proper. Values also serve as the criteria for evaluating our own personal actions and the actions of others. As marketers, we recognize that we not only serve our organizations but also act as stewards of society in creating, facilitating and executing the transactions that are part of the greater economy. In this role, marketers are expected to embrace the highest professional ethical norms and the ethical values implied by our responsibility toward multiple stakeholders (e.g., customers, employees, investors, peers, channel members, regulators and the host community).

Ethical norms

As marketers, we must:

1. **Do no harm.** This means consciously avoiding harmful actions or omissions by embodying high ethical standards and adhering to all applicable laws and regulations in the choices we make.
2. **Foster trust in the marketing system.** This means striving for good faith and fair dealing so as to contribute toward the efficacy of the exchange process as well as avoiding deception in product design, pricing, communication and delivery or distribution.
3. **Embrace ethical values.** This means building relationships and enhancing consumer confidence in the integrity of marketing by affirming these core values: honesty, responsibility, fairness, respect, transparency and citizenship.

Ethical values

Honesty: to be forthright in dealings with customers and stakeholders. To this end, we will:

- Strive to be truthful in all situations and at all times.
- Offer products of value that do what we claim in our communications.
- Stand behind our products if they fail to deliver their claimed benefits.
- Honor our explicit and implicit commitments and promises.

Responsibility: to accept the consequences of our marketing decisions and strategies. To this end, we will:

- Strive to serve the needs of customers.
- Avoid using coercion with all stakeholders.
- Acknowledge the social obligations to stakeholders that come with increased marketing and economic power.
- Recognize our special commitments to vulnerable market segments such as children, seniors, the economically impoverished, market illiterates and others who may be substantially disadvantaged.
- Consider environmental stewardship in our decision-making.

Fairness: to balance justly the needs of the buyer with the interests of the seller. To this end, we will:

- Represent products in a clear way in selling, advertising and other forms of communication; this includes the avoidance of false, misleading and deceptive promotion.
- Reject manipulations and sales tactics that harm customer trust.
- Refuse to engage in price fixing, predatory pricing, price gouging or "bait-and-switch" tactics.
- Avoid knowing participation in conflicts of interest.
- Seek to protect the private information of customers, employees and partners.

Respect: to acknowledge the basic human dignity of all stakeholders. To this end, we will:

- Value individual differences and avoid stereotyping customers or depicting demographic groups (e.g., gender, race, sexual orientation) in a negative or dehumanizing way.
- Listen to the needs of customers, and make all reasonable efforts to monitor and improve their satisfaction on an ongoing basis.
- Make every effort to understand and respectfully treat buyers, suppliers, intermediaries and distributors from all cultures.
- Acknowledge the contributions of others, such as consultants, employees and coworkers, to marketing endeavors.
- Treat everyone, including our competitors, as we would wish to be treated.

Transparency: to create a spirit of openness in marketing operations. To this end, we will:

- Strive to communicate clearly with all constituencies.
- Accept constructive criticism from customers and other stakeholders.
- Explain and take appropriate action regarding significant product or service risks, component substitutions or other foreseeable eventualities that could affect customers or their perception of the purchase decision.
- Disclose list prices and terms of financing as well as available price deals and adjustments.

Citizenship: to fulfill the economic, legal, philanthropic and societal responsibilities that serve stakeholders. To this end, we will:

- Strive to protect the ecological environment in the execution of marketing campaigns.
- Give back to the community through volunteerism and charitable donations.
- Contribute to the overall betterment of marketing and its reputation.
- Urge supply chain members to ensure that trade is fair for all participants, including producers in developing countries.

Implementation

We expect AMA members to be courageous and proactive in leading and/or aiding their organizations in the fulfillment of the explicit and implicit promises made to their stakeholders. We recognize that every industry sector and marketing subdiscipline (e.g., marketing research, e-commerce, Internet selling, direct marketing and advertising) has its own specific ethical issues that require policies and commentary. An array of such codes can be accessed through links on the AMA website. Consistent with the principle of subsidiarity (solving issues at the level where the expertise resides), we encourage all such groups to develop and/or refine their industry and discipline-specific codes of ethics to supplement these guiding ethical norms and values.

Code of ethics — International Association of Business Communicators

Preface

Because hundreds of thousands of business communicators worldwide engage in activities that affect the lives of millions of people, and because this power carries with it significant social responsibilities, the International Association of Business Communicators (IABC) developed the Code of Ethics for Professional Communicators.

The Code is based on three different yet interrelated principles of professional communication that apply throughout the world.

These principles assume that just societies are governed by a profound respect for human rights and the rule of law; that ethics, the criteria for determining what is right and wrong, can be agreed upon by members of an organization; and, that understanding matters of taste requires sensitivity to cultural norms.

These principles are essential:

- Professional communication is legal.
- Professional communication is ethical.
- Professional communication is in good taste.

Recognizing these principles, members of IABC will:

- Engage in communication that is not only legal but also ethical and sensitive to cultural values and beliefs.
- Engage in truthful, accurate and fair communication that facilitates respect and mutual understanding.
- Adhere to the following articles of the IABC Code of Ethics for Professional Communicators.

Because conditions in the world are constantly changing, members of IABC will work to improve their individual competence and to increase the body of knowledge in the field with research and education.

Articles

1. Professional communicators uphold the credibility and dignity of their profession by practicing honest, candid and timely communication and by fostering the free flow of essential information in accord with the public interest.
2. Professional communicators disseminate accurate information and promptly correct any erroneous communication for which they may be responsible.
3. Professional communicators understand and support the principles of free speech, freedom of assembly and access to an open marketplace of ideas and act accordingly.

4. Professional communicators are sensitive to cultural values and beliefs and engage in fair and balanced communication activities that foster and encourage mutual understanding.

5. Professional communicators refrain from taking part in any undertaking which the communicator considers to be unethical.

6. Professional communicators obey laws and public policies governing their professional activities and are sensitive to the spirit of all laws and regulations and, should any law or public policy be violated, for whatever reason, act promptly to correct the situation.

7. Professional communicators give credit for unique expressions borrowed from others and identify the sources and purposes of all information disseminated to the public.

8. Professional communicators protect confidential information and, at the same time, comply with all legal requirements for the disclosure of information affecting the welfare of others.

9. Professional communicators do not use confidential information gained as a result of professional activities for personal benefit and do not represent conflicting or competing interests without written consent of those involved.

10. Professional communicators do not accept undisclosed gifts or payments for professional services from anyone other than a client or employer.

11. Professional communicators do not guarantee results that are beyond the power of the practitioner to deliver.

12. Professional communicators are honest not only with others but also, and most importantly, with themselves as individuals, for a professional communicator seeks the truth and speaks that truth first to the self.

Code of conduct — The International Public Relations Association

Adopted by the International Public Relations Association (IPRA) Board, Nov. 5, 2010.

The Code consolidates the 1961 Code of Venice, the 1965 Code of Athens and the 2007 Code of Brussels.

1. Recalling the Charter of the United Nations which determines "to reaffirm faith in fundamental human rights, and in the dignity and worth of the human person;"
2. Recalling the 1948 "Universal Declaration of Human Rights" and especially recalling Article 19;
3. Recalling that public relations, by fostering the free flow of information, contributes to the interests of all stakeholders;
4. Recalling that the conduct of public relations and public affairs provides essential democratic representation to public authorities;
5. Recalling that public relations practitioners through their wide-reaching communication skills possess a means of influence that should be restrained by the observance of a code of professional and ethical conduct;
6. Recalling that channels of communication such as the Internet and other digital media, are channels where erroneous or misleading information may be widely disseminated and remain unchallenged, and therefore demand special attention from public relations practitioners to maintain trust and credibility;
7. Recalling that the Internet and other digital media demand special care with respect to the personal privacy of individuals, clients, employers and colleagues;

In the conduct of public relations, practitioners shall:

1. Observance

Observe the principles of the UN Charter and the Universal Declaration of Human Rights;

2. Integrity

Act with honesty and integrity at all times so as to secure and retain the confidence of those with whom the practitioner comes into contact;

3. Dialogue

Seek to establish the moral, cultural and intellectual conditions for dialogue, and recognize the rights of all parties involved to state their case and express their views;

4. **Transparency**

Be open and transparent in declaring their name, organization and the interest they represent;

5. **Conflict**

Avoid any professional conflicts of interest and disclose such conflicts to affected parties when they occur;

6. **Confidentiality**

Honor confidential information provided to them;

7. **Accuracy**

Take all reasonable steps to ensure the truth and accuracy of all information provided;

8. **Falsehood**

Make every effort to not intentionally disseminate false or misleading information, exercise proper care to avoid doing so unintentionally and correct any such act promptly;

9. **Deception**

Not obtain information by deceptive or dishonest means;

10. **Disclosure**

Not create or use any organization to serve an announced cause but which actually serves an undisclosed interest;

11. **Profit**

Not sell for profit to third parties copies of documents obtained from public authorities;

12. **Remuneration**

Whilst providing professional services, not accept any form of payment in connection with those services from anyone other than the principal;

13. **Inducement**

Neither directly nor indirectly offer nor give any financial or other inducement to public representatives, the media or other stakeholders;

14. Influence

Neither propose nor undertake any action which would constitute an improper influence on public representatives, the media or other stakeholders;

15. Competitors

Not intentionally injure the professional reputation of another practitioner;

16. Poaching

Not seek to secure another practitioner's client by deceptive means;

17. Employment

When employing personnel from public authorities or competitors, take care to follow the rules and confidentiality requirements of those organizations;

18. Colleagues

Observe this Code with respect to fellow IPRA members and public relations practitioners worldwide.

IPRA members shall, in upholding this Code, agree to abide by and help enforce the disciplinary procedures of the International Public Relations Association in regard to any breach of this Code.

Code of ethics — Public Relations Society of America

Public Relations Society of America (PRSA) code of ethics: preamble

This Code applies to PRSA members. The Code is designed to be a useful guide for PRSA members as they carry out their ethical responsibilities. This document is designed to anticipate and accommodate, by precedent, ethical challenges that may arise. The scenarios outlined in the Code provision are actual examples of misconduct. More will be added as experience with the Code occurs.

The PRSA is committed to ethical practices. The level of public trust PRSA members seek, as we serve the public good, means we have taken on a special obligation to operate ethically.

The value of member reputation depends upon the ethical conduct of everyone affiliated with the PRSA. Each of us sets an example for each other as well as for other professionals — by our pursuit of excellence with powerful standards of performance, professionalism and ethical conduct.

Emphasis on enforcement of the Code has been eliminated. But, the PRSA Board of Directors retains the right to bar from membership or expel from the society any individual who has been or is sanctioned by a government agency or convicted in a court of law of an action that fails to comply with the Code.

Ethical practice is the most important obligation of a PRSA member. We view the Member Code of Ethics as a model for other professions, organizations and professionals.

PRSA member statement of professional values

This statement presents the core values of PRSA members and, more broadly, of the public relations profession. These values provide the foundation for the Member Code of Ethics and set the industry standard for the professional practice of public relations. These values are the fundamental beliefs that guide our behaviors and decision-making process. We believe our professional values are vital to the integrity of the profession as a whole.

Advocacy

We serve the public interest by acting as responsible advocates for those we represent. We provide a voice in the marketplace of ideas, facts and viewpoints to aid informed public debate.

Honesty

We adhere to the highest standards of accuracy and truth in advancing the interests of those we represent and in communicating with the public.

Expertise

We acquire and responsibly use specialized knowledge and experience. We advance the profession through continued professional development, research and education. We build mutual understanding, credibility and relationships among a wide array of institutions and audiences.

Independence

We provide objective counsel to those we represent. We are accountable for our actions.

Loyalty

We are faithful to those we represent, while honoring our obligation to serve the public interest.

Fairness

We deal fairly with clients, employers, competitors, peers, vendors, the media and the general public. We respect all opinions and support the right of free expression.

PRSA code provisions of conduct

Free flow of information

Core principle
- Protecting and advancing the free flow of accurate and truthful information is essential to serving the public interest and contributing to informed decision-making in a democratic society.

Intent
- To maintain the integrity of relationships with the media, government officials and the public.
- To aid informed decision-making.

Guidelines
A member shall:
- Preserve the integrity of the process of communication.
- Be honest and accurate in all communications.
- Act promptly to correct erroneous communications for which the practitioner is responsible.
- Preserve the free flow of unprejudiced information when giving or receiving gifts by ensuring that gifts are nominal, legal and infrequent.

Examples of improper conduct under this provision
- A member representing a ski manufacturer gives a pair of expensive racing skis to a sports magazine columnist to influence the columnist to write favorable articles about the product.
- A member entertains a government official beyond legal limits and/or in violation of government reporting requirements.

Competition

Core principle
- Promoting healthy and fair competition among professionals preserves an ethical climate while fostering a robust business environment.

Intent
- To promote respect and fair competition among public relations professionals.
- To serve the public interest by providing the widest choice of practitioner options.

Guidelines
A member shall:
- Follow ethical hiring practices designed to respect free and open competition without deliberately undermining a competitor.
- Preserve intellectual property rights in the marketplace.

Examples of improper conduct under this provision
- A member employed by a "client organization" shares helpful information with a counseling firm that is competing with others for the organization's business.
- A member spreads malicious and unfounded rumors about a competitor in order to alienate the competitor's clients and employees in a ploy to recruit people and business.

Disclosure of information

Core principle
- Open communication fosters informed decision-making in a democratic society.

Intent
- To build trust with the public by revealing all information needed for responsible decision-making.

Guidelines
A member shall:
- Be honest and accurate in all communications.
- Act promptly to correct erroneous communications for which the member is responsible.
- Investigate the truthfulness and accuracy of information released on behalf of those represented.
- Reveal the sponsors for causes and interests represented.
- Disclose financial interest, such as stock ownership, in a client's organization.
- Avoid deceptive practices.

Examples of improper conduct under this provision
- Front groups: A member implements "grass roots" campaigns or letter-writing campaigns to legislators on behalf of undisclosed interest groups.
- Lying by omission: A practitioner for a corporation knowingly fails to release financial information, giving a misleading impression of the corporation's performance.

- A member discovers inaccurate information disseminated via a website or media kit and does not correct the information.
- A member deceives the public by employing people to pose as volunteers to speak at public hearings and participate in "grass-roots" campaigns.

Safeguarding confidences

Core principle
- Client trust requires appropriate protection of confidential and private information.

Intent
- To protect the privacy rights of clients, organizations and individuals by safeguarding confidential information.

Guidelines
A member shall:
- Safeguard the confidences and privacy rights of present, former and prospective clients and employees.
- Protect privileged, confidential or insider information gained from a client or organization.
- Immediately advise an appropriate authority if a member discovers that confidential information is being divulged by an employee of a client company or organization.

Examples of improper conduct under this provision
- A member changes jobs and takes confidential information and uses that information in the new position to the detriment of the former employer.
- A member intentionally leaks proprietary information to the detriment of some other party.

Conflicts of interest

Core principle
- Avoiding real, potential or perceived conflicts of interest builds the trust of clients, employers and the publics.

Intent
- To earn trust and mutual respect with clients or employers.
- To build trust with the public by avoiding or ending situations that put one's personal or professional interests in conflict with society's interests.

Guidelines
A member shall:
- Act in the best interests of the client or employer, even subordinating the member's personal interests.
- Avoid actions and circumstances that may appear to compromise good business judgment or create a conflict between personal and professional interests.

- Disclose promptly any existing or potential conflict of interest to affected clients or organizations.
- Encourage clients and customers to determine if a conflict exists after notifying all affected parties.

Examples of improper conduct under this provision
- The member fails to disclose that he or she has a strong financial interest in a client's chief competitor.
- The member represents a "competitor company" or a "conflicting interest" without informing a prospective client.

Enhancing the profession

Core principle
- Public relations professionals work constantly to strengthen the public's trust in the profession.

Intent
- To build respect and credibility with the public for the profession of public relations.
- To improve, adapt and expand professional practices.

Guidelines
A member shall:
- Acknowledge that there is an obligation to protect and enhance the profession.
- Keep informed and educated about practices in the profession to ensure ethical conduct.
- Actively pursue personal professional development.
- Decline representation of clients or organizations that urge or require actions contrary to this Code.
- Accurately define what public relations activities can accomplish.
- Counsel subordinates in proper ethical decision-making.
- Require that subordinates adhere to the ethical requirements of the Code.
- Report practices that fail to comply with the Code, whether committed by PRSA members or not, to the appropriate authority.

Examples of improper conduct under this provision
- A PRSA member declares publicly that a product the client sells is safe, without disclosing evidence to the contrary.
- A member initially assigns some questionable client work to a nonmember practitioner to avoid the ethical obligation of PRSA membership.

PRSA member code of ethics pledge

I pledge:

To conduct myself professionally, with truth, accuracy, fairness and responsibility to the public; to improve my individual competence and advance the knowledge and proficiency of the profession through continuing research and education; and to adhere to the articles of the Member Code of Ethics 2000 for the practice of public relations as adopted by the governing Assembly of the Public Relations Society of America.

I understand and accept that there is a consequence for misconduct, up to and including membership revocation.

And, I understand that those who have been or are sanctioned by a government agency or convicted in a court of law of an action that fails to comply with the Code may be barred from membership or expelled from the society.

_____

Signature

_____

Date

The Page principles — The Arthur Page Society

Seven proven principles that guide our actions and behavior

Arthur W. Page practiced seven principles of public relations management as a means of implementing his philosophy.

Tell the truth. Let the public know what's happening and provide an accurate picture of the company's character, ideals and practices.

Prove it with action. Public perception of an organization is determined 90 percent by what it does and 10 percent by what it says.

Listen to the customer. To serve the company well, understand what the public wants and needs. Keep top decision makers and other employees informed about public reaction to company products, policies and practices.

Manage for tomorrow. Anticipate public reaction, and eliminate practices that create difficulties. Generate goodwill.

Conduct public relations as if the whole company depends on it. Corporate relations is a management function. No corporate strategy should be implemented without considering its impact on the public. The public relations professional is a policymaker capable of handling a wide range of corporate communications activities.

Realize a company's true character is expressed by its people. The strongest opinions — good or bad — about a company are shaped by the words and deeds of its employees. As a result, every employee — active or retired — is involved with public relations. It is the responsibility of corporate communications to support each employee's capability and desire to be an honest, knowledgeable ambassador to customers, friends, shareowners and public officials.

Remain calm, patient and good-humored. Lay the groundwork for public relations miracles with consistent and reasoned attention to information and contacts. This may be difficult with today's contentious 24-hour news cycles and endless number of watchdog organizations. But when a crisis arises, remember, cool heads communicate best.

GLOSSARY

 A

Analytical process
A process in which action in each step is determined by the information acquired and decisions made in previous steps.

Attitudes
Collections of beliefs organized around an issue or event that predispose behavior.

 B

Beliefs
Inferences we make about ourselves and the world around us.

Big idea
A creative, overriding strategy and message that provides direction to a campaign.

Brainstorming
A structured group creative exercise to generate as many ideas as possible in a specified amount of time.

 C

Channel
The conduit or medium through which messages are sent to a specific public to accomplish a specific purpose.

Communication confirmation table
A visual tool used to validate the logic of a communications plan.

Confidence level
The percentage of certainty that the results of a survey would be the same if replicated.

Creativity
The process of looking outside ourselves and our routine to discover new ideas and innovative solutions.

Crisis management
The process of anticipating and mediating problems that could affect an organization's environment and profitability.

CTR (click-through rate)
A way of measuring the success of an online advertising or communications campaign by the number of users that click on a specific link.

 D

Demographic data
Information used to segment publics according to tangible characteristics such as age, gender and socioeconomic status.

Disinformation
Information that is intentionally inaccurate or misleading.

Diversity
Appreciating differences in culture, gender, race, background and experience.

 E

Ethical codes
Written and formalized standards of behavior used as guidelines for decision-making.

Ethics
Personal and professional value systems and standards that underlie decisions and behavior.

Evaluation criteria
Metrics or standards set to measure success.

Evaluation tools
Methods used to gather data needed to assess whether evaluation criteria were met.

 F

Focus group research
Moderator-led discussions with fewer than 15 participants providing in-depth information on attitudes and behaviors.

Formal research
Data gathering structured according to accepted rules of research.

Frame of reference
The collective influence of experiences, knowledge, culture and environment that forms our perceptual screen.

Framing
Designing a message to influence how an issue or event is perceived.

 G

Gen X
Generation born between the early 1960s and 1980s.

Gen Y
Generation born between the early 1980s and 2000s, also called millenials.

Goal
The result or desired outcome that solves a problem, takes advantage of an opportunity or meets a challenge.

 H

Hyperconnected
When people are connected to organizations and society through multiple means such as email, phone, social media and instant messaging.

 I

Ideation
The formation of new ideas.

Informal research
Less-structured exploratory information gathering.

Interactivity
The degree to which the tactic provides interaction between the sender of the message and the receiver.

Intervening public
An influential individual or small group of people used to carry a message to a key public.

Issue management
A long-term approach to identifying and resolving issues before they become problems or crises.

 K

Key public
Segmented group of people whose support and cooperation is essential to the long-term survival of an organization or the short-term accomplishment of specific objectives.

KPI (key performance indicator)
An important measure tied to a campaign or social media objective and used to evaluate its success.

 M

Microblog
A type of blog that lets users post short text updates. Microblogging features are often embedded in social networking sites.

Misinformation
Information that is unintentionally inaccurate or misleading.

N

Nonsampling error
Mistakes made in designing and implementing a questionnaire that may include definitional differences, misunderstandings and misrepresentations as well as coding errors and/or a failure to represent all populations.

O

Objective
Specific, measurable statement of what needs to be accomplished to reach the goal.

Omnibus survey
An ongoing, open survey to which a company or organization may add a few proprietary questions at a reasonable cost.

Opinion leader
A trusted individual to whom one turns for advice because of his/her greater knowledge or experience regarding the issue at hand.

P

Panel study
Respondents who have agreed to be surveyed repeatedly to track opinion and attitude change over time.

Partnership
A mutually beneficial short- or long-term cooperative relationship to reach common goals.

Persuasion
Disseminating information to appeal for a change in attitudes, opinions and/or behavior.

Persuasive appeals
Appeals to self-interest to enhance persuasion and motivate behavior.

Pinboard
Pages on Pinterest where users can save individual pins organized by a central topic or theme.

Planning
The process of using research to chart the step-by-step course to solve a problem, take advantage of an opportunity or meet a challenge.

Priming
Increasing the salience of a public issue through strategically timed media coverage.

Primary messages
Sound-bite statements that encompass what you need the public to do and an appeal to the public's self-interest to act.

Primary research
Firsthand information gathered specifically for your current purpose.

Professional courtesy
Exhibiting good manners by being thoughtful and considerate of others.

Professionalism
Characteristics and behavior befitting a professional.

Psychographic data
Information used to segment publics according to values, attitudes and lifestyles.

Public opinion
What most people in a particular public express about an issue that affects them.

Public relations
Strategically managing communication to build relationships and influence behavior.

Purposive sampling
Identifying and surveying opinion leaders to determine attitudes and behaviors.

Q

Qualitative research
Using research methods that provide deeper insight into attitudes and motivations but don't provide statistical significance.

Quantitative research
Using research methods that yield reliable statistical data.

R

Relationship building
A return to the roots of human communication and persuasion that focuses on personal trust and mutual cooperation.

Research
Gathering and using information to clarify an issue and solve a problem.

Research-based
When decision-making in the planning and implementation process is based on the acquisition, interpretation and application of relevant facts.

S

Sampling error
Measured as margin of error, it indicates the possible percentage variation of the sample data from the whole population.

Secondary messages
Bulleted details that include facts, testimonials, examples and all other information or persuasive arguments that support a public's primary message.

Secondary research
Information previously assimilated for other purposes that can be adapted for your needs.

Segmentation
Defining and separating publics by demographics and psychographics to ensure more effective communication.

Selective perception
The subconscious function of selecting from the millions of daily stimuli only those messages one chooses to perceive.

Selective retention
The function of selecting from the stimuli perceived only those messages one chooses to retain.

Self-interest
The fundamental motivation for an individual's behavior.

Slogan
A short, memorable phrase that integrates primary messages and appeals to several publics.

Social media
A collective of online communications channels that enables users to create and share content and participate in community-based input, interaction and collaboration.

Sponsored content/native advertising
Online editorial content paid for by a company that is designed to feel more like regular editorial content so it is less intrusive.

Strategic communications planning
An approach to communications planning that focuses actions on the accomplishment of organizational goals.

Strategic cooperative communities
Relationship-based interaction among all members of a community to achieve individual and collective goals.

Strategic function
One that contributes significantly to the accomplishment of an organization's mission and goals.

Strategic management
The process of evaluating all proposed actions by focusing on organizational goals, usually defined in short-term contributions to the bottom line.

Strategies
Public-specific approaches specifying the channel to send the messages to achieve objectives.

Strategy brief
An analytical tool that infuses strategic planning into the creation of effective tactics.

Stratified sampling
Selecting the sample to ensure proportionate representation of segments within the universe.

Subjective norms
Perceived behavioral expectations.

SWOT analysis
A structured analysis tool set up in a 2-by-2 table that examines strengths, weaknesses, opportunities and threats.

T

Tactics
Strategy-specific communication products that carry the message to key publics.

Triggering event
An event that transforms readiness to act into actual behavior.

Trust
An emotional judgment of one's credibility and performance on issues of importance.

Tweet
A publicly visible, 140-character text message sent through Twitter.

V

Values
Core beliefs or beliefs central to an individual's cognitive system.

W

Web analytics
The measurement, collection, analysis and reporting of Internet data for the purpose of understanding and optimizing Web usage.

Webinar/Web conference
An online conference or workshop where participants can all see and hear a presentation simultaneously and interact with the presenter and each other.

Wiki
A Web app that allows users to add, modify or delete content in collaboration with others.

INDEX